Praise for *The M*

"Insightful, enlightening, and practical, *The Magic Words* is a book that belongs on every writer's shelf. Loaded with concrete examples and specific strategies, it's likely to end up dog-eared and well-worn—that favorite book on craft that writers revisit again and again with each new project."

—Kate Messner, author of *The Seventh Wish* and
the *Ranger in Time* series

"What Cheryl B. Klein talks about when she talks about writing is what every aspiring children's and young adult novelist needs to hear. She offers generous insights, frank talk, nuts and bolts advice, editorial wisdom, and ample encouragement. *The Magic Words* is all the inspiration and guidance you'll need to get your novel started, and more importantly, to get it finished."

—John Dufresne, author of *The Lie That Tells a Truth: A Guide to
Writing Fiction* and *I Don't Like Where This Is Going*

"*The Magic Words* manages to articulate, in clear and compelling language, what others rely on intuition to understand. The result is a comprehensive and engaging examination of what readers will recognize to be true about the best novels—and yet have never heard expressed."

—Eliot Schrefer, two-time National Book Award nominee
for *Endangered* and *Threatened*

"Inspiring, comprehensive, and insightful, *The Magic Words* ably fills a gaping hole on the shelves of developing and experienced writers alike. An essential guide to the art and craft of writing for young readers."

—Anne Ursu, author of *The Real Boy* and *Breadcrumbs*

THE
Magic Words

THE
Magic Words

*Writing Great Books
for Children and Young Adults*

Cheryl B. Klein

W. W. NORTON & COMPANY

INDEPENDENT PUBLISHERS SINCE 1923

NEW YORK · LONDON

For information about permission to reproduce selections from this book,
write to Permissions, W. W. Norton & Company, Inc.,
500 Fifth Avenue, New York, NY 10110

For information about special discounts for bulk purchases, please contact
W. W. Norton Special Sales at specialsales@wwnorton.com or 800-233-4830

Manufacturing by LSC Harrisonburg
Book design by Fearn Cutler de Vicq
Production manager: Julia Druskin

Library of Congress Cataloging-in-Publication Data

Names: Klein, Cheryl B., 1978– author.
Title: The magic words : writing great books for children and young adults /
Cheryl B. Klein.
Description: First Edition. | New York : W. W. Norton & Company, [2016] |
Includes bibliographical references and index.
Identifiers: LCCN 2016014423 | ISBN 9780393292244 (pbk.)
Subjects: LCSH: Children's literature—Authorship. | Young adult fiction—Authorship.
Classification: LCC PN147.5 .K59 2016 | DDC 808.06/83—dc23
LC record available at https://lccn.loc.gov/2016014423

W. W. Norton & Company, Inc.
500 Fifth Avenue, New York, N.Y. 10110
www.wwnorton.com

W. W. Norton & Company Ltd.
15 Carlisle Street, London W1D 3BS

1 0 9 8 7 6 5

For my parents,

Alan and Rebecca Klein,

who let me read and helped me go.

Contents

The Magic Words

An Introduction, and How to Use This Book

"What was your favorite book when you were a kid?"

Among writers, that's the best conversation starter I know. *Matilda. The Secret Garden. Bud, Not Buddy. Harry Potter and the Prisoner of Azkaban.* People remember how they found the books: this class, that librarian, that former best friend. They remember what the books meant to them: laughter, heartache, recognition. And they remember how the books changed them: how the characters modeled the courage to stand up to oppression; how a novel became a safe space, a home.

Through the invocation of the right words in the right order—the magic words—books can change lives. And that is never more true than in childhood and young adulthood, when books introduce their readers to worlds both fantastical and right next door, inhabited by characters who share their challenges and joys.

You doubtless have a favorite novel yourself—a story that changed *your* life, that made you a reader and writer, that perhaps even inspired you on the path you're on today. In this book, we'll talk about how such wonderful novels work: how novelists create an alternate reality, bring it to life for their readers, and set a story ticking within it. We'll discuss structures and techniques for carrying these feats off within your own novel, and we'll look at some of the particular requirements of writing for a younger audience. I've worked as an editor in children's and young adult (YA) publishing for more than fifteen years, and I believe the magic starts with these five essential qualities:

- **Good prose:** This means the strength and integrity of the writing on a sentence-by-sentence level. Sometimes this strength lies in lyricism; sometimes it comes from personality (especially for a first-person voice); sometimes it's just plain cleanliness, where the text conveys its information clearly and succinctly. As a reader, I always love discovering a distinctive voice, where the thoughts and the manner of expressing those thoughts could belong to only one writer or character.
- **Rich characters:** Whether human, animal, inanimate, or alien, the characters are figures with multiple dimensions and desires, who are engaged with and take action in their worlds, whom I come to care about, and who show depth and change as the book progresses.
- **Strong plot construction:** The events in the book are compelling enough that I want to read on and see their consequences, which usually happens because I feel invested in the characters and what they're striving for. These events should make logical and emotional sense given who the characters are and the world they live in, but I also want the plot to surprise me at times, so I can't always see what's coming. The action of the book should conclude in some form of emotional consummation, whether satisfying me with its wholeness, or tantalizing me into the next volume.
- **Thematic depth:** The writer is interested in more than just telling a story; she's trying to make that story mean or say something about being in the world. What she has to say is original, or a familiar thought newly revealed in an original way.
- **Powerful emotion.** The writer catches me (and most readers) up in what the characters are feeling, particularly the viewpoint character. Or, if we have some distance from those characters, the writer can get us to experience the particular emotion he intends at each moment in the narrative, from sadness to terror to hilarity to peaceful quiet. These

emotional reactions usually (but somehow not always) grow out of all the preceding elements mentioned here; and as they accrue over the course of reading, their authenticity and integrity become a key measure of the quality of the book.

This last point is worth expanding on, because I believe great fiction (and indeed great art in general) creates a deliberate emotion in the person experiencing it—"deliberate" meaning it's the emotion the author of the book set out to create, so well as that intention can be discerned by the reader. This emotion is achieved authentically through immersing us in the protagonist's real experience, not through cheap manipulation. And while every reader's interaction with a text will be different, in great books, the emotion the author intends is experienced by a substantial majority of the people who come in meaningful contact with the work. Otherwise, the author isn't achieving what he or she set out to do.

In good children's and young adult books, the emotional experiences offered by the book will be appropriate to the reader's age, and then will speak to or expand the reader's own emotional experience—often at least partly through a connection with the main character. The winners of the Newbery Medal usually excel at creating emotion, especially sad feelings; the grief I felt in reading *Bridge to Terabithia* and *The Crossover* transported and elevated me, following the Aristotelian model, where tragedy cleanses the spirit and creates great art. But kids don't want to experience sadness all the time, and who can blame them? So they love *Captain Underpants* and *Divergent* and *Diary of a Wimpy Kid* and the Percy Jackson series, and many other books that make them feel more pleasurable emotions, like humor or warmth or excitement or safe (controllable) fear.

I believe an artistically successful book will demonstrate strength in at least four of the qualities I named above. It doesn't have to have strength in all of them, because that last category, emotion, will determine the depth of the other qualities needed: If you want to write an exciting book, you'll need an exciting plot, while you might be able to let thematic depth go by the wayside. Different readers will also value these qualities in varying measures depending on personal taste and mood; sometimes I love a good plotty mystery and sometimes I want a novel with gorgeously lyrical writing. And the presence of all five equals, I would say, masterpieces, like the Harry Potter series and *The Westing Game* and *One Crazy Summer* and *Clementine*. These authors are wizards: They found the magic words.

∾

All writers must discover the stories they want to tell, refine their own unique points of view, and figure out methods of getting their stories and voices down on the page in a manner that communicates their intent. I believe writing guides are most useful to this process when they offer some ground rules or guidelines for writers' explorations, and suggest narrative techniques or exercises that can help writers dig deeper and channel their multifarious creativity into focused novels. But in putting forth those ground rules, techniques, and even exercises, a guide is also setting forth its particular values for what makes a good book, so I want to be forthright about mine here.

Most of those values I've already stated earlier, in describing the kinds of books I love and have had the privilege to edit. I'll add that, besides pleasure, the thing I seek most in fiction is a new reality I can believe in: truth as polished by one particular writer's art. I want to be sucked into this imaginary world and believe these characters and their actions are real, and I want the flow of language to be like water to a fish—transparent, so I see right through it to the action, and so immersive that I take it for granted. When I edit a novel, nearly everything I suggest aims for more truth or more transparency. In this book, I'll lay out the principles that guide my editing toward those ends, and show you how to apply those same principles to your work.

You may disagree with these principles or other techniques put forward in this book, and if so, I hope the conflict will be intellectually and creatively stimulating for you. I will also say up front that I am a very structure-oriented person, and much of the content and a lot of the exercises here reflect that—they're all about anatomizing, classifying, mapping, designing. To me, structure provides a scaffolding for creativity: Once you've constructed your narrative skeleton, you can build all kinds of awesome and crazy things on top of it, and they retain an organic wholeness because you have that underlying organization and strength.

But some people—including some of the authors I've worked with— *hate* this kind of structural analysis. Doing some of these exercises would completely kill the joy and excitement of writing for them. And while I do believe in structure, I also believe artists must protect their creativity, because all their work flows from that spring. If you find anything I suggest is ruining your book for you and draining all your energy, so you don't have any enthusiasm for writing or revising; or, worse, if you're doing all these activities to put off the actual work of writing or revising . . . move on! Take what's useful to you, ignore the rest, write the story you need to tell, and enjoy the process as best you can. Or as Charlie Parker put it: "You've got to learn your instrument. Then, you practice, practice, practice. And then, when you finally get up there on the bandstand, forget all that and just wail."

Alas, there are no magic words that can transform any of us into great writers, or turn our books instantly into beloved bestsellers. Speaking personally, I've found writing a book on "how to write children's and young adult fiction" as humbling and delightful as writing about "what humanity is like" or "how you should live your life": the topic is hopelessly broad; the choices mind-blowingly varied; the richest and best answers are always the ones you discover yourself. But even with so many possibilities, we can find insights to share with each other, stories to tell one another, that can help us live better lives or write better books. And with time, heart, and hard work, I know writers can find their own magic words, so their books live on and become favorites for decades to come. I hope you find some inspiration and aid here, and I thank you for reading *The Magic Words*.

CHAPTER 1

Clarity and Connection

Principles of Good Writing

As I was writing this book, I found I kept coming back to fourteen key principles that I'll lay out now for future reference.

Intentionality. What do you want to do with your book? Or what do you want your book to do? How should the book feel, and what should the reader feel within it? Once you know the answers to those questions, every choice you make as a writer, from the point of view to the plot structure to the comma placement, should go toward serving those intentions.

Credibility. The entire effect of any fiction depends on belief: readers' faith in the world and the people that the writer is creating for them. Weaken that faith and you threaten the whole religion; break it, and your characters are statues in a church where readers don't worship. The good news is, readers are endlessly credulous, willing to put their trust in anyone who will show them one true or new thing. Keep that faith by keeping the true things coming.

Reality. The true things—that is, things that chime with the world the reader knows outside the book. On the most basic level, a writer must create a fresh physical world within our heads, populated with items we know (a banana) or can imagine (a ray gun), shown to us in details that evoke our senses (an overripe yellow banana, its flesh bruising at the touch), and abiding by known scientific laws (for instance, what goes up must come down—at which point the banana goes splat).

On the next level, the writer must create real people moving through this physical world, who will have their own distinct personalities, physicalities, histories, desires, passions, patterns of speech, roles in society, and all the other dimensions that make up a human being. These people can be utterly unlike anyone the reader knows in "real" life and still remain credible, so long as they have some kind of consistency to their internal makeup, and that makeup is consistent with their physical and temporal world. If I were writing a historical novel set in eighteenth century Cornwall, I could certainly create a carefree child character who longs to ignore his responsibilities and play in the surf, as children always have. However, that child should not say, "Tubular!" as that purely twentieth century word would render him instantly unrealistic—in-credible, in the old sense of the term.

On the third and final level, those characters must display an emotional reality of actions, feelings, and reactions, according to the particular emotional standards set up by their character and the society they live in. Suppose that carefree eighteenth century child has a responsible older brother who wants to be a shepherd when he grows up. If their father orders them to clean the sheep pen, neither brother might be particularly excited about the task, but the younger brother is more likely to complain, rebel, and run away to sea, in keeping with both the author's definition of his tastes and the emotions that arise from them. No matter how fantastical your material is—superheroes, time travel, antimatter, unicorns—your story should be grounded in the emotional reality of your characters.

Specificity. Reality comes about through specificity—through the details that root your characters in a particular time and place, and show the texture of your protagonist's unique life and mind. As an example, take these lines from the first chapter of *If I Ever Get Out of Here* by Eric Gansworth (‡),* narrated by a twelve-year-old Tuscarora American Indian boy named Lewis, just after he cut off his long ponytail:

> I left a few minutes later, starting my long walk home across half the reservation, still gripping the hank of hair. I opened my fingers a little every few yards to let the August breeze take some for the birds. As I turned the corner at Dog Street, where I lived, I could see my old elementary school. The teachers would be in their classrooms now, decorating bulletin boards with WELCOME TO THE 1975–76 SCHOOL YEAR! in big construction-paper letters. They were going to be puzzled by the fact that the United States Bicentennial Celebration wasn't exactly a reservation priority, since *we'd* been here for a lot longer than two hundred years.

Eric makes every detail count in establishing our vision of Lewis and his environment. His releasing his hair to help the birds make their nests, rather than just throwing it away, shows us his deep sensitivity to others, and this will indeed be a book full of Lewis watching and calibrating his reactions to other people. Identifying the road he lives on as "Dog Street" assures us that the author has imagined this reservation right down to its street layout. Every kid who's ever stepped foot inside a school on the first day will recognize that eminently teacherly welcome message and the construction-paper letters—a recognition that reinforces the reality of this story. Eric also works in the fact that the novel begins in August 1975, which is important for both the context of the period and the details of the characters' lives and thinking. Finally, the last line again shows us Lewis's sensitivity to other people and conveys some of the dry humor and wry observation that will characterize him as a narrator throughout this book. In sum, every specific choice here contributes to establish the reality of this boy and his place.

---

* Throughout this book, I use ‡ to denote novels I edited and published.

Clarity. Clarity in writing is the expression of an idea in a manner that best conveys the truth of that idea. Consider this sentence:

> Choosing this two-story Victorian with its dingy blue columns and faded shutters, wedged between two even more run-down houses, was especially odd since every business worthy of the name had long ago deserted the street.

The central idea of this sentence is that some unnamed person has made an odd choice in deciding to locate a business in "a tiny, two-story Victorian with . . . dingy blue columns and faded shutters," on a run-down street that has no other businesses. However, it takes the reader a few seconds to discern this central idea, as the structure of the sentence turns the verb "choose" into a noun phrase, and separates those key ideas of "choice" and "oddness" with several distracting details. A clearer form of this sentence would be:

> It was an odd choice of location for a bookstore—a two-story Victorian mansion with dingy blue columns and faded shutters—especially since every other business worthy of the name had long ago deserted the street.

Now the central idea of that odd choice comes through immediately, and the information that follows supports the central idea rather than obscuring it. The addition of "location for a bookstore" helps define why the odd choice matters, while the word "mansion" provides a stronger, clearer mental image of this place for a young reader than just the word "Victorian" might. But this revision isn't the only way that sentence could have been improved. Here are some other examples:

- A dingy Victorian house seemed like a bizarre location for a bookstore, especially since it was the only business on the street.
- Joe wondered why his mother put her bookstore here—a tiny, two-story Victorian house with dingy blue columns and faded shutters.

- It seemed very odd to Joe that his mother chose *this* place for her bookstore—a faded old mansion on a silent street.

Which expression of the idea is the best choice for the book? Well, that depends on our connection to the protagonist, how this sentence nests in among the sentences before and after it, the tone and specific details that best support the overall world this writer is building—all things that only the writer can know and determine. (Which points to another principle we'll return to throughout this book: There is no ultimate right or wrong in any writing, only choices that work better or worse for your particular project.) But all of the options here are an improvement in clarity over the original, as they express the central idea of the sentence with more energy and exactitude.

Transparency. If clear writing reflects the optimal expression of an idea, transparent writing offers the optimal depiction of the images and objects within your fictional world. You, the writer, can see your imaginary reality in your head; can we readers see it as well through your prose? And I do mean "see through" here—I want the words to create that reality in my head, too, not get in the way of that vision with awkwardly constructed sentences, poor word choices, vague details, or unnecessary explanations that pull me out of the flow of action. For instance:

> A rich woman stood in the center of the room. She had a brightly colored dress on. She looked around. Everyone was cowed by her. She touched her necklace.

What is this room like? How do they know she's rich? What color is her dress? Who are the "everyone," and why were they cowed by her? What's the significance of the necklace? How should we feel about this woman? We readers can't see any of these details because the text obscures them—unintentionally, one hopes, but frustratingly nonetheless. Focus the camera lens, clear away the fog, and the result is Anne Ursu's elegant original of this example, from *The Real Boy*:

A lady from the City had come in, her jewel-blue dress a violent gash of color against the white, brown, and black of the villagers. The lady stopped and looked around at the crowd, as if it were so terribly odd to find people in a store. The villagers bowed their heads. Her eyes searched the room, and she sighed heavily, fingering the green amulet around her neck.

Ursu doesn't even have to *say* the lady is rich (and note the power of "lady" vs. "woman"): The "jewel-blue" of her dress and the green amulet show it to us, while the "violent gash" and her hauteur establish an ominous atmosphere without the author having to say "everyone was cowed." Thus we readers can see through the transparent prose to understand the plot dynamics and emotional tenor of the scene, and feel the uneasiness the lady brings with her very presence.

Sensibility. Good writing is alive to the emotion in each moment, and seeks to capture that emotion and make it present for the reader through the action. I adore this passage from *Eleanor & Park* by Rainbow Rowell:

> "You don't like me," he said, leading her, pressing the base of the phone into his lowest rib.
>
> "I don't like you, Park," she said, sounding for a second like she actually meant it. "I . . ."—her voice nearly disappeared—"I think I live for you."
>
> He closed his eyes and pressed his head back into his pillow.
>
> "I don't think I even breathe when we're not together," she whispered. "Which means, when I see you on Monday morning, it's been like sixty hours since I've taken a breath. That's probably why I'm so crabby, and I snap at you. All I do when we're apart is think about you, and all I do when we're together is panic. Because every second feels so important. And because I'm so out of control, I can't even help myself. I'm not even mine anymore, I'm yours, and what if you decide you don't want me? How *could* you want me like I want you?"

He was quiet. He wanted everything she said to be the last thing he heard. He wanted to fall asleep with *I want you* in his ears.

This confession feels as headlong, breathless, and risky to readers as it does to the characters because the emotion of it is so uncut and the prose is so utterly transparent: The passage consists entirely of Eleanor and Park's actions and speech, and their own moment-by-moment reactions to each other's actions and speech, with no narrative explanations or intrusions to distract us from the purity of their emotion. As a result, we feel as if we're living through this intense moment with them, and we share their desperation and wonder. *Eleanor & Park* (and *Twilight* and *The Fault in Our Stars* before it) became a bestseller because readers young and old *love* experiencing the emotions of falling in love via a book. Indeed, readers love being hooked into heightened emotions in general: the terror of a haunted house, the thrill of a hunt, the exhilaration of a victory won. Try to capture and create those strong feelings through your writing.

Personality. Of course, many, many, *many* books show characters falling in love—probably half of all YA novels, for that matter—and very few of them go on to be bestsellers. When that does happen, as with *Eleanor & Park*, it's usually because both the characters and the prose display some fresh personality: They have an energy or flavor or perspective unique to the literary sphere, with people we haven't seen before (in this case, a zaftig redhead, a quiet half-Korean comics nerd), and feelings or insights we discover anew when revealed from the author's perspective ("He wanted everything she said to be the last thing he heard. He wanted to fall asleep with *I want you* in his ears"). The nature of that energy will be determined by the author's own personality, creativity, and outlook on the world. When agents and editors say we're looking for a strong voice, what we're really looking for is this unique personality, combined with the discipline of all these other virtues.

Activity. Like wild creatures on the hunt, readers are madly attracted to movement: a protagonist taking action, a villain threatening apocalypse, a team on its way to the big game, two friends in conflict, a character changing her mind. We like secrets, mysteries, the promise of things to be discovered; we like to see characters in jeopardy, because we also like to see them get out of it. Moreover, a narrative is defined by change, so if nothing changes in your story, you don't actually have a story. Give us movement and changes to watch.

Originality. If personality is the fresh expression of an idea, originality is a fresh idea itself, ranging from the thing nobody's ever tried before (a whole novel told from the point of view of a virus) to a new combination of established narrative elements (a murder mystery set in Antarctica). Originality connotes movement—something new coming into the world—and editors and agents, who are particularly rapacious forms of wild readers, will often spring at it. But the idea does have to be executed with credibility and sensibility; if you have a fresh idea, but you can't make us believe in its reality or feel its implications, it's almost worse than no idea at all.

Poetry. I don't mean here that your writing must be poetic, especially as poetry is stereotypically conceived—that is, full of metaphor, obscure references, and supposedly meaningful line breaks. Rather, I'm thinking of Tom Stoppard's definition of poetry: "the simultaneous compression of language and expansion of meaning." The more resonance you can get out of the use of a particular word at a particular time, and the tighter you can keep the rest of your prose, the richer your work as a whole will feel, as every word counts.

Honesty. The author of books for children and young adults implicitly accepts the responsibility of telling them the truth about the world—its joys and losses, its injustices and possibilities. I could say this truth must be told for the betterment of that world, as Mabel Louise Robinson put it: "Only as we give children the truth about life can we expect any improvement in it." But I think it's actually more of an artistic principle, that our audience deserves the respect signaled by the truth, rather than the condescension of cute lies or cheap happy endings. We do agree as a society that some truths need to be paced out through children's lives, for their emotional health or social development, and we also think carefully about how we express these truths in general: "You get seventy-nine years and then you die" may be true for the average American, but only a jerk would say that to a kid! Still, within those boundaries, we do our audience the honor of honesty.

Empathy. Thinking about the right way to express a truth to a child requires empathy—that is, as per the *American Heritage Dictionary*, "the ability to identify with or understand another's situation or feelings." Writing for children and young adults means a writer must practice empathy on four different levels:

- **Identifying with your intended reader.** More than perhaps any other genre of writing, children's and YA books are about emotion: recognizing a child's feelings and affirming them through their documentation within a book, saying, "You are seen, your feelings are real and important, you will get through this, and this book can show you one way." Children's and YA fiction thus requires writers to identify with the emotions, experiences, and interests of a reader of a very particular age, and then try to mirror those in their books. To accomplish this, you must understand and be able to imagine or imitate the general level of intellectual, emotional, and psychological development that a young person might have at seven, or thirteen, or seventeen, or whatever age you choose.

- **Understanding your protagonist.** And then you must turn those generalities into specific characters that you understand down to their heartbeats. You can hear these characters' thoughts, envision the other people in their lives, write out their histories, recognize the fears and desires and joys and need for love that all mix together to make them who they are. This does not mean that you approve of them or even *like* them, necessarily; you can certainly write a bully who beats up other children without thinking he's a great kid. But you do have to understand where that viciousness comes from, and know the points of vulnerability in him that might humanize him for the reader.

- **Rendering the protagonist's emotions on the page**. This often requires feeling the character's feelings along with them—which can be hard for a writer, truly, if a character is in a dark place, especially one that has resonance in the writer's own life. But as you empathize with this person, you must make readers empathize as well. That necessitates giving us the full sensibility of his emotions as they play out.

- **Taking the protagonist's side (which is taking the reader's side, too)**. In any conflicts shown in the novel—between a child and parent, say, or a transgender boy and his transphobic town—the narrative sympathies should flow toward the protagonist. This does not mean you give him a free pass out of trouble or let him get away with doing stupid things; you need to be honest about both the challenges he might face and the consequences of his actions. Rather, it means that you don't judge or belittle your protagonist for being who he is, and that you treat his concerns as valid and fair.

Done rightly, all of this can create the very best kind of empathy within both writer and reader: a stronger, wider connection with the world, forged through imagining and coming to understand more of the people who inhabit it, in all their weaknesses and glories.

Harmony. Finally, all of these principles must be integrated into and balanced within the book as a whole. Sometimes having too much specificity can get in the way of activity, weighing the novel down with unnecessary detail; sometimes you're so caught up in sensibility that you sacrifice credibility, writing dialogue that no rational character would ever say. Judge everything against the goals set up through intentionality, and that will help your work achieve harmony in the end.

Experience and Emotion

Ages in Children's and YA Literature

Children's and YA novels bear a rare distinction among all published books: They come with a ticking clock of societally acceptable reading. If you're nineteen or ninety, you can read whatever you want, and everyone will admire you for choosing a book over Twitter. But if you're eight, some adult will have an opinion on whether you should still be reading picture books, or if that chapter book is too long for you. If you're eleven, another adult might weigh in on whether the content of the novel you're reading is morally appropriate, whether you asked their opinion or not. Once you're fifteen, critics can worry that the "dark" themes of your favorite YA novel are infecting your brain, encouraging you toward antisocial behavior or self-harm. At the moment you blow out eighteen candles, snobs will announce you shouldn't read YA anymore, because that contributes to the infantilization of America. ("But I just wanted to finish the Chaos Walking trilogy . . ." you say.)

What underlies all of these opinions is a societal sense of a right age to read certain books, based on the reader's reading ability, the perceived age level of the book in question, and what we want children or teenagers to do, feel, think, know, or not know. In many of these cases, the naysayers are just patronizing buttinskis: If you meet someone who thinks YA fiction is less intelligent than adult fiction, for instance, please smack them down with *The Astonishing Life of Octavian Nothing, Traitor to the Nation* by M. T. Anderson. (Literally, if you choose, though be careful: It's a heavy book.)

But indeed, some novels *are* more appropriate than others for young people at various ages, mostly because kids' lives and perspectives can change so drastically with every turn of the calendar. While grown-ups can work the same job with the same people doing the same tasks for a decade or more, a child's world can explode and remake itself every year, as he graduates to a new grade with a new teacher and a new set of possible friends and enemies; acquires new siblings or responsibilities or skills; and becomes aware of more of the world, in all its beauty, possibilities, and ugliness. As a result, an effervescent nine-year-old who loves horses can be a very different person three years later, when she might skulk about on a skateboard for hours; and those two different people would require different books for their divergent interests, emotional concerns, and levels of reading proficiency.

Age Bands in Children's and Young Adult Publishing

So how do we define these age bands in publishing? While no one in the industry will say the following six categories are perfect, they reflect generally agreed-upon stages of child development, literary ability, and social approval. I am borrowing the word counts from agent Jennifer Laughran's excellent "Wordcount Dracula" post at literaticat.blogspot.com.

- **Board books:** Ages 0–3; 0–100 words. These books feature thick cardboard pages—the better to be drooled or chewed on—and often include special visual or textural elements to attract and hold little ones' interest.
- **Picture books:** Ages 3–8; 0–1,300 words, with a sweet spot of 300–550 words. Most picture books are written to be read by adults to children, so they may use language that falls outside the vocabulary of the children themselves. The illustrations tell the story in concert

with the words, and profoundly shape the emotional experience of the text.

- **Early or easy readers:** Ages 4–7; 100–2,500 words, depending upon the reading level. These are carefully written and designed to promote children's reading skills and confidence, usually featuring large text with a prescribed number of words or lines per page. The color illustrations will often be deliberately redundant with the story, so a young reader who is struggling with the words "purple scarf" might see that bright violet neckwear in the picture and take a cue from it. Because children read through easy readers quickly and primarily to gain skills, they are usually published as paperbacks, with occasional hardcover editions for libraries.

- **Chapter books:** Ages 7–10; 4,000–13,000 words, with a sweet spot of 6,000–10,000 words. These retain the larger text size and illustrated format of easy readers, but the pictures will be less frequent—a few per chapter, usually in black-and-white. Chapter books are also often published in series, which allow children to have the familiarity of reading about beloved characters while enjoying new adventures for them each time.

- **Middle-grade novels:** Ages 8–12; for realistic novels, 25,000–60,000 words (sweet spot: 30,000–45,000); for fantasy, 35,000–75,000 words (sweet spot: 45,000–65,000).

- **Young adult novels:** Age 13–18; for realistic novels, 35,000–75,000 words (sweet spot: 45,000–70,000); for fantasy, 50,000–150,000 words (sweet spot: 65,000–85,000). Editors and agents definitely side-eye anything over 100,000 words in any category, so if your manuscript is that long, the story needs to justify its length.

- **New adult novels:** Ages 18–30, same word count as YA. These books have the emotional intensity of young adult novels but are focused on the experiences of college or early adulthood, often including the additional "content" (as defined on p. 17) that comes with those experiences. Some YA editors occasionally handle new adult, but the genre is more often published by an adult house.

The chapter book, middle-grade, and young adult categories are the object of our investigations in this book. These are my basic expectations for what these novels will do:

- **The book will be centrally interested in the life, experience, and growth of its young protagonist.** This may sound like an obvious statement, but many adult novels use young protagonists as a lens on the corruption or danger or wideness of the world, and I often feel those books aren't interested in the protagonist so much as the "innocent" contrast he provides.
- **It will have a fully developed story, with a beginning, middle, and end,** in which most of the action is dramatized on the page for us, and those events have shape and meaning. (Nihilism can be a hard sell in children's and young adult publishing.)
- **The protagonist will contribute to the action,** consistently doing things or making choices that move the narrative forward.
- **The novel will be narrated with relative immediacy to the protagonist's youthful perspective,** and not with the distance of, say, an adult looking back at his preteen years.
- **In more literary novels, the protagonist will be different at the end of the novel than he was at the beginning,** and usually for the better, as he will have gained some new understanding, wisdom, connections, or security within himself or the world. Richard Peck offers the excellent dictum that a YA novel ends "not with happily ever after, but at a new beginning, with the sense of a lot of life yet to be lived"; and in a children's or YA novel, I want to see the events of the book prepare the protagonist for that future.
- **Finally, the book should give pleasure to its young readers in some way**—by making them laugh or cry, or involving them in an adventure, or introducing them to new fictional friends, kids whose lives and feelings resonate with or expand their own. Adults will read a book for the prestige of its literary merit, or solely for the beauty of the prose; but most child and teen readers want a good story, with characters and a

situation that will catch their imaginations and prove the book is worth their time.

Once a book satisfies all of those considerations, it does have to be assigned an age category, because it has to be shelved in and sold from a specific section in a bookstore, and we publishers want to place it in the section where it will have the most appeal to readers. When we're making a determination about whether a book is YA or middle-grade (which includes chapter books), we look at five major factors that are all deeply interconnected:

The Physical Age of the Protagonist. It is a publishing rule of thumb—so ingrained that it's practically a rule of the whole hand—that children and teenagers want to read about people their own age or older, and they will not read about people younger than they are. (The truth of this rule varies wildly with individual readers, of course, but it gives us publishers a useful basic guideline.) As a result, the first thing we look to in setting an age category for a book is the age of the protagonist: If he is twelve or younger, the book belongs in middle-grade; thirteen or older, it's young adult. (I should note that these are the standards set by bookselling retailers, as the American Library Association offers slightly different guidelines for its age-based awards.) Additionally, if the protagonist is older than eighteen or in college, conventional wisdom holds that the novel should be adult fiction, though YA publishers sometimes push this bromide with new adult material.

Writers learning these guidelines often ask questions like, "What if I'm writing a five-book series where the first book features the protagonist at ten, but she ages two years in each novel, so the series will start as middle-grade but end as new adult? J. K. Rowling crossed age categories like this; why can't I?" Well, if the first book in your series is as delightful and sells as well as *Harry Potter and the Sorcerer's Stone*, then yes, you can. Until that happens, you might want to reconsider your series plans, as publishers and retailers will want to be able to group all the books together in one section, and the section changes could create difficulty in our selling the series as a whole.

The Emotional Age of the Protagonist. You might know a ten-year-old girl with the attitude and wardrobe of a fifteen-year-old, or a fourteen-year-old boy who secretly still loves to play Legos. (No judgment, in either case!) If a character's physical age is determined by her birth certificate, her emotional age is how old she feels and acts mentally and emotionally—the age to which her interests and emotions are cued.

What distinguishes the emotional ages of a middle-grader versus those of a young adult? Well, just about everyone who works in children's and YA literature will offer you a different formula, though they all run along the same lines. Novelist Laura Ruby observed once, "Middle grade is about ability; YA is about identity"; that is, in middle-grade, a character gains skills, knowledge, or perspective, while in YA, she refines what she has learned into a particular worldview and chooses a path of action for the future. The agent and writer Michael Stearns says that in YA, "*how* a character feels about what is happening is as important as *what* is happening," while middle-grade tends to be more outwardly focused.

When I'm thinking about the middle-grade/YA distinction for novels I edit, it often comes down to the characters' relationship to the idea of home. Middle-grade protagonists are acquiring some independence, certainly, but they still need the anchor that "home" and all it represents provides. When they participate in a grand adventure, it usually ends with the promise of a return home to a safe space, the status quo. If their family or home situation is a bad one, they'll want to find a new home, as they're looking for security, not seeking to strike out on their own. In general, if a novel focuses strongly on its protagonist's relationship to his family, school, or animals, or if the protagonist *is* an animal, then my first instinct will be that it belongs in middle-grade.

Meanwhile, YA protagonists are interested in the world beyond home: friends, romance and sex, independence, travel, the future. Most times the protagonist's driving ambition or desire will lie in something that will help them establish an independent identity from their home, and the action will take place outside the domestic sphere. If family or home do come into the story, it's usually either as an obstacle (parents or circumstances that keep the protagonist from achieving her dreams), or, interestingly, as stakes, where she has to fight to protect her home or family from threats in the wider world. Think about your protagonist's relationship with home to help determine her emotional age.

The "Content" of the Book. I'm using the word "content" here as a catch-all term for language or subjects that American adults often wish to keep young people away from: swear words, sex, drug use, and violence and the effects of violence. Just as certain words, images, or subjects will earn a movie a PG-13 or R rating, the appearance of those words, images, or subjects in a book for young readers can push its classification from middle-grade to YA. (You can write pretty much anything in YA besides erotica.) This troublesome content and the politics of this content have been widely debated within the industry, as they are in American culture as a whole. Writers who choose to include such content in their books should be aware that it might limit the book's audience, as some adult gatekeepers (and some young readers themselves) don't want kids exposed to what they regard as corruptive influences.

From a publishing perspective, editors want content at every level to be justified by the reality of the characters and story line, and to be in tune with the ethos of the overall book. (Put another way, if you're adding content just to seem cool or edgy, it shows.) If it *is* necessary for the story line, theme, or art of your book, then you absolutely *should* include that edgier content. Often you can't write the truth of a place or a life without swearing, sex, drugs, or violence. Indeed, in both YA novels and many people's adolescences, coming of age is often defined by first encounters with those things. Don't shy away from such material, but don't be salacious about it, either. Just treat it with the same matter-of-factness you'd apply to any other element of the character's life, and write it true.

The Subject Matter of the Book. Some novels presume a level of pre-existing knowledge about or interest in their subject matter. Romances that go beyond first kisses are almost always YA, in keeping with teenagers' awakening sexuality. A novel about the Civil War could work just fine for middle-grade, as many young readers first hear about it in their introductory American history classes; but one about a soldier in Alexander the Great's army might be better suited for YA, after readers have studied world history. A book that deals with an older sister's teen pregnancy could have a ten-year-old protagonist and no mature content on the page, but it might still be better served as a YA novel if it gets into abortion and the politics surrounding it, as most middle-graders have probably not encountered the topic. If you're trying to determine what academic subjects a young reader might know or not know, you can look at curriculum guidelines to see when certain eras of history or other subjects are taught in schools.

The Prose Style and Reading Level. Compare these two passages:

> Arrietty wandered through the open door into the sitting room. Ah, the fire had been lighted and the room looked bright and cozy. Homily was proud of her sitting room: the walls had been papered with scraps of old letters out of waste-paper baskets, and Homily had arranged the handwriting sideways in vertical stripes which ran from floor to ceiling. On the walls, repeated in various colours, hung several portraits of Queen Victoria as a girl: these were postage stamps, borrowed by Pod some years ago from the stamp box on the desk in the morning room.

> We're late, near the last: Hide is already shuffling back-forth back-forth on his little patch of ground, and Heather's fingers are tapping 'gainst the arm of her wheelchair, the one that used to belong to Reynard before he died and we put him in the ground. Seed's hand's caught her other, fingers tangled together, talking broad-smile low to Jiéli's ma Kimmie, while the little girl squirms and fidgets and makes her sing-

ing noises in her mama's arms. I count heads: near the full forty-three people who shelter in Safe. Forty-three Tales in the back of my head; forty-three offerings to make a Tale of tonight.

The first passage is from a classic English middle-grade novel called *The Borrowers* by Mary Norton; the second is from a contemporary magical-realist YA novel called *Above* by Leah Bobet (‡). While the two books are both about communities of people who live hidden away, the writing alone signals their different audiences and intentions. *The Borrowers* offers up straightforward sentences—long, but not difficult to detangle— with an emphasis on explanation and description, so a young reader can easily envision this charming room and feel oriented in the comic action that will take place there. *Above*, on the other hand, is written in a dense, evocative, world-specific dialect that concentrates on the details of the scene more than the overall setting. It also drops a thicket of proper nouns and relationships for the reader to figure out and keep track of—a strategy that is important long-term for the book's themes of community, diversity, and inclusivity. The mere fact that *Above* involves those themes means it needs a reader sophisticated enough to appreciate their complex treatment here, as well as one with a high degree of reading ability and the patience to decipher the language and find pleasure in it. All of that points to YA.

Obviously these two examples come from extreme ends of the literary spectrum, and there are plenty of YA novels with straightforward declarative sentences, and plenty of middle-grade books with an extraordinary level of literary sophistication. Perhaps the true distinguishing factor here is intensity: YA often burns white-hot emotionally, dramatically, even linguistically, while middle-grade holds itself at more of a comforting simmer.

═ EXERCISES ═

If you're concerned about the right age category for your work-in-progress (WIP), let's see how these principles apply to your book. Answer the following questions:

- **How old is the protagonist at the beginning of the book?** If twelve or younger, write "MG"; thirteen or older, "YA."

- **What are his or her emotional concerns?** List them all. Do they feel more like the problems of a middle-grader or a YA reader, according to the standards set out above? Write "MG" or "YA" appropriately.

- **Is there any mature content, beyond the occasional punch or minor swear word?** If yes, write "YA" as a default.

- **How much preexisting knowledge does the subject matter require?** This might have to be a gut-level call. Again, write "MG" or "YA."

- **And the prose style?** Are there many complex sentences and difficult words? Is there a sophistication in the prose that might leave a younger reader behind? Again, choose "MG" or "YA."

If all of your answers line up in the same age band, congratulations! Your work here is done. If your answers split between "MG" and "YA," you should just be aware that such books can be harder for agents and publishers to sell, as any disjunction within those categories means the book might struggle to find its right audience. If you can pick a category, stick to it, and revise the manuscript accordingly, it will go easier for you. Maybe your fourteen-year-old protagonist could actually be twelve, or vice versa. If every plot element points toward YA, but your prose is more middle-grade, perhaps you could find ways to increase the temperature and complexity of your writing. (Or you may want to start a new project that *is* appropriate for middle-grade; it can be very hard to change your voice.)

If you truly can't decide on an age band, here are some additional questions that might point you toward a final answer:

- Which kind of book did you *think* you were writing? What aspects of it indicated that answer to you?
- When you envision yourself giving the book to a young reader, or visiting schools or doing signings, how old are the kids you imagine?
- How old do you feel *you* are, emotionally? Do you still relish the drama and crises of adolescence, or seek out safety foremost? What was your favorite age as a child? How old are your favorite young people to talk to now?

Again: The more you can harmonize all of these elements within the story you want to tell, the more easily the publishing journey will go for you and your book.

Writing from the Mind-set of a Child or Young Adult Character

As young people are not yet fixed into one way of being, they constantly explore their worlds and test who they might become. Most children's and young adult fiction dramatizes one subset or strand of these explorations and tests. Children and teens may lack wise judgment or the ability to articulate their emotions within certain situations (though so do many old adults, to be fair). But they feel, think, and act with the same seriousness and intensity that grown-ups do, and the best books for young readers honor that emotional reality.

In his book *Feeling Like a Kid: Childhood and Children's Literature*, scholar Jerry Griswold identifies five key themes that recur throughout books written for children: *snugness, scariness, smallness, lightness,* and *aliveness.* These all ultimately point to children's concern with power and uncertainty, and their desire to have some measure of control within their environments. In their daily lives, children are constantly negotiating with, or being subject to, the authority of their parents, teachers, and siblings over their rights, responsibilities, and pleasures. They must navigate the power of the popular kids at school, and of bullies, who have the social or physical power to enforce their dominance. Kids from nondominant cultures also witness all the ways in which their culture is subject to the dominant one. As children become teenagers and gain more physical freedom, they often negotiate to gain power or rebel against those who hold it. When you craft children or teen characters, recognize the many figures that assert power in their lives and their complex relationships with them, and think about the myriad ways they can respond to authority.

When you're trying to connect with a younger mind-set, it's often useful to start from personal experiences—the memories, emotions, and relationships that may feel long forgotten, but often rise to the surface with just a little digging.

═══ EXERCISES ═══

Freewrite for at least ten minutes regarding your memories and feelings at age eight. Then do it again for age twelve, and again for age sixteen. (It will probably help to identify what grade you were in at the time.) If you have a WIP, try freewriting about yourself at your protagonist's current age, or imagine your protagonist at eight, twelve, or sixteen in order to flesh out her backstory. When you finish, look over your notes and think about the key emotions and dilemmas that absorbed you at each age, alongside the specific incidents and details that embodied these emotions for you. (If you're part of a writing group, it might be interesting to try this exercise together and see how universal or unique your answers are.) Some questions that can serve as prompts:

- **You.** What scared you most at each of these ages? What made you angry? What did you worry about? What did you want for your birthday, and if you had a party, what was it like? If you had a free Saturday to yourself,

what did you do with it? What occupied your time besides school—
sports, music, hanging out? What did you want to be when you grew up,
and what inspired you toward that desire?

- **Family and home.** What did your parents represent to you at each age—
idols, dangers, obstacles, friends? How did you and any siblings relate to each
other? What did your room look like? How did everyone negotiate time in
the bathroom? What were your chores? How did you feel about visiting your
grandparents? Who were your favorite cousins? How did you spend holidays
or vacations? What was your favorite place to get away from everyone?

- **School.** Who was your homeroom teacher, or your favorite teacher? What
did his or her classroom look like? Where did you sit in it? What were your
relationships like with most of your other teachers? How did the school cafe-
teria smell? What was your favorite lunch? How did you and your parents feel
about your grades? What do you remember about being on a school bus?

- **Social life.** Make a list of all of the friends you can remember at each of
those ages. Who was your best friend? What did you like to do together?
Did you have a nemesis—either individually or as a group? What caused this
enmity, and how did you interact with him or her? Who was the most popular kid in your class and why? The meanest one? Who was your first crush?
What attracted you to this person? How did your first kiss come about?

- **At eight.** What were you allowed to do by yourself? What couldn't you
do? What was your favorite toy, stuffed animal, or game? What did you do
at recess?

- **At twelve.** What freedoms did you have at this age that you didn't have
at eight? What additional responsibilities? How had your relationship with
your parents changed? Where did you sit in the lunchroom? What were
the social groups in your grade? What new friends had you gained and
what friends had you lost since you were eight, and why?

- **At sixteen.** What freedoms and responsibilities did you pick up since you
were twelve? What relationships changed notably in the past four years

and why? Where did you go after school and on weekend nights? If you drove, what was your car like? What was your first job, and how did you feel about working?

Choose one of your friends from each of those years, and write a brief character study of that person.–How did you get to know each other? What did you like about your friend? What did you do together? What was this friend's family situation like? Were the parental rules for this friend more or less restrictive than yours, and how did he or she react to them? If you compared those to your own home and family at the time, what did you take away from that comparison? When you compared yourself to this friend, what did you see?

Write about a first. Children's and YA fiction often dramatizes firsts: first pet, first mean teacher, first big game, first evidence of unreliability from a parent, first driving lesson, first kiss. Choose one of those firsts and freewrite about your experience for ten minutes.

On YouTube or in your music library, find your favorite songs at ages eight, twelve, and sixteen. As you listen to the song now, try to remember listening to the song *then*. Where did you listen to it—in your room, in a car, with friends? Identify one specific time you heard it and write down all the situational and sensory circumstances of that moment. What was the appeal of this particular song? How did it make you feel? What does it show you now about what you liked or wanted then?

Obviously, your child and teenage characters should not be just like you, especially if they'd have musical tastes from another era. But if you can reconnect with your younger emotions, priorities, and sense of possibilities and boundaries—the size of the world around you, the things that most concerned you, how you understood yourself and other people—those memories can inform all your characters of that age.

Now the bad news: Your childhood and teenage experiences likely *were* in another era, and certain parts of being a child or teenager have changed enormously in just the last fifteen years, particularly thanks to technology and the Internet. If you are a parent or you work with children or teenagers, then you may be around young people enough that you know about these developments naturally. If not, and you plan to write a contemporary child or teenager in the United States, these steps might be useful in observing the mind-sets of young people today:

- Talk to—and even more, listen to—actual kids. What activities are they involved in? What do they and their friends do together for fun? What technology are they using? What are they thinking about on the personal, national, and global levels? What is their current favorite thing?
- Look at the media marketed to people of your protagonist's age. Check out magazines and websites aimed at the appropriate demographic. Watch the Disney Channel or MTV. For kids, wander Toys "R" Us and note what toys are marketed to the age group; for teenagers, visit Forever 21, H&M, and Hot Topic, and see the images they're selling. What messages do you see coming out of these media? What is their appeal to kids in general? How are they like and unlike the media of your youth? What would your protagonist think of those messages? How would he respond to them? *Note:* Try not to include current slang, TV shows, or musicians' names in your book, because trends can change with enormous speed, and while *The James Games* may be the number one show for kids eight through twelve this week, it could disappear forever in the time it will take for your book to come out. Make up your own versions of these things if you need them for your plot.
- **Be aware and beware of these trends.** News sites frequently post articles on supposed trends in children's and teenagers' lives—overtesting, screen use, the rise of cyberbullying, college pressures—and those can be compelling starting points for a contemporary novel. Do remember that such articles are often deliberately alarmist, designed to get clicks from or sell magazines to a particular adult advertising demo-

graphic; and again, these trends can easily change in the period before your book comes out. If the idea interests you, try to find out if and how it resonates in the lives of most children or teenagers. Then write the nuanced truth of that story, not the alarmist.

See Chapter 9, "Power and Attention," for further discussion of writing from a different mind-set.

CHAPTER 3

Proficiency and Practice

Using and Developing Your Gifts

Thus far, I've laid out some principles of what good writing should accomplish, and what a good book for children or young adults should achieve. Now let's make this personal: What do you want *your* particular book to do? What are your especial interests, skills, and talents as a writer? How can you maximize those gifts within the story you wish to tell? How can you develop them across what will hopefully be a long career?

In thinking about what makes a writer "talented," I actually don't think "talent" as a term is very useful, because talent breaks down into a number of constituent elements that are more interesting and helpful to discuss. To wit, I believe talent is actually a combination of:

Imagination. The writer is capable of envisioning and rendering in words something new on this earth: a new human being, a new form of magic, a new planet, a new story. Of course, this is what most writers do by definition, but writers who are gifted with original imaginations take that a step further, to put together elements no one else has thought to join before, and then render those inventions thrillingly real and meaningful. Think of M. T. Anderson's vision of a world consumed by the Internet in *Feed*, or

Shaun Tan's faceless exterminators in one nightmare world of *The Arrival*, or Neil Gaiman's boy raised by cemetery denizens in *The Graveyard Book*, or J. K. Rowling's conception of wands as indicators of personality.

These gifted writers might also demonstrate great depth in what they imagine, bringing a prodigious and wonderful specificity to their reality. To cite two of my favorite adult writers, half of *Americanah* by Chimamanda Ngozi Adichie is set in a cramped African hair-braiding shop shown in such well-chosen detail that readers can see the wavery fluorescent lights and smell the oils in the air. Or Patrick O'Brian created Stephen Maturin, a short half-Irish, half-Catalan doctor, naturalist, spy, violin player, Catholic, opium addict, faithful lover, terrible husband, worse housekeeper, excellent friend, and awful seaman, who is more real to me than half my acquaintances, because O'Brian imagined him so deeply and wonderfully. An original imagination, as with Anderson or Gaiman, will attract readers for the chance to expand our minds beyond the familiar; a deep imagination, as with Adichie or O'Brian, will attract readers for the chance to dwell in these authors' interpretations of the real world. Either way, they offer the pleasure of discovery to readers, who then feel they can confidently come to this writer to see something new.

Observational Skill. The writers I admire most, like the late Mr. O'Brian, create human beings I believe in as real people, like the eternal Stephen Maturin. To accomplish that, writers have to observe human beings carefully, and then remember and reflect upon what they observed, so they can combine their reflections with their imaginations, and create characters with the histories, personalities, and complexities of actual people. This means writers need to have an interest in human beings to start with, and the skill and patience to observe and try to understand their behavior. Not all people have that interest or those qualities.

Insight, Understanding, and Wisdom. I also love writers who have something to say about our world, about race, or death, or growing up, or war, or how love feels, or the pleasure of hating something. This wisdom can come about through observation or reading: Philip Pullman's lifelong engagement with the work of William Blake and Heinrich von Kleist, for instance, eventually grew into his iconoclastic vision of religion and God in the *His Dark Materials* trilogy. Insight can also be hard-won through life experience—especially pain, if you can reflect on it and use it well. J. K. Rowling has said that after the death of her mother in 1991, her conception of the Harry Potter series suddenly took on new richness and meaning, because her understanding of death was so much more intimate and profound. Every writer has a well of experience and knowledge to draw on, and the great ones can transform that personal reality into a story and characters that feel universal.

Dramatic Skill. This is the ability to make characters within a world move together in some emotionally compelling action. It requires first a sense of what *is* emotionally compelling, to you or to others, and then the ability to create that drama in the plot, through generating interesting conflicts and dilemmas and playing them out through compelling scenes and characters. It's also useful to have a strong sense of timing, to know just how long to let the lovers stare into each other's faces before a kiss, or how to make a fight scene move at the proper speed.

Writing Craft. Finally, writers must put the results of all this imagination, observation, insight, and dramatic instinct down on the page in a story that communicates those thoughts and feelings to a reader. The task is quite simple. The work is astoundingly hard.

≈

A gift for each of these aspects of writing could be inborn, and the more instinctively each of these things come to you, the more "talented" you are considered to be. But gifts also germinate through the years in combination with one other element that is essential to a writer's development:

Subconscious Reading. If you want to write well, you must get good prose and story structures into your brain so they flow naturally onto the page. You can only do that through massive amounts of reading. The younger you start, the better; the more you read, the better. Your reading helps form your sense of sentence rhythm and define your vocabulary, which in turn defines the store of words available to you to express what you want to say. If you're reading within a specific age range or genre, you'll imbibe its tropes and learn how to craft a satisfying narrative inside or against its bounds. The content of what you read subconsciously often determines what defines a good story for you—whether it's giant wham-pow fights or witty banter or two characters having long philosophical dialogues. You will likely end up writing the kinds of stories you read, because it is what you know or what makes you happy as a reader. Or you may react against a story you've read and want to tell it *your* way, or just better.

(As a side note to this point about reading, I always encourage writers for children and young adults to continue reading adult fiction, and/or to read wonderful adult nonfiction about whatever subjects interest them— space exploration, poetry, literary biography, politics. Such reading keeps writers engaged with the world beyond the insular limits of children's and YA publishing, and can often inspire new insights and stories along the way.)

Your reading combines with all of the elements of talent identified above, especially dramatic skill and writing craft, to form the base level at which you work, the moment you pick up a pen. And then you have to:

Practice. So. Much. Practice. "I know what I think when I see what I say," E. M. Forster said, and a writer's unique personality and the range of her abilities can emerge only through a lot of saying—writing, and writing, and writing, and then revising, revising, revising. Practice requires the discipline to sit down in front of a blank page and put words on it, which can be much harder than it sounds. But if you have that discipline and put in that time, the words eventually become both a story you can revise now and a light forward into the future: Its weaknesses will show you what aspect of writing you need to work on next, while its strengths might inspire you to try it again, differently. And your voice—your writerly personality; the way you put your imagination, observation, and insights on the page; your overall genius, truly—will come to you only if you practice. It doesn't matter how much talent you have, if all the fluency and wisdom and imagination of Laurence Yep and Katherine Paterson and Julius Lester bubbles in your mind and heart: You will never become a good writer without practice and then more practice.

~

Let's say you have talent and you're practicing regularly in order to get better. The following tasks can then help you improve and/or increase your odds of writerly success:

Read Consciously. Separate from the "Subconscious Reading" discussed earlier, this is the reading you do to study the techniques other writers use to achieve their emotional effects—how they bring off a romantic dialogue scene, or make you weep silent, salty tears at the death of a favorite character, or even how they turn a character into a favorite in the first place. You can then imitate or steal those techniques and effects for your own ends. When I wrote "So. Much. Practice." above, I was stealing an effect I have seen in many, many places, where the one-word sentences give the point about the necessity of practice extra weight by virtue of their brevity. An MFA or resources about writing and storycraft (like the book you're holding) also fall into this category.

Cultivate a Process. Write longhand first, then dictate that writing into a computer. Type 50,000 words in thirty days. Create a detailed outline of each scene and plot point, then flesh it out in prose. Imitate Anthony Trollope and write precisely 250 words every fifteen minutes from five-thirty to eight-thirty in the morning. Every writer has a different method, and there is no wrong way to approach the task. Just find a writing and revising process that helps you do your best work.

Cultivate a Purpose. Why do you write? Do you need to see a story completed, or get paid, or receive praise, or teach a lesson, or simply think out loud? If you can identify your reasons, they can help keep you going through the long trek to finishing a story or novel. The more you can make your purpose depend on you alone—that you want to work through your own questions about the afterlife, say, or your magical forest on the page is more of a home to you than your actual house—the easier it will be to carry out that purpose, as you won't be reliant on other people to get what you need emotionally from writing.

If your sole purpose in writing is to be published, I would encourage you to think further about this, particularly about what you believe you will get out of being published. It is meaningful and exciting to see a book with your name on it and your thoughts in it, and to get paid for those thoughts, and being a published writer can certainly change your life. But it's equally important to recognize that publication in and of itself will not solve your problems or make you happy long term, and it may even create more stress about the book's success or your future work. (Note that "getting published" is a purpose that is entirely dependent on the decisions of other people.) See if you can find a purpose for your writing that will make the process worthwhile for you even if you never publish the book.

Find Congenial Sources of Feedback. Look for people who understand what you're trying to do, and who can tell you where you succeed and where you're falling short. This could be a writing group or critique partner when you're starting out, or an agent or editor when you're closer to publication. Such smart companions are essential for giving you a reader's response to your work, offering course corrections when you lose sight of what you're trying to achieve, and providing you with emotional support.

Persevere. It requires sheer cussedness, frankly, to stick with the practice and the submissions, the slowness and the unfairness, the dissatisfaction and jealousy, the reviewers who don't get it and the reviewers who correctly identify all the places where you screwed up. The lovely moments in writing are truly lovely—when you nail that complex thought in a few perfect words, or when readers write to thank you for your book. You need perseverance to pull you through the many moments in between.

If you have all of these qualities and complete all these tasks, two more things can help you write a great novel:

Choose the Right Material. In 2007, I signed up *Marcelo in the Real World*, a novel about a teenage boy with a condition similar to Asperger's syndrome who works in his father's law firm one summer. Marcelo spoke in plain, straightforward sentences that reflected his place on the autistic spectrum, and he wrestled deeply with the intricacies of human behavior and our responsibilities for one another. When the book was published in 2009, the novel received five starred reviews and was optioned for film. (I'll discuss it at length later in this volume.) The author, Francisco X. Stork, has a naturally spare and beautiful writing style, a deep love for humanity, an amazing gift for writing distinct characters and realistic dialogue, and a fascination with the same philosophical questions that consumed Marcelo. Thus, in developing *Marcelo in the Real World*, Francisco created a character whose first-person voice suited his writing style, who was involved in a plot that spoke to his own purpose and interests as a writer, and whose story expressed some of his personal truths. That celestial alignment of author, character, story, voice, and values led to a marvelous book.

So what is the right material for *your* fictional values and range of practice, *your* strengths and boundaries? What do you enjoy writing, and what are you good at writing? Finding a subject matter and style that bring all of these factors together will vastly increase your odds of writing a satisfying book, especially if it's also material that works with the strongest element of your talent. And to do that:

Work with What Makes You Weird. What are you passionate about? Write a novel about that. What sets you apart from everyone you know? Write a novel about that. What do you see in the world? What do you believe is true? Write a novel about that.

I'll even add: What experiences have hurt you? Confused you? What are you still in pain over? Write a novel about that. This is obviously tricky territory, if the material is too tender, or if you're too close to it to be able to render it honestly in fiction. But Emily Dickinson wrote, "I like a look of agony— / Because I know it's true," and readers have that same heartlessness and hunger for what is real. If you can give that reality to them, they'll respond to your work.

This advice is exactly as prescriptive as everything else in this book, meaning it comes with the silent parenthesis "(if that works for you)." And if you're writing out of a painful experience, I absolutely don't mean you should write that exact narrative, the roman à clef of the time your friends abandoned you or you were betrayed by the person you loved most. But perhaps you can transpose that feeling of abandonment or betrayal into a different situation or a fantasy world. Perhaps you can draw on your experience to say something fresh about power or relationships. Those electric-fence emotions can power your fiction, if you can plug in safely.

The best fiction happens when writers pair their unique worldviews and experience with a story that reaches beyond their singularity. Don't run away from your individual strengths toward the latest trends, what everyone else is doing, or "what the market wants." Rather, look for ways to translate your uniqueness so it speaks to others, to extend a hand to readers through your writing. Find a place to dig deeply with your imagination, a character who fascinates you, a situation with layers upon layers to unfold. Remember that incident that gave you wisdom, that insight you'll bring to life with your drama and craft. Apply the theories and techniques discussed in this book to it, and write the novel that could only be yours.

═══ EXERCISES ═══

What makes you weird? Answer that question, and the rest of the questions in the "Work with What Makes You Weird" section above.

Describe the qualities of your dream novel–the book that would satisfy your every wish as a reader.–What genre would it be in? Who would the main character be? Who would that character's key relationships be with—friends, comrades, parents, romantic partners? (It doesn't have to be a children's or YA book.) Would the characters be engaged in a great battle against an enemy, living everyday domestic lives, or both? Would there be a lot of dialogue, or a lot of action, or gorgeous writing, or brilliant descriptive passages? What would its tone be? What might this book say to you or show you? How would it make you feel?

- Could you write this book? Why or why not?
- If you don't conceive the book as a kids' or YA novel, could it be one? How would you do it?

Think over your reading from childhood to the present day.–From a strictly artistic perspective (not awards, prestige, or sales), pick out four books that you wish you could have written, and four books that left you dissatisfied. Write down their titles, then answer the following questions about each one:

- What one element in the book gave you the most pleasure?
- Who was your favorite character in it, and why?
- What elements of talent (as listed earlier in this chapter) particularly distinguished this book?
- What question did this book ask and answer?
- For each of the books you wish you could have written: What impressed you about this book? What made it so special? Do you think you *can* write

a book like this eventually? (Do you want to?) What qualities would you need to work on to write a similar novel?

◅ For each of the books that left you dissatisfied: How did this book disappoint you? How could that dissatisfaction have been addressed?

Look over your answers for all eight books. What do they have in common? Do those commonalities make sense with what you already know about your individual personality, your writing personality, and your interests? If so, you might write along that more satisfying direction. If not, it might be interesting to explore those disjunctions further.

Consider the qualities identified at the beginning of this chapter: imagination; observational skill; insight, understanding, and wisdom; dramatic skill; and writing craft. How much value do you place on each of those qualities in the books you read? On a scale of 1–10, with 1 as a tapeworm and 10 as Toni Morrison, how would you rank your skills in each of those qualities? Which ones do you feel confident in? Which skills do you want to work on?

To develop your imagination:

◅ Here's a trick I learned from the novelists Ammi-Joan Paquette and Bruce Coville: For each of the three fictional problems listed below, brainstorm twenty ways you could solve it. Having to come up with so many ideas will force you to push past obvious answers and dig down to something truly creative, so it's a useful technique to try whenever you feel stuck.

 ∿ You must cross a ravine twenty feet wide and forty feet deep, with a tiger at the bottom.

 ∿ The Crown Prince of the realm has asked you for the fifth dance on your card—the same dance you already promised to your true love.

 ∿ Your mother catches you in a lie, and she *hates* lying.

To develop your observational skill:

- Search online for the work of photographers Diane Arbus, Rineke Dijkstra, William Eggleston, or Carrie Mae Weems. Choose a photograph and study it closely. What are your initial impressions of the person or situation it presents? As you look closer, longer, do those dynamics continue to hold true? Name the people in the picture and their relationship to one another. Where are they? When? What can you learn from the background of the photo? How do the people in the picture feel about the photographer? Write a brief scene encompassing the taking of this photograph.

- Go to a public place where you can sit quietly and write. For ten minutes, describe everything happening around you, from the wind blowing through the trees to the dialogue of a husband arguing with his wife. At the end, choose one item or situation and write exclusively about it for five more minutes—describing it in detail, transcribing any dialogue, noting both your own associations with it and how it belongs or doesn't in this environment. Try practicing this regularly to move beyond surface observations to more specific sensory details or insight.

To develop insight, understanding, and wisdom:

- List twenty things you know to be true in life. How did you learn they were true for you? Perhaps your characters can travel similar journeys to their own insights.

To develop your dramatic skill and writing craft:

- The best way to improve these skills is to read everything you can and write and revise even more. Everything you read and write has something to teach you, even the things you hate. (Why do you hate something? Why do other people like it? What can you learn from that?)

- Think of a moment in a movie, play, or TV show that took your breath away. What dramatic elements combined to cause that emotional effect?

If it involved a revelation: How were the characters and plot constructed to lead to that reveal? If a culmination: What made the coming-together of these things so satisfying? Try to reproduce that same effect in a scene with your own characters and setting.

To practice subconscious reading:

ᴥ Linda Sue Park, the Newbery Medal–winning author of *A Single Shard*, tells all aspiring children's writers that they need to read at least five hundred books in the age band they hope to work in before they sit down at a keyboard. That seems like a smart guideline to me. You can simply read your way through the children's or YA section of your local library, or look at the ALA Notable Children's Books, the YALSA Best Fiction for Young Adults lists, and Elizabeth Bluemle's "A World Full of Color" database to find quality titles. (A full list of all of the titles mentioned in this book is included in the "Recommended Reading" section.)

To find congenial sources of feedback:

ᴥ If you aren't already a member, look into the Society of Children's Book Writers and Illustrators. SCBWI offers multiple resources, conferences, and benefits for children's and YA writers, including the chance to connect with like-minded creative people online or in person.

To practice:

ᴥ Do it.

CHAPTER 4

Promise and Premise

Crafting a Strong Story Concept

Readers buy books for the promise of a particular experience. If they want to be scared, they'll buy a horror novel. If they want to learn about squids, they'll find a nonfiction book on cephalopods. If they want to live in the warm and orderly world of Sarah Dessen's characters, they'll pick up the next Sarah Dessen book. Often readers—and we editors and agents, too—have no idea what experience we want until we see a book that provides it. (For instance, it had never occurred to me to want to edit a novel about a boy with Asperger's syndrome, and then I was profoundly moved and surprised by *Marcelo in the Real World*.) This is why it's hard for editors to spell out what we're looking for explicitly, and why publishers put out so many books on such an astonishing array of subjects: When we enjoy a reading experience, we imagine other readers might take the same pleasure in it, and we want to share that pleasure with as wide an audience as possible.

However, given that more than 300,000 new books are professionally published each year, we publishers often don't have much time to convince booksellers and readers of the pleasures of a particular project—why they should purchase *this* book over *that* one. Thus the easiest way for us to articulate a book's promise is through a strong premise, that is, a strong story concept that will attract readers to its characters, action, or big ideas.

Constructing a Saleable Premise

Consider these sample premises from children's and YA fiction:

- Tired of being known as the "gay boy" in his town, an out teenager decides to become "openly straight" when he transfers high schools.
- A girl sets off on a journey to meet the Old Man in the Moon.
- A brother and sister run away to stay in the Metropolitan Museum of Art.
- A teenage girl, slowly dying of cancer, meets a boy with the same (imperial) affliction.
- Cleopatra's daughter is forced to build a new life in ancient Rome after her mother is murdered by those very Romans.

As you can see, from a practical perspective, a premise is a one-sentence description that defines the protagonist of the book and the overarching action and conflict. Each of these premises also makes promises, for hijinks, high drama, or heroic action. Editors love to publish novels with both rich emotional promise and what I call a saleable premise.

A saleable premise is a book concept that can find a satisfactory audience of book buyers.

To explain this in more detail, I'm going to break this definition down to its constituent elements.

"Book": The idea is capable and worthy of filling out an entire book. Suppose you feel very strongly that nose-picking is bad, and to help people understand that, you're going to write a whole novel where a boy gets his finger stuck in his nose. This might turn out to be a great absurdist project, if it's developed right. But if it's not, and the story just makes the same point over and over again—that "Wow, nose-picking is disgusting in multiple ways!"—then the idea belongs in a public-health brochure, not a book.

"Concept": The concept is the thing that will get readers' attention and make them want to buy the book. This concept might be a desire to show, explore, or teach a particular idea. It might be a new approach to a familiar subject; adult publishers put out new diet books every year in the hopes that *this* technique, *this* idea, will capture readers' attention, just as the readers buying those books hope that *this* one will work. With certain brand-name authors, like James Patterson or Danielle Steel, the authors are more or less the concept, the premise, *and* the promise—readers will buy these authors' new books because they've had a good relationship with their work in the past. Most often this concept is indeed a story concept, a conflict or mystery or relationship. We'll go into more depth on what kind of concepts qualify as "saleable" below.

"Can find": There are no guarantees in publishing, but we publishers believe an audience for a book we choose to publish is out there. Often we believe it because we've reached that audience before, or because we are that audience ourselves, or, with kids' books, we *were* that audience ourselves.

"A satisfactory audience of book buyers": A certain number of people willing to spend the money required to purchase the book; a certain level of sales that make publishing the book financially worthwhile to this publisher. If I receive a middle-grade novel written in Elizabethan blank verse with sixteenth century spelling, vocabulary, and philosophy, it might be a literary masterpiece, but it is also going to be a hard sell for middle-grade readers and the adults who buy books for them, simply because very few people have the knowledge or patience to navigate the archaic language and ideas. So I wouldn't call that audience "satisfactory," however brilliant the book itself might be. On the other hand, if you pitched me a middle-grade novel about two sisters who are the only survivors of a small plane crash in the Alaskan wilderness, and they have to work together to get home, that book would appeal to any reader who appreciates adventure or great stories about strong girls and their relationships—a very satisfactory audience. It could be *Frozen* meets *Hatchet* by Gary Paulsen, and if it were written well, I'd sign it up tomorrow.

~

Successful "saleable premises" go in and out of fashion. In the year or two immediately after *Twilight* became a smash, publishers rushed out novel after novel featuring vampires, many of which were successful, if not to the same degree. A whole wave of other paranormal projects followed—angels, werewolves, heroines with the ability to kill with a touch—to the extent that Barnes & Noble established a section entirely devoted to "Teen Paranormal Romance." Cut to the mid-2010s: It's certainly not impossible to publish a book on those subjects anymore, but it's very easy for them to be regarded as *so* 2008, and no editor wants to be ten years behind in their publishing. (And, for the record, Barnes & Noble has now taken that section down.)

So, how do I personally know when a manuscript is saleable?

- **When it is *great*.** Emily Dickinson said, "If I feel physically as if the top of my head were taken off, I know that is poetry." When I read a manuscript that performs a similar partial decapitation on me—where I love the characters, where I'm moved by the language and caught up in the action, where the book fulfills and exceeds all of its initial promises—I want to tell everyone about it and have everyone read it.
- **When it puts a new spin on already successful material, particularly a new approach to a proven emotion.** One of the reasons zombie/werewolf/angel novels followed the vampire trend is because they took the love story at the center of *Twilight* and combined it with other supernatural beings that presented new and different challenges for a romance. Readers like to read more of what they already know and love, so a story that promises both fresh action and a familiar emotion will often grab their attention. This combination is often conveyed through the "meets" formula, as when I said "*Frozen* meets *Hatchet*" above. If you have a sense of the premises of those two stories, you instantly think sisters and survival. (Maybe also singing.)

- **When it is new, period.** In 2010, a writer named Karen Rivers queried me about a middle-grade novel called *The Encyclopedia of Me*, which focused on a twelve-year-old girl who gets grounded for the summer and decides to create an encyclopedia of her life. The novel was actually written in alphabetical encyclopedia entries, from "Aa" to "Zoo," with some lovely, funny, heartfelt action with the protagonist's family, best friend, and the cute boy next door worked in. The originality of the A–Z structure immediately grabbed my attention as an editor, because it distinguished the book from the usual run of domestic middle-grade novels, while the rich voice and characterizations made the novel more than just a clever trick. Editors and agents love original premises like this because they make a book extremely easy to describe and therefore sell.

- **When the premise pairs compelling external action with the opportunity for strong character development.** If you look back at the list of sample premises I offered earlier—from *Openly Straight* by Bill Konigsberg (‡), *Where the Mountain Meets the Moon* by Grace Lin, *From the Mixed-Up Files of Mrs. Basil E. Frankweiler* by E. L. Konigsburg, *The Fault in Our Stars* by John Green, and *Cleopatra's Moon* by Vicky Alvear Shecter (‡), respectively—they all feature a powerful challenge posed to their protagonist's original life or way of being, matched with compelling or exciting physical action, as we see the effort of living a deception, the adventure of a long journey with dragons and friends, the sophisticated pleasure of hiding in an art museum, the drama of love in the face of death, and the glamour and heartbreak of having one of history's most famous women as your mother. That pairing of internal and external drama promises readers both rich substance and high entertainment—a hard-to-resist combination at any age.

- **When it fills a hole in the market.** In *Divided We Fall* by Trent Reedy (‡), Danny Wright is a seventeen-year-old boy who likes his truck, his girlfriend, country music, and guns, and serves in the National Guard in his native Idaho. I knew a lot of guys like this while growing up in a small town in Missouri, but there are very few YA novels that might speak to this kind of country boy. As a result, I was excited to publish *Divided We Fall* for that guy and others like him.

- **When it works well for an editor's publishing house.** No matter how terrific I think an adult novel manuscript might be, it will never, ever work for me at Scholastic, because our expertise and sales and marketing infrastructure point entirely toward publishing children's and YA books. On the other hand, if I receive a great middle-grade fantasy, I know we can sell the heck out of it, thanks to both our proven track record with such books and our school book clubs and book fairs. Every publisher has its own particular strengths and weaknesses, and if a premise suits a house's strengths or special markets, it becomes especially saleable to the editors there.

So what makes premises *less* saleable? Note I am not saying *not* saleable; all of these terms will be in the eye of the beholder, and novels in any and all of the following categories get published every day. But when one of these situations applies to a manuscript, publishers might decide that its "satisfactory audience of book buyers" is not quite satisfactory enough:

- **When the concept has been overdone.** If I've seen a manuscript's central premise before, and the project doesn't distinguish itself through fresh characterizations, excellent writing, or new twists on the plot or theme, it's easy to turn it down.
- **When the concept is written for the wrong age group.** A picture book about losing your virginity, say.
- **When the premise is too dense, quiet, or nebulous.** This can happen when a premise requires three sentences of backstory to set up the central conflict; the external action isn't all that dramatic or interesting; the stakes are extremely low; or it's difficult to define or explain either the internal or external action.

These situations absolutely do not mean the novel would be *impossible* to sell, either to an editor or in the marketplace. After all, the premise of

Eleanor & Park is that two outsiders fall in love, which could easily be dismissed as both quiet and overdone. But the richness of the characterizations and writing in the book made the novel so extraordinary that it became a word-of-mouth phenomenon and a beloved bestseller in spite of its softer premise. It's extremely useful to have a strong premise for all the reasons I've listed here. But if you don't have one—if you're writing a book where the premise doesn't get across the actual promise of the book—your novel can still succeed, so long as other aspects of the text offer readers a compelling and pleasurable experience.

- **When a publisher can't envision or reach the audience.** Again I'm going to cite that middle-grade novel in Elizabethan blank verse. Are there a thousand readers in the United States who would be up for that? Yes, as it might get great reviews, or people might buy it out of curiosity. If I were going to publish it, are the book sales from those one thousand readers enough to pay the author a decent advance, cover my time costs in editing it, and cover my company's publishing costs in designing, proofreading, printing, marketing, and distributing it? Well, no.

This is why it's terrific that there are so many different publishers in the world, because a smaller, more literary independent press, like Soft Skull or Graywolf, might know how to reach those exact readers through its very specialized marketing to very literary audiences. They would also pay a smaller advance and have a smaller print run at first, but the book would be present in the world, where it would have an opportunity to break out and find more readers. Or, if you are the author of this book and you know exactly how to reach those thousand readers yourself, self-publishing might be the right choice for you, because you get to connect with those readers directly and keep all the profits. So I'm not saying the premise isn't saleable for anyone ever. I'm just saying it wouldn't be saleable for *me*, at the publisher I work for at the moment, at the present time in the middle-grade publishing market. Saleability depends very much on time and place.

Agents and editors love to find a saleable premise that's right for us because it makes it easy for us to do the sales parts of our jobs. Help us out and write a story that has that saleability built in.

═ EXERCISES ═

Write down the promises of the novel you're working on now. What emotions does it offer to a reader?

Write the premise of the novel in one sentence. You may be able to create several premises here, each highlighting different story lines or other aspects of the book, but ideally each should show the book's central internal dimension and external action, and its promises, freshness, or accomplishments.

Identify three comparison titles for the book—that is, books to which your book might rationally be compared, because of similarities in their action, promise, or overall spirit. Comps are often phrased in the "meets" terms above, and they're extremely useful in describing or positioning your novel to others.

Developing an Idea into a Premise and Story

Developing a story is a continual process of figuring out the answers to five interrelated interjections:

- **"Who?"** Who is our protagonist, the person we will follow through the story? What milieu does he come from? What does he want?
- **"Ouch!"** Once you know who that person is, you need to find obstacles that will stand in the way of his desire, as well as other factors that will create internal and external drama for him. These obstacles will make him and us readers say, "Ouch!" (sometimes literally)—and we will then read on, to see how he escapes that painful situation.

- **"What?"** This protagonist and his obstacles must be integrated into a coherent reality, and every part of that reality should be interconnected and organic. As a result, when you create any item in this world, you need to ask what its relationship is to the rest of that world, and find those connections.

- **"Why?"** You also must keep asking "why" of everything you discover, to develop both the causes of the action and appropriate obstacles to it. Let's say you want to write a story where a boy is kidnapped by pirates. Why would the pirates want this child? They might seek revenge against his parents (or maybe his nanny, a former pirate herself). They might want a ransom from the parents (or maybe the country, if he is a prince of the realm). Perhaps he has a treasure map tattooed on his back. (And how would this have come about?) Perhaps they need a cabin boy and they saw him sweeping the sidewalk outside of a bakery in exchange for bread. (Why didn't he just steal the bread? Who or what in his past gave him the moral character to work for food instead?) Each answer will open up further questions that reveal more about the personality and circumstances of your protagonist and his world, and thus more possibilities for his story to follow.

- **"So?"** What is the effect of this emotionally on the character and reader? What does it mean thematically to all of us? Why would we care?

If you start out with an answer to any one of these questions, or a situation to inspire the "Ouch!," an entire novel can unfold before you—but it will take some digging. Let's walk through the development of a story from each interjection.

Starting from "Who?": Turning a Character into a Story

Perhaps you have a vague idea for a character—some human figure or detail that has caught at your mind and made you want to know more about this person. It might be a line of dialogue, overheard or imagined; an action, like a mountain biker crashing at the bottom of a hill, but getting up and pushing on anyway; a real person you glimpsed across a coffee shop; or a childhood friend who moved away. Start by taking a close look at the details you know and extrapolating more information from them. Perhaps this person in the coffee shop was wearing motorcycle boots under yoga pants and a *Doctor Who* T-shirt. What do each of those individual items tell us about him? What does the whole ensemble say? If he has bright red hair, what might that indicate about his family history? Perhaps your childhood friend loved to jump off swings at their highest point. What qualities gave her that daredevil attitude? What consequences followed from it, if any?

Using the twenty-things brainstorming method (see p. 36), make a list of at least twenty items you know or can imagine about this person. They can be as small as his love of broccoli or as large as being abandoned by his dad when he was six. They don't have to be big, definitive, or final, either, as you can always change them later, as you get to know this person better or find he needs to have different qualities in order to suit your story. The goal is to bring that vague image into sharper focus. Once you feel you've brainstormed enough to have a decent sense of who this person is, assign your character a name and a setting, and fill out the following chart for him. (You can have more than one answer in each category—you should, in fact.)

	WHY?
WANTS	
NEEDS	
FEARS	
LOVES	
HATES	

The "Why?" in all of this should flesh out her backstory—the history, personality quirks, and circumstances through which she developed the wants, needs, fears, and so on. Once you have those things, it should be easy to identify an "Ouch!" for the character: Create an obstacle to her getting what she wants or keeping something she loves. Confront her with her fear or something she hates. Or figure out a story that will give her what she needs, however painful that might be, and whether she knows she needs it or not. Indeed, your plot will often be driven by the character's wants—the action she takes to achieve her desire—while the deeper emotional development of the book will come about through the fulfillment of her needs, as she gains some new dimension she truly requires to become a more complete human being. When both the character's wants and needs have been addressed, the story is over.

Back at the beginning: What will happen when the character is confronted with that "Ouch!"? What will she do next, and how might that change her circumstances? Follow the consequences of her character and how she seeks to get past the obstacle, and you should be well on your way to a novel.

Starting from "Ouch!": Turning a Situation into a Story

A boy is kidnapped by pirates. A girl's mother is dying of ovarian cancer. A brother and sister are caught in a hurricane in 1926 Miami. Our world, but suddenly everyone has ESP. All of these situations have an "Ouch!" built in: the potential for conflict within a character's life, thanks to a challenge or loss.

To develop that conflict into a story, again, start with some brainstorming. List at least twenty things a character might encounter in navigating this situation, ranging from the everyday—having to swab the decks of the pirate ship—to the apocalyptic—flooding might overtake the entire Floridian peninsula. (If the action is set in a fantasy world or at another time in history, you may need to do some world-building or research before you can make this list.) Keep going as long as you can. When you feel like you've exhausted your powers of invention, look at your list. Which possibilities interest you? What potential scenes are you most excited to write? If the story might have a natural climax—for instance, the passing of the hurricane—what would that be? If you struggled to come up with this

An Aside: Character- vs. Premise-Driven Books

I've heard writers say that sometimes as they're writing merrily away, their protagonists will take on independent life and want to go chasing after something not provided for in the plot. Should they follow the protagonist, these writers ask, or should they stick with their planned plot?

There is no one-size-fits-all answer here, but I would say you should write toward whichever element you care about more—the protagonist or the situation. Still, even if the situation would win that battle, I suggest giving your protagonist free rein for five pages just to see what might happen. This whim might end up connecting back to the situation in a new and interesting way. Or it might turn out to be more intriguing than your original conception of the situation, and it will be deeper and more emotionally powerful, too, because it comes from the protagonist's character and heart.

While books on writing (including this one) will tend to praise character-driven plots over premise-driven ones (as I just did), readers themselves don't much care so long as they get a good story—and premise-driven plots are excellent at delivering story. I think of character-driven books as ones in which the protagonist and his/her nature and desire bring about the central action, while in premise-driven books, external forces or other characters bring the action to the protagonist. If Katniss Everdeen founded the Hunger Games and made everyone participate, it would be character-driven; as it is, it's more premise-driven, because she must join the Games against her will, and most of the challenges within the arena are imposed by the gamemakers. *The Fault in Our Stars*, on the other hand, is character-driven, because beyond the original setup, Hazel and Augustus constantly make the choices that take their relationship deeper, thus driving the plot.

Nobody's life is 100 percent character-driven: We are all always creating the action in our lives and reacting to outside forces at the same time. If you have a premise-driven book, be careful that your protagonist and his choices generate enough action in the book that he doesn't seem passive, which equals boring. If you have a character-driven book, make sure interesting things happen in it.

list, then the idea might be too thin to sustain an entire book. But if you can find at least ten potential points of action, danger, or conflict for your characters, then you can turn those into scenes, arrange them in order of ascending drama, and have a rough outline for a novel.

Another thing to pay attention to within this list: Can you see any thematic ideas or connections emerging from it? A novel about a boy who joins up with pirates could very easily be about family—whether he belongs with his family, or whether he can create a new family with the pirates, or whether he needs a family at all. It might also be about freedom, and where people truly find their freedom: in civil society, or outside of it, as the boy chooses between a life of relative order vs. rampaging around the high seas. If different thematic directions like these are possible, which ones speak to you most? How could you develop the story further to address them?

Finally, think about the kinds of characters who might be involved in this situation. What range of ages, occupations, abilities, or talents would be necessary to navigate it? For instance, in the ovarian-cancer situation, the girl would probably meet her mother's doctor and nurse, and have to work closely with other family members in caring for her; in the ESP situation, someone with strong mental discipline or an inquisitive brain might be especially gifted at mind-reading. Assemble your cast, then choose or shape a protagonist through whom the story will be told. If a protagonist does not immediately present himself, ask yourself, "Who would suffer most from this situation?" and build a character from the answer. Note that I'm not referring to physical suffering here, because most physical suffering isn't very interesting or distinctive—*nobody* likes swabbing the deck. I mean emotional, mental, or moral suffering, the kind of experience that will be unique to every individual in a particular circumstance, which then forces that character toward growth and change. This sort of suffering lifts your premise from a story, which is a sequence of events, to a plot, which imbues those events with meaning. (We'll explore these ideas more in the plot section.)

So what kind of boy would suffer from being kidnapped by pirates and grow in an interesting way?

- A spoiled brat made to swab the deck would suffer because his ideas of his own importance would be challenged.

- A son of a Royal Navy captain who was raised on his father's ship would suffer because he might hate the pirates' disorder; he'd have to work through the competing value systems of what he was taught growing up and how he has to live now.

- A kid who grew up boasting his father was a fearsome pirate captain, and then discovers Dad is actually the mediocre scallywag Yellowbeard, would suffer from the loss of that illusion, and the pain of having to rebuild his vision of his father, and who he is in turn.

Each possibility suggests further refinements on the original kidnapping situation or directions it could go. There is no shame in jerry-rigging a character to serve a situation or plot; there is only shame in not doing it well. And once you have the basic concept for your protagonist established, you can go back to the ideas suggested in the previous section, about starting a novel from "Who?," and use those to develop the protagonist into someone who can function well within this plot. Take those character points and your list of scenes, and you've made a strong start.

Starting from "What?": Turning a Line, Emotion, or Image into a Story

You hear someone say on the street, "So when Sweetpea ran away, Lucille *LOST. HER. MIND.*"—and as a writer, you can't help wondering: "Who's Sweetpea? Who's Lucille?" From this, you start thinking about times you lost your own mind, more or less—the grief that got you there, the situation that occasioned it, the doubled pain of that situation plus the fear and misery of your own breakdown. Then you see a LOST DOG poster on a telephone pole with a picture of a German shepherd snarling at the camera. She's standing on a pink gingham blanket with some hunting rifles propped in the background. The dog's name? Sweetpea.

Every element in this situation could make a great start to a story. To develop a specific situation or feeling into a narrative, don't brainstorm outwardly, but dive deep. *For a line of dialogue*: Who said it? Why would they say it, and to whom? If these two interlocutors are talking about a third person, like Lucille, what's the relationship between Lucille and the speaker? How would Lucille have acquired Sweetpea? Why might Sweetpea have run away? What did both characters do next? *For an image*: Look back at the photographer exercise under "Observational Skill" at the end of Chapter 3, "Proficiency and Practice," and ask the questions there (and above about the line) to start a story. What can that pink gingham blanket tell you about Lucille? What does Sweetpea's snarl reveal? *For a feeling*: Sit with this emotion and note all of its dimensions. When you lost your mind, for instance, was it entirely awful? Or might there have been some release in the wildness, some pleasure in the complete letting-go? What caused the loss? What happened afterward? What might the relationship between Lucille and Sweetpea have been like, to inspire a similar loss in her? Then replace the word "idea" with "feeling" in each of the questions in the "Theme" section that follows, and work through your answers.

Starting from "So?": Turning a Theme into a Story

Suppose you have a philosophical idea you want to explore through a story, like the extent of our ethical responsibilities toward people we don't know, or the ability of humans to fully conquer nature.

✎ **Is this an idea you want to explore, or one you want to illustrate?** (That is, do you feel you already know your answer to the theme's question?) If you want to explore the idea, try to restate it as a question: "What are our ethical responsibilities to people we don't know?" If you have an existing opinion that you want to illustrate, make this thematic idea into a statement: "We have no ethical responsibilities toward people we don't know." (Oh, look! You're writing Ayn Rand's lost YA novel!) It's understandable to want the story to express and support your point of view, whatever it may be. The great danger here is that the novel might become didactic, as it exists to illustrate your point of view, and then antidramatic or boring, as all of the action will barrel toward your already determined conclusion. To counteract that, you will need to flesh all of your characters out as fully as you possibly can, including the characters who oppose your opinion, and develop a strong plot in which your perspective doesn't automatically win in every situation.

⮑ **What situations might enact this idea?** Either way, try the twenty-point brainstorm by coming up with twenty situations that might dramatize your chosen idea. The question about humans' control of nature, for instance, could resonate in stories involving genetics (see *Jurassic Park*), physics (the atom bomb), home construction (as tree roots can displace a house's foundation), climate change, animals (*The Yearling*), psychology and physiology (what are the long-term effects of a drug that suppresses a basic human need?), and politics (as politicians debate infrastructure projects that one big storm might destroy). Once you have that list, look for the situation that interests you most, and one where a child or YA character could realistically be involved and take action. (What if he was the subject of the genetics experiment? Perhaps she owns the animal?) With your situation in hand, consider:

⮑ **What are the range of possible reactions to this thematic idea/statement?** Brainstorm a list of those, and then you can create your cast of characters to embody those different reactions. For instance, in a story about our responsibility toward people we don't know, you could have a teenage girl who spends every afternoon volunteering at a local homeless shelter; a teenage boy who is devoted only to himself and having a good time; a reporter for their school paper, who sees himself as performing a service with his journalism; a teacher who disapproves of the girl's volunteer activities, as they distract her from the academic work she needs to do for college; the girl's aunt, a Catholic nun, who encourages her to think about not just local work but about structural change to combat poverty; the guests at the shelter, who are each unique individuals with complex histories . . .

Once you have a wide-ranging cast, choose the two characters who are most diametrically opposed and set them in conflict. As they work out that conflict, they will end up dramatizing the idea and its complexities. Or take the character whose opinion fascinates, compels, or repels you most, and run the Wants/Needs/Fears/Loves/Hates/ Why chart on him or her. Turn the opposite opinion into that character's "Ouch!," and you can tie it back to this thematic idea.

∾

Where do writers get their ideas? Everywhere. But the actual magic lies in making one idea real—specific in your mind and solid on the page. Are you ready for that? Let's get to work.

CHAPTER 5

Effort and Flow

How to Write a Novel

Writer, Know Thyself. Think about how you wrote papers in school or how you like to approach any large task. Do you prefer to blast through a project and clean up the details later? Or do you like to polish things piece by perfect piece? Are you disciplined about setting aside writing time? Motivated by deadlines? Or do you need to be responsible to someone, like a writing partner or group? Whatever your style is, try to set up a working method that suits it. There is no shame in any habit that helps you get the work done.

Invest the Time. Many writers establish a routine with a set time of day, a place, and a goal—a word or page count, a scene, a time period. (As Robert Pinsky said, "Take the time to write. You can do your life's work in a half hour a day"; Richard Rhodes adds, "A page a day is a book a year.") But if a fixed routine isn't possible with your life circumstances or just isn't the way you work best, that's fine too. The only requirement for becoming a writer is doing the writing.

Defeat Distractions. Put your phone in airplane mode and leave it in another room during your writing time. Download an Internet blocker for your computer (Mac Freedom, Anti-Social, WasteNoTime) and use it as necessary. Some writers keep a notebook by their computer or a journal/freewrite file on the desktop that allows them to note passing thoughts and reminders without leaving their working document. If you have a hard time getting started, try the Pomodoro Technique: Set a timer for twenty-five minutes and force yourself to write until it rings. Or end each day's work in the middle of a sentence or scene, so you always have something obvious to complete when you come back to the manuscript.

Develop a Framework. Before you dive in, it is useful to have at least a general sense of the premise, your protagonist, his or her desire, a couple big scenes, and the climax or ending. All of those things can absolutely change in the writing, but setting out with them in mind will give you a character and situation to play with up front, and something to write toward in the long term.

Finish a Draft. Your first major goal is to finish a first draft of a novel, and you must complete a first draft of one of the first four novels you start. No matter how messy the book itself is, the accomplishment and discipline of writing all the way to the end will teach you things about novel writing that you can only learn through that act.

Explore. In the meantime, your job for the first draft is to explore: to find out what characters spark both for you and on the page, what the story is, what the book is about—to locate the heart and spirit of the project. If you can find that spirit and keep to it as you write your first draft, feel free to ignore mechanical issues like changing a character's name halfway through, or the fact that you didn't really set up that plot twist you now love. You can easily tidy up those details in revision, but you can't revise text that hasn't been written, and right now you just need to get that text on the page. As Jane Smiley says, "Every first draft is perfect, because all a first draft has to do is exist."

Expect and Accept Bumps in the Road. It is 99 percent guaranteed that at some point in this process, you will feel lost, overwhelmed, worthless, talentless, stupid, stuck, or all of the above. This is an absolutely normal stage in writing, and stressing about these emotions will only pull you deeper into the spiral. Step away from the manuscript itself for a while to get a little clarity.

- Feeling stuck usually comes from dishonesty, confusion, or fear: You aren't telling the truth about your characters or their situation; you've either lost or never found the spirit of the novel; or you fear being judged or you're judging yourself in every line—a sure formula for writerly paralysis. Do some freewriting or journaling about your problems to suss out your concerns and find your way back to that spirit. What inspired you to write this novel in the first place? What are you afraid of now? What would help you overcome that fear?
- Give yourself permission to write badly. Again, all you're doing in this first draft is exploring, playing, making things up. You will have many opportunities to revise this text, and even then, nobody else has to see this book unless you choose to publish it. Be kind to yourself. It's okay not to have it right.
- Bookmap the material you already have. (For a description of a bookmap, see p. 157.) This will reacquaint you with what you've written so far while also giving you some distance to look at it objectively. Where does the story truly start? What ideas, characters, and developments in it do you really like? What isn't working so well for you? How can you build on the good stuff?
- Forget the plot and just hang out with your characters for a while. Your protagonist: What is she excited about at the moment? Who's her best friend? How's her relationship with her dad? Go for a walk and daydream conversations with her, or what she'd say about what you see around town. The more you know about her, the more possibilities might shake loose for her story.

- Read a book that isn't in the same genre/age group as your novel, and isn't directly related to it, but speaks to its spirit in some way. (Poetry can be good to get thoughts and images flowing.)

Trust the Flow. Once you develop a writing process, trust it. If you get in a flow, don't break it. You can write scenes out of order if you like, but in doing so, you are making a promise to your book that you will go back and fill in the missing scenes, and revise the scenes you wrote first so the whole narrative hangs together. If you don't have the discipline to do this, try not to write scenes out of order.

Don't Be Afraid to Ask for Help. If you're puzzling over something, call up your critique partner or editor and take a half hour to talk through a difficulty. You will need to define the problem you're facing in order to describe it to them, which can be useful on its own, and then they can help you untwist its knots or brainstorm solutions. But do this sparingly; often the value of solving a narrative problem lies in the struggle of it, and if an author was calling me every week, I'd start to think he needed to do more of his own thinking.

Secure Your Data. Back up your computer frequently, or e-mail your working files to an account in the cloud. Paste anything you must cut into an outtakes file. This costs you very little in time and digital space, and it allows you the security of knowing nothing has been lost if you want to use it later.

Celebrate Completion! It is a real accomplishment to finish a first draft, and many wannabe writers never even reach that step. Treat yourself to a massage, a new book, a nice dinner out.

Take Time Off. Unless you require momentum to keep working on a writing project, put the manuscript away for a minimum of two days and a maximum of two months before revising it, so you can approach it with a reader's fresh eyes instead of a writer's fond heart. To clear your mind, work on a different writing project in the meantime.

Reread. Your second major goal is to revise the first draft you completed. When you're ready to dive back in, change the font of the manuscript and then print it out on paper. Do not start actual revisions as yet; instead, require yourself to read all the way through the draft, taking notes on both the material you like and what needs work. (At this stage, you could also try some of the techniques from Chapter 17, "Vision and Revision.")

What should you revise toward? Try to maximize the principles from Chapter 1 as applied to your particular project. Here those principles can be shorthanded to four Ds: Revisions should increase the *drama* of your action, *dimension* of your characters, *distinction* of your prose, and *depth* of your themes and the reality of the whole.

Create a To-Do List. Based on your notes from your reread and other observations, create a to-do list of tasks you want to accomplish in the manuscript in order to stay focused through the morass of revision. Only once you have that full view, and possibly the opinion of another reader (see the next point in this list), may you go back and start revising the text itself.

Solicit the Opinions of Others, but Cautiously. Be careful when you get feedback, and from whom. If you're the kind of person who wilts under criticism, it may be worth trying to get a whole draft done and even revised before you seek outside counsel. When that time comes, try to choose a person who thinks critically, who is on your wavelength literarily, who will be both kind and honest with you, and who can articulate feedback beyond "I liked it" or "I didn't." (If you don't have a friend like this in your social circle, find a critique partner in person or online.) If you receive the critique in person, don't speak while the critiquer offers their initial response; this is your opportunity not to say what you meant in the text, but to hear what an unbiased reader took away from it. When it is your turn to talk, ask the critiquer to tell you what they see as the key idea or point of the manuscript, then what is serving that idea or point vs. what isn't. (This goes for professional critique as well: If an editor or agent has a different vision of the project than you do, and you can't see your way to happily combining their vision with yours, it's probably not going to be a productive relationship.) If your critiquer doesn't offer any positive feedback, ask what they like about the present manuscript so you know what *is* working for them, and you can get a sense of the standard you should be aiming for. Take careful notes or use an audio recorder to tape the critique so you can review and process what was said in a calm frame of mind. Once you've sorted out the feedback that seems useful to you, incorporate your plans for responding to it in your to-do list.

Everything Can Change. In revising, remember: *You* made all of this up. Nothing in the book is set in stone, and you can rewrite any or all of it at any time to make its pieces snap together more elegantly. I call this idea the "Bechard Factor" after the experience of an author I work with, Trent Reedy. Trent wrote the early drafts of his book *Words in the Dust* while completing his MFA at the Vermont College of Fine Arts, where he was mentored for one semester by the novelist Margaret Bechard. In one of those drafts, a supporting character named Meena lived in a cave, which required the protagonist to spend a lot of time sneaking out of the village to visit her. Bechard asked Trent why Meena couldn't just live in the village, and Trent said, "Because she lives in a cave." That was the way he had first imagined her, and he hadn't had any reason to rethink his initial instinct. But the cave wasn't essential to either Meena's characterization or the role she played in the plot, and when Trent revised the novel, he brought Meena into town, which allowed the action to flow more easily. Keep an eye out for moments where some aspect of your first conception of the novel is getting in the way of larger and more important plot, character, or thematic dynamics or goals, and revise accordingly.

Keep Your Eyes on the Prize. And the prize is not making the text "perfect"—an impossible and illusory goal—but finishing a manuscript to the best of your present writing abilities, and sharing it with readers. That's really it.

Skip the Comparison Game. You will end up comparing yourself to other writers—it's an inescapable feature of the literary life. Remember that *everyone* finds the process difficult at times. *Everyone* has to revise. Katherine Paterson, John Green, Jacqueline Woodson, Sherman Alexie, J. K. Rowling: All of them were once where you are now. They all have bad writing days, they all have to toss material, they all get edited, and they probably all grump about the process. What makes them successful is that they put in the time and do the work—and you can do that, too.

Choose Your Shots. Any piece of writing can be made better through the application of time, thought, heart, and effort. Not all writing is worth these resources. The only way to learn which work is worth it is by doing a lot of writing, getting feedback on it, figuring out what most pleases both you and your readers, and moving in that direction.

If You Enjoyed the Process and Created Something You Love: Repeat.

CHAPTER 6

Intention and Invention

Identifying Your Points

At this moment in the book, we're going to transition from talking about the act of writing to the art of craft—how to use the elements of fiction to create a satisfying and artistically whole novel. As writers may be reading this at many different stages in their processes, I'll note that there are some things you can't know about or shouldn't ask of a novel until you've completed a first draft of it, and that's especially true of this chapter, where identifying your points too early may shut off some useful avenues of exploration. If you're reading this before you have a finished draft, try to hold the ideas lightly until they might become useful.

When I sit down to evaluate a manuscript I'm editing and figure out how I want to respond to the author, the first thing I do is identify the book's point. The "point" is my personal term for the idea or experience that the novel has been written to convey. It might be to scare the bejee-zus out of your reader, or make him fall on the floor laughing or crying. It might be a moral lesson, like that cheating on a test is bad. It might be the exploration of an idea: why people have to suffer, what happens after we die, whether the joy caused by love is worth its pain. And it might be—indeed, probably ought to be—more than one of these: a whole nexus of ideas, emotions, and intentions that together create the ethos of the book.

Every decision that you make as an author should ultimately be in the service of this nexus, going toward the ends you want to achieve for yourself and for the reader. These decisions get made in three main areas:

- **The plot**—the structure of the book's story.
- **The characters**—the people who bring that story to life, and who must come to life themselves.
- **The voice**—the human intelligence and personality behind the story's telling. A wise person once said, "All art is where you put the camera," and we're going to explore that idea in detail later.

A lot of these decisions are made unconsciously: You hear a voice in your head, and that naturally becomes the voice of your narrator. Or you're writing about a magnetic older man, and you automatically give him aspects of your incredibly charismatic father. But these unconscious choices don't always suit the larger needs of your story. To know whether they work for those larger needs, you first need to know what those larger needs *are*; and that requires defining the points of your book.

So, to repeat the questions I posed when discussing intentionality earlier: What do you want to do with your book? What do you want your book to do for readers?

Over time, I've found four useful ways to break these huge questions down into more manageable pieces, addressing in turn the writer's heart, the reader's experience, the protagonist's growth, and the book's philosophical issues or themes.

1. What about this book is making you write it? This is the *core* of the book.
2. What is its overarching emotional experience for the reader? This is its *experiential point*.
3. What does the main character discover through the events of the book? This is its *emotional point*.
4. What idea do those events come together to show? This is its *thematic point*.

You might know your exact answers to each of these questions from the moment you pick up a pen, or—far more likely—you'll discover them in the course of writing, or as you reread, consider, and revise your first draft. Looking at a completed manuscript from all of these angles ensures that you're writing the book you want to write, which offers a satisfying experience to its audience, takes its protagonist on a complete emotional journey, and finally strives to say something about the way we live in the world. We'll return to these ideas often throughout this book.

The Core

This idea comes directly from Maggie Stiefvater, the *New York Times* bestselling author of the Shiver trilogy, *The Scorpio Races*, and the Raven Cycle, among other books. She defined the term "core" with characteristic punch in a 2010 blog post about revision:

> Core is what your novel is. It's not what your novel is *about*. It's the thing that made you want to tell this story and no other. It's the theme, or the character, or the setting that made you love it. You have to know what the specific core of your novel is, because that's all that you're going to consider sacred. *Everything* else is negotiable.*

To put this concept into questions: What powers this book for you? What within the story gets you to the computer each morning? What is the most important thing you want your novel to convey or to accomplish? What is the thing you will not give up in it, no matter who tells you to do so?

As Stiefvater goes on to say, you don't get to reply to that last question with "Everything"—you get, at most, *two* answers here, two things that are inviolate. After that, you have to be willing to change just about anything in the novel if those revisions will get you closer to conveying that core to the reader. Thus it can become a powerful anchor through both

---

* See http://maggiestiefvater.com/blog/revision-nothing-is-sacred-except-for-the-stuff-that-is/ for the full and excellent post.

the writing and revision processes, when so much else is up in the air: As you have to make choices about the characters, story, or voice, you always have your core as a pole star, the thing you most want to reach and serve.

=== *EXERCISE* ===

What is your novel's core?

_____

The Experiential Point

The experiential point is what you want readers to *feel* as a result of the book, the emotional experience you want them to have in reading it. Clearly readers' emotions will vary with events from scene to scene. But you will likely have some overarching emotional tone and purpose for the entire novel: Do you want readers to be terrified? Swooning? Exhilarated? Do you want them to learn something? Think about an idea or issue? Or just have a good time?

As an example, consider *The Fault in Our Stars* by John Green, a novel about two teenagers with cancer, in love, and facing death. While I don't know John Green's intentions (and he would say the author's intentions don't matter once a book is in a reader's hands), given his choice of subject matter, it feels safe to theorize that his experiential points were (a) that we readers should fall in love with Hazel Grace and Augustus as they fall in love with each other, and (b) that we should cry our eyes out. (As a reader, I did both.) Since Green is a writer of a more literary bent, he also poses and answers enormous questions about the marks we leave on the world, what true heroism looks like, how much writers and readers each own a story, and what happens after that story ends. Another experiential point, then, surely, was (c) to inspire readers to reflect on these questions—and, for Green, it was likely a core value to work out and put forth his answers to them.

After the core, your experiential point should guide your narrative choices above all else, as you should always turn toward creating or sustaining that overarching feeling. If you're writing a horror novel, you should make plot choices that jeopardize your protagonist's safety and thus terrify or unbalance your reader. If you're writing a realistic, thoughtful novel, its voice should reflect that thoughtfulness more than emotional extremity. Calibrate everything in the novel to work toward your experiential ends.

═══ EXERCISE ═══

What is your novel's experiential point?

The Emotional Point

What does your character learn or discover emotionally between the beginning and ending of the novel? How does that character change as a result? Your answers are your emotional point. At the beginning of *The Fault in Our Stars*, Hazel Grace is depressed, in part because she is dying of cancer—a fact that does not change by the end. Yet through falling in love with Augustus, and the conversations and further experiences their relationship incites, she comes to a better understanding of and more peace with her place in the universe. Discovering that peace is her emotional journey, and the emotional point.

Emotional points matter to readers because of the readers' own connections to the character. If the character perceives something incorrectly throughout the novel—seeing herself as more influential than she is, let's say—then we readers will often make that mistake alongside her, especially if the novel is written in first person or stays relatively close to her point of view. Then, when she recognizes her real place in the world, we share all of her feelings at that discovery: the humiliation and pain of the mistake and its consequences, perhaps, but also the wisdom and humility she might have going forward. The character's emotional journey thus forms a second experiential track in the novel that can work in harmony or counterpoint with the overall experiential point.

=== EXERCISE ===

What is your novel's emotional point?

The Thematic Point

The writer David Lodge said, "A novel is a long answer to the question, 'What is it about?'"—and the thematic point is, indeed, that larger philosophical subject of your book. In *The Fault in Our Stars,* it's the many thematic ideas I listed earlier—the marks we leave on the world and so forth—which Green raises through the action and the characters' own discussion of them. You could phrase the ideas in your thematic point as questions: For instance, as I said earlier, you might write a novel to dramatize the question, "Is the joy caused by love worth its pain?" Or if you feel you know the answers from the beginning, you can write forth accordingly: "The joy caused by love is *not* worth its pain, and I'm going to write a novel to prove it!"

In all cases, the events of the novel should come together to show the thematic point. If you felt strongly that the joy caused by love is not worth its pain, you might show your protagonist falling in love, and the incredible bliss it brought him for a brief time. His beloved could then depart—via death, or betrayal, or frankly whatever will hurt the protagonist most—and we'd see the even more incredible suffering he goes through because of the beloved's exit and the bleakness of that unloved state. If reading your novel then makes a reader feel that love would surely never, ever be worth it, congratulations! You have achieved your thematic point. (You have also likely depressed everyone involved, but so it goes.)

EXERCISE

What idea do the events of your novel come together to show? What is your thematic point? (Alternatively or additionally here: Make a list of all the thematic ideas or questions you'd like your novel to explore, or that it already does.)

As you can see from the examples I've cited, you can have more than one answer in each of these categories, if you're exploring a lot of different ideas, or if your protagonist is working through a number of different issues emotionally. Indeed, the more you're exploring, the richer and more complex your novel can be. Still, if you do have multiple ideas in your book, try to have a nexus of no more than four main points (let's say) in each category, and to look for as many connections among your core and those points as possible. The more closely you can make your core, points, action, characters, and prose work together toward similar ends, the more aesthetically integrated and satisfying your book will be.

Caveats and Process

Having said all this, I'll admit it is entirely possible to write a novel without building in emotional or thematic points, and furthermore, the resulting book can be really enjoyable. The *Goosebumps* books don't end with the protagonists recognizing any larger philosophical truths; the heroes of *Captain Underpants* don't grow emotionally; and if we widen the field to include adult novels, probably about half of all fiction skips these categories entirely. That's because emotional growth or thematic complexity isn't where the pleasure of fiction comes from for many readers. Rather, they choose novels for the explosions or chase scenes, the world-building or kissing, the joys of the adventure, or the humor or vicarious glamour or thrills. I'd go so far as to say that often readers don't *want* the challenge that emotional concerns or larger philosophical questions bring up; they just want to be lost in a story.

I think that is perfectly fair. We all read fiction for pleasure foremost, and if a book lives up to the promises it sets out for us—if it fulfills its experiential point—we usually call it a "good book." Still, because the kind of fiction I read, edit, think about, and love most reaches for emotional and thematic points, those are the expectations and standards I'm going to talk about going forward. The adult novelist Caleb Crain defined literary depth as writing that has "a sense of the complexity of reality," and literary fiction will often display that complexity via a plot driven primarily by the characters; characters who are themselves complex and interesting; and distinctive writing, where the thoughts and the expressions of the thought are original and could belong only to this one writer or character. If you're writing a book where you're not striving for those qualities or emotional or thematic points, then you can just tune out anytime I mention them and focus on the structural ideas here instead.

I put a lot of emphasis on figuring out the core and points of your novel because, in revision, they become a yardstick by which you can measure everything else in the book. (And I emphasize "in revision," because I think most writers discover their points as they write their first drafts, which is as it should be.) Once you've identified these ends, you can take a second look at the characters, plots, and voice, and see how each of them is contributing—or not—to what you want to accomplish. Alternatively, you can take what you love within the characters, plot, and voice, and adapt your points to fit. If your experiential point is to write a rip-roaring adventure, but your main character spends most of her page time brooding over her relationship with her best friend, you're either going to need to kick that character into action, or refocus your intentions for the novel to explore her friendship instead. Or suppose you want to delve into the familial themes brought up by losing a baby brother, but you can't help cracking potty jokes every four lines; again, you'll likely have to adjust either your point or your voice to tell an emotionally integrated story.

After I identify the points of a manuscript I'm editing, I have a conversation with the author, where we dig into our visions of the book and discuss what revisions are necessary to achieve those goals. This diagram summarizes the overall process:

Points / Goals / Big Ideas

What do we want this book to do?

Plot & Character Definition

What characters and events do we need to achieve that aim?

Plot & Character Mechanics

*How can those best work together
to maximize sensibility, credibility, and elegance?*

Scene-Level Polishing

Let's make the prose shine.

Of course, the actual work is never that simple and clean; we're constantly talking about definitions during the mechanics step, and checking in with our points throughout. But it all starts with getting a clear sense of what the book should be, so the author can revise toward those long-term aims alongside immediate narrative necessities.

To that end:

═══ *EXERCISES* ═══

What inspired you to write this novel? Write that out in a paragraph.

Write a letter to a sympathetic reader about the book. The ideal time to complete this exercise is after you've completed a first draft, but before you've gone back and reread the whole manuscript. However, you can use it at any point in the writing process where you want to reconnect with the heart or spirit of the book. Write an informal letter to a sympathetic reader (a friend, a writing partner) in which you describe:

- What you wanted to do with the book, and/or wanted the book to do.
- What the story is, briefly.
- What the book is "about" in a larger sense.
- What you love about it.
- What you suspect (or know) needs some work.

You can keep this letter for yourself, or give it to that sympathetic reader to discuss with you—a conversation that can be especially useful if they've read the manuscript as well. (I often ask my authors to write this kind of letter for me after their first drafts, and it's always enlightening for both sides.) The letter can anchor you throughout the revision process, to remind you of your vision and overall story; to identify the good parts, so you can bring the rest of the novel up to those standards; and to start to articulate a to-do list for an eventual revision.

Find a physical object that reminds you of the core or spirit of the novel, or your intentions or goals in writing it, and keep that near you as a touchstone as you revise.

Create a collage of your book. The novelist and literary theorist Jennifer Crusie—one of my very favorite writers—creates collages for every book she writes.* She collects objects and images, then moves them around in a frame until they achieve what feels like the right balance to her, finding new connections, motifs, backstory, and themes along the way. You could also just pin interesting and relevant images on a Pinterest board. Either way, this is an opportunity to let your inner visual artist and/or subconscious instincts play with the material of the book, and see what happens.

---

* Ms. Crusie has written about this with instructions at http://www.jennycrusie. com/for-writers/essays/picture-this-collage-as-prewriting-and-inspiration, and, with visuals, at http://www.jennycrusie.com/morestuff/book-collages.

Assemble a playlist (a) reflecting the emotional journey of your protagonist, or (b) with a theme song for each main character, or (c) with a song for the dominant emotion of each chapter or scene. Listening to these songs might help you key back into the emotion you intend for that scene during revision, or turn up new connections as you figure out why you chose that song for that character or moment.

CHAPTER 7

Identity and Choice

Creating Multidimensional Characters

My name is Cheryl Beth Klein, and I'm the writer of the book you hold in your hands now, *The Magic Words*. I am also the wife of James Monohan; the daughter of Alan and Rebecca Klein; the older sister of Melissa Jackson; the best friend of Katy Beebe; the editor of many excellent books; and the maidservant of Marley the cat. I was born September 22, 1978, in Warrensburg, Missouri. I graduated from Raymore-Peculiar High School and Carleton College in 1996 and 2000, respectively. I'm white, a Virgo, a runner, a Ravenclaw, a feminist, a Democrat, a knitter, and a blonde.

Every day I put on a watch and two rings. I love reading more than any other activity on earth. I attend church, even though I struggle with my faith. I want to eat tacos for lunch, achieve a headstand in yoga, and edit a book that wins the Newbery Medal. I will work until things are right. I can be easily distracted. I love the fifth, sixth, and seventh *Fast and the Furious* movies. I take care of my friends. And I have secrets I'm not telling.

I have just listed these things in such detail because this is my character—who I am, as best I can define it in words. I could go on for much longer, of course, naming all the books I've read, the places I've traveled, the people I've been in love with and why, and describe how each of those experiences has changed me over time and affected the way I will act in the future. But those details wouldn't advance the narrative of this chapter, which should be all about your fictional characters, and not my real one.

And that is the challenge writers face with characters every day: to create people who are rich with possibilities and complexities, and make that richness pay off in a narrative, a chain of events that will change those characters' lives. That involves knowing *which* possibilities and complexities out of the billions of available human details are right for these particular characters in this particular narrative, especially if you want these characters to be liked by readers. It requires making these characters real enough that they seem to make decisions independently of you, their creator, yet using their personalities and actions in service of a plotline *you* determine. The goal is always to get all of these complexities working together, to create characters readers believe in, having experiences that make them laugh, cry, gasp, and, in a word: feel.

So, first of all, what is a character? It is a human being who inhabits a story. The character may actually be an animal, or a doll, or an amoeba, but it must have some form of human language, desires, and motivations in order to function in a narrative, so we'll count it as one of us. I believe a character can further be defined by what he is (essence) and by what he does (action)—very much like a spoon. According to Webster's, a spoon is "an eating or cooking implement consisting of a small shallow bowl with a relatively long handle." But it is just an oddly shaped little basin on a stick until it is used. The thing that transforms it from that basin into a spoon is its action in stirring, measuring, and eating.

A character in fiction functions the same way. She can have plenty of charming quirks, a distinct cultural heritage, all the personality and kindness in the world—a truly wonderful essence—but they'll just sit on the page until she does something within the novel—her actions. Yet at the same time, if she didn't have that depth of personality and background, there would be nothing to distinguish her from a robot or any other creature capable of carrying out the function she serves in the story.

What makes a character come alive on the page is the unity of essence and action.

You probably already have a spoon in mind—that is, a protagonist you've been developing for some time. Take a moment now to picture that character, either their outward appearance, or what you know of their (for lack of a better word) soul, that complicated mélange of passions and vulnerability, beliefs and history that makes them who they are. If you skipped the character-focused exercises in Chapter 4, "Promise and Premise," I encourage you to try those before moving forward here, as the answers will set up some useful basic dynamics that we'll consider further in this chapter. We'll also think about the depth of development each member of your cast might require, and all the dimensions a character might encompass. And I will continue to use myself as an example in this chapter, I'll admit, because I'm the character whose complexities I know best and about whom I can speak with the most authority.

Essence

Who is your character? There are five categories that prove useful in my experience in fleshing out a character's nature and personality. (This is an aspect of *my* personality, as you may have gathered by this point in the book: I love lists.)

Groundwork

This is my term for the facts of your protagonist's life situation at the outset of the novel. Is the character a boy or girl, intersex or transgender? How old is he/she at the time your book takes place? What is his/her racial or ethnic background? Sexuality? Who is in his/her immediate family, and what is their socioeconomic status? Where and when do they live?

These questions are the roots of your protagonist's being, the decisions that define their basic makeup and the boundaries of their world. Age will determine some of their physical, mental, and emotional capabilities. Gender, race, and socioeconomics can bind characters into certain societal expectations or free them from others, just as their place on the globe and moment in history will calibrate their freedoms further. Their connections with their family can establish their base level of psychological and physical security. Each of these elements are so intrinsic to a character's life that you probably knew them before you set fingers to keyboard—but they should each still be considered carefully, to check the ways that groundwork might echo throughout their nature and world. (It's also good to keep in mind the power dynamics created by these elements, as we'll discuss at more length in Chapter 9, "Power and Attention.")

═══ *EXERCISE* ═══

Write down the groundwork of your character's life. (You can also find a chart with these categories and all the qualities we'll discuss here on p. 100.)

Identities

Identities are the roles that characters play in their lives. (I learned about this concept from Kathi Appelt, author of *The Underneath* and *The True Blue Scouts of Sugar Man Swamp*.) In the introduction to this chapter, when I called myself writer, wife, daughter, sister, cat servant, friend, editor, runner, and knitter, among other things, I was listing the identities I cycle through regularly, depending upon the circumstances and my responsibilities moment by moment. At any point in the day, I have a primary identity I prioritize above the others—or other people might prioritize for me—which directs my actions in that particular situation. When I'm with my cat, taking care of his needs is my most important function; when I go shopping, I might receive preferential treatment because I'm a well-off white woman; at work, my running is irrelevant; and so on.

In a novel, a protagonist will generally have one primary identity that reflects the central action or relationships he pursues in the book, and a number of secondary identities in his other roles or relationships. The more identities he has, the more multidimensional and real he feels. Those competing identities can then become a wonderful driver of plot conflict, if another character or the society at large disagrees with his definition of himself; if the protagonist is forced to prioritize one identity over another, to the latter's detriment; or if the protagonist's identity is threatened or changes according to outside factors.

I'll offer two examples. In the chapter book *Bobby vs. Girls (Accidentally)* by Lisa Yee (‡), one of Bobby's identities is "Holly Harper's best friend"—in secret, of course, because boys and girls can't be best friends in public. As they head into fourth grade, however, the gender roles are getting more calcified and contentious, so Bobby and Holly are each coming to define themselves more as "boy" and "girl" than as "best friends," and suffering from the resulting loss of their connection. In the YA fantasy *Graceling* by Kristin Cashore, Katsa has always defined herself as a fighter, even a killer, foremost. When she falls in love, she's forced to consider an identity as a lover instead, with the possibility of eventually becoming a wife and mother, which causes her considerable distress. In both of these novels, internal and external conflicts arise organically out of the characters' shifts in identity, as the protagonists wrestle with how others perceive them and what kind of people they ultimately want to be.

═ *EXERCISE* ═

List all of the identities of the protagonist of your WIP at the beginning of the book. Next, rank them by their importance to that character at that point. How will those identities or priorities be challenged in the plot? How will they change by the end of the book?

Internal Qualities

With apologies for the vague name, "internal qualities" are any aspect of your character's psychology that determines how he acts and reacts. Such a determinant might be in his DNA, or it might have been learned through or created by external experiences, or the causes might overlap—a result of both nature and nurture. Internal qualities can be as all-encompassing as paranoia or as isolated as a fondness for Manx cats, and they can be further categorized into five loose buckets, which might also overlap with each other, as each reflects a facet of the same essential whole.

The first category is basic *personality postulates*: the combination of deep-seated desires, needs, and fears that drive an individual's approach to the world. A postulate, in scientific terms, is "something taken as self-evident or assumed without proof as a basis for reasoning." Within a novel, postulates are the core beliefs on which a character has built his entire theory of himself, his relationships with other people, and his place in the world. "Everyone deserves sympathy"; "I'm going to have to fight for everything I get, because other people don't want me to have it"; "I should be the star in every situation": These are all postulates that will play out through the characters' action in the novel, showing us people who will behave kindly or combatively or seek the spotlight in turn. Characters often have more than one postulate at work in their thinking. I said of myself earlier that "I will work until things are right," and that behavior is a manifestation of two of my personality postulates—the beliefs that there *is* a distinct, recognizable "rightness" that can be divined and achieved in most books or situations, and that we humans (and I specifically) were put on this planet to bring our lives and art more in tune with that rightness.

Does that sound highfalutin, self-centered, and quite possibly wrong? Well, postulates often are! Because they describe a character's deepest beliefs, they tend to be BIG ideas that then have BIG behaviors and feelings attached when they're activated or violated by events in the story. That leads us to the second category of internal qualities here: the *person-*

ality behaviors that result from the postulates. If I can't figure out how to help an author get a manuscript to "rightness," for instance, my husband and friends know I can be depressed or snappish, because I feel like I haven't completed my purpose on earth. If this again sounds high-falutin and a little ridiculous to you, it's worth recognizing that postulates are often tied to love—both what a character loves and wants to honor in their life, and what they think will make them worthy of love overall. Many people believe in the postulate "If I am not _____ or do not _____, then no one will love me" (or its inverse, "If I am _____ or do _____, then everyone will love me") on some level at some point in their lives. How might your protagonist fill in those blanks?

Both personality postulates and the behaviors that result from them could be described as weaknesses or flaws, because they often lead to avoidable mistakes of interpretation or action. As with most characteristics, however, they can also be great strengths. Working all the time means I get a heck of a lot done; that value for and sense of rightness means I pay a lot of attention to details; the books I edit have been critically acclaimed because of their authors' genius way more than my efforts, for sure, but I often helped those authors find their own rightness in some way. Yet at the same time, it might take me longer to finish things because I'm trying to do so much; I can obsess over those details and miss the larger picture; I feel stressed most of the time, as I'm trying to live up to that sense of "right" in all aspects of my life. As you create your protagonist's postulates and resultant personality behaviors, be sure to think about both the positive and negative ways they can play out in his/her story.

Here are three more postulates that are always worth completing for a character, as they help define his wants, needs, and fears:

- "The most terrifying thing in the world is _____."
- "I was put here on earth to _____."
- "The most important thing in the world is _____."

═══ *EXERCISE* ═══

You can do this either for yourself or for the protagonist of your WIP: List seven of your postulates and seven personality behaviors that result from them. These beliefs can be as everyday as, "Food will make me feel comforted," with the accompanying behavior of, "When I am upset, I will eat"; or as deeply rooted as, "God loves me and will protect me no matter what," and therefore, "I can handle snakes, climb volcanoes, or go skydiving, and I will always be safe." Once you've done that, list at least two possible consequences—one positive, one negative—for every behavior you've included.

As you might see from that exercise, to create a plot, you don't need to do much more than find a character's deepest personality postulates and follow them over time to their logical conclusions, especially as they come into conflict with other characters' postulates. If a character truly believes God will protect her in every situation, almost like a superpower, then she might also be called to go where her superpower is most needed, like leading her country into war against an oppressor. If something then happens to test this belief—she's captured during a battle, for instance—more than her physical safety will be in question, as her entire belief system will suddenly be in doubt. Or perhaps she passes unscathed through that bloody war, but then attracts trouble of another kind, as observers could be suspicious about how she survived, what sort of bargains she made, and whether she can be trusted. Will she be able to convince them of her goodness and God's role in protecting her? (If this plot sounds unlikely to you, note that it's the story of Joan of Arc—a character who has fascinated readers for six hundred years because her postulates and resulting behavior were so extreme.)

When one particular postulate emerges for a character within a book, and then becomes the guiding star for their action throughout the book,

I call that the character's *compulsion*. A compulsion is the one postulate most strongly called forth by the situation the book presents, which will drive the choices the character makes at every turn in the plot. If I were the protagonist of a novel set at my workplace, let's say, my postulate about needing to work until I get things right would probably serve as my compulsion for that book.

Once a compulsion has been established, you can plot the whole novel by simply bringing that compulsion up against obstacles ("Ouch!'s") and seeing how the character navigates them. Will the postulate—this character's beliefs about the world—be proven true and right? If it's shown to be false, how will the character react? In the Joan of Arc example I just gave, the compulsive postulate that "God will protect me" comes up against both the fact of her capture and her captors' own postulate that God is on *their* side. In a novel, such obstacles create both great conflict and the opportunity for great growth within the protagonist, as she might then evolve away from her compulsion, or come to recognize the limits of it, or find new dimensions within it. If this evolution happens, that will usually be the emotional point of your book. (We'll discuss this idea of "compulsion vs. obstacles" in more depth in Chapter 10, "Structure and Sensibility.")

As we think about a character's personality postulates and behaviors, we also encounter the limits set upon those postulates and behaviors, which form the third category of internal qualities: the character's *ethics, morals, or values*. What will they do, or won't they do, to get what they want? Will they steal, lie, cheat, kill? Where are their boundaries, and what determined those boundaries? I suppose you can regard these as postulates upon postulates—that is, if the character's compulsion is, "Food will make me feel comforted," let's say, he might still have the moral belief that, "I should not shoplift it from the bodega at the corner, because shoplifting is wrong." With that in mind, you can again plot a novel quite simply by determining the character's ethical limits, and then giving him a motivation that will push him up against those limits. Maybe at the beginning of the book your protagonist is willing to steal money to fund his grandma's cancer treatment, but by the end he's found someone he can't steal from. Or maybe he's not willing to steal at the beginning, but it seems perfectly justifiable to him by the end, as his grandmother gets sicker and suffers more intensely. Choosing between two values (love of grandma vs. wrongness of theft) creates a plot concept called "moral dilemma," and again, we'll discuss this at more length in Chapter 10.

When contemplating character misbehavior, it's also useful to determine our fourth category of internal qualities: the character's *degree of self-awareness*. Suppose your protagonist becomes a thief in the situation above. Is he aware that stealing is bad and he gets a charge off it? Aware it's bad, but he's able to rationalize it? Or does he just not think about it at all? This self-awareness comes into play in everyday life as well: Is he paralyzed by self-consciousness in talking to his crush? Does he weigh every move before he makes it? Or does he charge into situations with either confidence or a complete obliviousness to social cues? The degree to which readers are tuned in to his consciousness makes a huge difference in how they react to his behavior and understand his actions. As an example, in *The Hunger Games*, Katniss spends a lot of time thinking about (even agonizing over) the fact that she's taking others' lives. Because of this, we can accept the deaths as an unfortunate necessity in her life rather than gleeful or mindless cruelty, which would make many readers stop reading.

The last internal qualities category I'll mention here is *tastes*: your protagonist's favorite food, color, video game, sport, movie star, sneaker, vacation spot, breed of chicken, you name it. Specific tastes can make a character feel real through their very human irrationality or uniqueness— that he wears red on days when he needs luck, say, or that she loves ginger ale but hates Fresca. (Nobody expects me to love the wham-bam-all-about-the-fam *Fast and the Furious* films, and that's part of the great pleasure I take in them.) Tastes can also provide a useful reflection of the character's identities and groundwork. In *P.S. Be Eleven* by Rita Williams-Garcia, Delphine's adoration of the Jackson 5 echoes her identities as a girl of 1968, a sister fascinated by sibling relationships, and an African American eager to see people like her on TV. With that said, a very few such favorites go a very long way, and overloading a character with specific tastes (especially by using brand names) can weigh down the action or inadvertently date the book. Show us just two to four specific tastes that will resonate with the character's everyday reality and larger plot concerns, and you will have fulfilled this category admirably.

=== **EXERCISES** ===

Consider Howard Gardner's seven types of intelligence. In his book *Frames of Mind,* Gardner theorized that human nature could be categorized into seven types of intelligence: bodily-kinesthetic; interpersonal (a value for interactions with others); intrapersonal (in tune with and a value for the inner self); logical-mathematical; musical; verbal-linguistic; and visual-spatial. Which would be your protagonist's dominant type of intelligence? How might that type resonate through his thinking, his activities, the metaphors he'd use, his decision-making process? Rank the remaining types from strongest to weakest for him. What might these rankings show you about him and his preferences for action?

Four other fun and telling measures of personality: What is your protagonist's Myers-Briggs type? Where would he fall in Gretchen Rubin's Four Tendencies framework? How would he be sorted at Hogwarts? And what would his alignment be in Dungeons and Dragons?

Go to an Internet personality quiz site and take a few quizzes as your character to practice making decisions as your protagonist would and fleshing out his tastes. Do any of the choices he'd make surprise you? What can you learn about his larger personality from them?

External Qualities

Just as internal qualities show us a character's interior makeup, external qualities encompass the aspects of the character that can be observed from the outside. We base our first impressions of strangers in part on their *physical appearance*, so we expect a description of a character to tell us a great deal about this person. Here, for instance, is our introduction to the supporting character Tina in Pamela Dean's *Tam Lin*:

> Janet went on smiling, but her stomach protested a little. This roommate—probably the Chicago one, who had written, since she had a tennis racket under one arm and a tape recorder under the other—was about six feet tall and looked perfectly pleased with this condition. She was dressed more or less as Janet was, except that her blue corduroy pants had been ironed; her Oxford-cloth shirt was not only ironed, but pink, and tucked in, too; her tennis shoes were of a dazzling blueness. She had a nice healthy face with large blue eyes, and a head of straight blond hair, cut just above the shoulders.

From this, we can divine that Tina is nearly a stereotype of the "all-American girl"—neat, athletic, and popular, not particularly intellectual or deep—and these impressions more or less hold true in the early stages of the novel. But note that descriptions like this actually characterize everyone involved in the transaction, both the seer and the seen. At this point in *Tam Lin*, we readers have not gotten a comparable description of our protagonist Janet—we still don't know what her hair color is, for instance, or its length. Yet thanks to this description of Tina, I can tell you that Janet is short, and sensitive about it; she's wearing cords, a button-down shirt, and sneakers, but she doesn't take particularly good care of them, perhaps because she values inner intellectual worth more than external appearances (in fact, she's a snob about it); her beauty (if she is beautiful) isn't of the same all-American vintage as Tina's; and given all of these differences, there will probably be tension between the two girls. This description of Tina thus makes for brilliant, two-for-the-price-of-one characterization and plot foreshadowing.

Physical description of characters will always help solidify them in readers' minds and ground the story in a visual world. Lengthy portraits are especially common in fantasies like *Tam Lin* or in historical fiction, where authors want readers to be immersed in these unfamiliar worlds as fully as possible, and make our mental movies of the action unspool in high-res detail. Still, realistic contemporary fiction often doesn't include such thorough descriptions as the example above, because the book's focus is less on the details of a world most readers already know than on the personal interactions taking place there. Thus just a few revealing or significant physical details might stand in place of an extensive catalog. (In chapter books, any kind of description like this could also prove redundant with the illustrations.) At the same time, if the character in question isn't the default figure we see in most major media—that is, white, able-bodied, slender, and attractive—a description can count as almost a political act, declaring the presence and importance of this figure within both the book and the world. Whether you'll want to linger on characters' appearances depends on the point you're trying to achieve.

The second category of external qualities is the character's *manner of speaking and patterns of behavior,* which are often outward manifestations of the smaller personality behaviors we discussed above. Because I want things to be right, for instance, and I'm easily distracted, I will often stop myself in the middle of saying something to correct a previous thought or chase down another idea. Within fiction, these patterns are often embodied in small distinctive gestures that we might see again and again: Marcelo in *Marcelo in the Real World* opens and closes his hands when he feels stressed, to help him physically release tension; and in *Clementine* by Sara Pennypacker, our heroine says, "Okay, fine," when she's forced to admit to one of her (many) questionable actions. I actually think this category is much more important than the character's physical appearance, because these specific patterns and gestures provide the little details that, in their humanity and recognizability, make a character real.

EXERCISES

Draw a portrait of your protagonist.

Write a paragraph describing your appearance at this very moment from the point of view of one of the characters in your WIP. What feature would she notice first? What details would she pick up on—the fit of your clothes, their brand names, the dog hair on your T-shirt? How would she feel about this entire exercise of paying attention to someone's appearance?

Watch several episodes of a video blog of your choice with the sound off. Write down the vlogger's actions (beyond talking and looking at the camera). What expressions do you note? What gestures or movements does this person make often? What impression do they create? Watch the episodes again with the sound on. How do the vlogger's movements relate to the content or emotion of what s/he's saying?

Backstory

Where was your character born? When is her birthday? Who was her first crush? What was her biggest success, her greatest failure, her first betrayal? Where did her mother grow up? What kind of relationship did she have with her grandparents? The answers to all of these questions are part of her backstory, as each of them could have affected who she has become, and influenced how she will act and think in the future. The more important a character is to a novel, the more depth she should have, and the more backstory I expect the writer to know about her.

For plot purposes, a non-point-of-view character's backstory can be used to create a mystery around him, as other characters wonder what drives his behavior now or how he became who he is. Indeed, a great part of the brilliance of the Harry Potter series is that every book works in two opposite directions: Harry's frontstory—what happens during his school year—often involves investigating the backstories of Voldemort, his parents, or his professors. Backstory can also be used—and *should* also be used—as emotional context for the characters' relationships or actions. There's a terrific example of this early in *The Hunger Games*, when Katniss reflects on what she knows about a young man named Peeta, who will be her fellow representative of District 12 in the games. She remembers a time when she and her family were starving and she came to his family's bakery to beg bread. His mother turned her down, but shortly thereafter, Peeta deliberately burned two loaves of bread, suffering a beating in consequence, in order to be able to give them to her. That backstory makes us readers like Peeta a great deal, however much Katniss professes to be neutral about him.

In general it's good to know as much backstory as you can about your characters, because it helps them acquire dimension and reality in your mind. However, the only history your readers need to know—the only thing that should be on the page—is what's relevant to either your plot or how your character will act in that plot. If you were writing a middle-grade novel about a softball star and her quest for the state championship, for instance, it would be important to mention the team's performance the previous season, because that will influence the character's drive now. But you don't need to include her spotty GPA, unless that's something that will keep her off the team this year or it's causing tension with her academically overachieving family.

Too much backstory can easily swamp your main plot. Concentrate on getting the frontstory out to the reader, then use backstory anecdotes or details to show the reader the context of the characters' lives and relationships, and why the frontstory is important.

═══ *EXERCISES* ═══

Write a Wikipedia-style biography for your protagonist, the antagonist, or one of the supporting characters in your WIP, from their birth to the time your book begins. (Look at the Wikipedia entry for "Malala Yousafzai" for a good example.) This is a great way to firm up a character who feels a little vague in your mind, or keep track of the facts of a character with a complicated or hidden history.

Choose one of the following elements and write a short scene showing your protagonist's first encounter with it: His best friend; his pet; his current love interest; his favorite food; death; the ocean. (It does not count if this scene is dramatized within your book.)

Before I go on to the action side of the essence + action pairing, it's important to note that when editors say we want you to "show, not tell," in relation to a character, we mean we want the character's internal qualities to be demonstrated through their external qualities and action rather than through blunt statements of fact. For instance, rather than your saying, "Pablo hated to deal with anything related to his father's death," we want you to dramatize a scene where Pablo's mom or cousin tries to approach the topic, and we see Pablo pull away or change the subject repeatedly. You *can* get away with telling if you have showing to back it up. For instance, if you spent a paragraph talking about how Pablo couldn't think about the accident his father was in, that he couldn't even mention the place or the month or the make of the car without freezing up, you would have earned the right to say at the end, "Pablo hated to deal with anything related to his father's death," and the sentence would serve as the conclusion to your argument. (Or you could put it at the beginning of the paragraph, and it would serve as a thesis statement that you then support with evidence.) But you would still need to be careful that your telling sentence feels like a conclusion or thesis statement, and doesn't repeat what the reader already knows. The rule of thumb here: Let your characters' words and actions speak for themselves.

Action

And that leads us nicely out of the essence side of the character equation—who that character is—and into the action qualities—what that character does. The essayist Michel de Montaigne wrote, "Anything we do reveals us," and the following three qualities all reveal the essence of your characters through the actions they take.

Desire

What does the protagonist want? To defeat the curse, to get the boy, to get a dog, to steal a million dollars, to find their father, to kill the queen, to dance onstage, to go to Arby's, to make straight Bs, to live a normal life. . . . These could all form the protagonist's desire, which I define as some perceived good a character wants to achieve for herself or the world. By "perceived good," I mean that the character sees this thing as good, not that it *is* good; the theft of a million or the murder of a queen are morally questionable at best. But if the protagonist wants something, and we connect with her enough to want to read about her, then we also accept her perceptions and values enough to follow her wherever this desire leads.

As a rule of thumb, every major character in your novel should have a desire, because people with desires are people who are engaged with the world and DO THINGS within it, and those are the kind of people most readers want to read about. (I put DO THINGS in all caps every time it appears in this book because I feel so strongly about this principle.) These desires will often be rooted in what I think of as the "primary value": If a rock fell on your protagonist's head and knocked her out, when she woke up—after her basic needs were met and she knew everyone around her was okay—what would be the first thing she thought of? Her art, her work, her sister's mental illness, her own secret dream of becoming a star? (You may have considered this already thanks to the "most important thing" postulate on p. 80.) That primary value will likely point the way to her desire, as she faces a new opportunity to get her wish, or a new challenge in protecting what she has already.

Jennifer Crusie points out that desires need to be positive goals that look forward and allow the character to drive the action, not negative statements dependent on others, or about going backward or staying in the same place. "I want a dog"; "I want to find my father"; "I want to dance onstage": All of these will make the protagonist move toward some drama and change. Contrast those to, "I don't want to leave Tinyville"; "I want my life to return to the way it was when I was best friends with Ayesha"; "I want my mother to stop drinking." In the first two cases, the negative desires leave your protagonist with nothing to do but mope about their present circumstances, which is the opposite of interesting. (Change these to, "I'll run away to Tinyville," and "I'm going to make Ayesha be friends with me again," and instantly we have more action, energy, and narrative possibility.) In the last example, while the protagonist could certainly help Mom move toward sobriety—throw out her liquor bottles, drive her to AA meetings every day—the achievement of that desire is ultimately dependent upon *Mom's* desire to be well, which is something our protagonist can neither create nor control.

That points us toward another rule of desire: It should be something the character can realistically DO on his own within the scope of the book. If a character says, "I want to become an astronaut," that would take a lot of hard work and luck, but with those things and a talent for science, it's in the realm of rational possibility. "I want to fly to Mars in this special jetsuit I've built myself at the age of ten," on the other hand . . . that could be a fun fantasy picture book, but it wouldn't be credible to readers of a realistic novel, since it would violate scientific laws and our understanding of age-based mental development. "I want everyone around the globe to get out of poverty" is a similarly sticky situation, because such an effort would be dependent upon the cooperation and work of millions of people, including governments and corporations, over the course of decades. Revise that to, "I want to start a food bank in my town," and it's much more doable and believable within the limited scope of a novel.

Because the desire should be such a central concern for the character, it will likely align in some way with their primary identity. At the same time, because most characters have more than one identity, they usually have more than one desire as well. As a boy who feels he belongs on the autism spectrum, Marcelo of *Marcelo in the Real World* wants to attend his specialized private school, Paterson; but as a son, he also wants to keep a good relationship with his father, who thinks he should attend a regular public high school. Katniss wants to survive the Hunger Games, which requires the deaths of all of the other tributes; but she also wants Peeta and Rue to live, which would necessitate her own demise. This doubled desire is a tremendously effective narrative device not only because it's realistic—don't we all want more than one thing in our lives?—but because it instantly creates internal and external conflict, when the character has to choose to pursue one desire over another, or choose among the people who represent those different values and desires to him, or decide what happens when his desire clashes with another character's desire.

In this way, desire serves as a plot engine in the novel like few other story elements can, because once we have a character to invest our interest in, and this character *wants* something, that creates stakes—will she get it?; tension—can she overcome the obstacles in her path?; and action—what will she do to make it happen? A desire can be established implicitly through the character's situation; for instance, we know that Harry Potter wants a happier home life simply from witnessing his treatment by the Dursleys. Or you can dramatize a moment like this one in Jenny Han's *Clara Lee and the Apple Pie Dream*, where Clara first conceives her royal ambitions:

Last year, Trudie Turner from the fifth grade was Little Miss Apple Pie. Since I'm only in the third grade, I don't know her, but she looked pretty good up there on the float. . . . Miss Apple Pie was a high school girl with long blonde hair and she wore a red dress and high heels. She looked like a girl in a commercial.

If I won, I knew just what I'd wear. The dress Grandpa bought me in Korea last year. It's Korean style, with a skirt the color of fruit punch and a white jacket with rainbow-striped sleeves and, best of all, a long bow. . . . I could almost picture it: me, in my Korean dress, on that float.

Whether the protagonist's desire is implicit or explicit, as a rule of thumb, it should be revealed within the first three chapters, so readers know your protagonist is involved with the world, might DO THINGS within it, and is thus worth following.

The establishment of the desire makes a promise to readers: by the end of the novel, this desire will be resolved. It might be fulfilled, as Clara Lee does indeed become Little Miss Apple Pie. Alternatively, it might be frustrated or changed, as the character is forced to accept he won't achieve the desire, or the values that created that desire in the first place shift within him. In Lisa Yee's *The Kidney Hypothetical*, Higgs Boson Bing wants to win "Maverick of the Month," the only award he hasn't yet captured during his four years at Sally Ride High School. But in the last week of his senior year, as he campaigns to become the Maverick, he's rocked by a series of revelations and adventures that reveal the empty nature of his pursuit of academic prizes, and point the way toward a more truly fulfilled life. Because we readers experience Higgs's change in values alongside him, we don't mind that his initial desire to be the Maverick falls away. (We root for it, in fact.) If that change didn't happen, we wouldn't be satisfied with the book. (As a side note, the "Maverick of the Month" award here is what film critics call a "MacGuffin"—an object or goal that sets the characters or story in motion, but ultimately becomes unimportant in the scope of the overall plot. It is perfectly fine to have a MacGuffin so long as it points the way to greater growth.)

In conclusion: Give your characters something to want, and we'll want good things for them, too.

=== *EXERCISE* ===

Make a list of all your protagonist's desires in the book. Which one is most important to her at the beginning? If those priorities change, what causes those changes? Which desires are fulfilled, and which not? Is the desire at the beginning a positive goal that the protagonist can accomplish herself within the scope of the book? If it's a negative goal, is there a way you can restate it and reposition the action so that it becomes a positive goal that gets her moving?

Attitude

Attitude is the basic energy and outlook a character brings to the world. Take all the personality postulates that we discussed back in the discussion of internal qualities, roll them into a ball, put them inside the character's brain, and send him out into the world. With that ball knocking around in his head and driving his actions, how will he engage with others? Who will he connect with? How will he express himself? How will he react when faced with a challenge? As an example, suppose your character is the new kid in school and he's heading into the lunchroom. His interior monologue could be, *Oh, gosh, will anyone ask me to sit down?* Or, *Which of these losers has earned the right to my presence at their table?* Or, *I have to find that cute Jamie—I'd love to eat with him.* All three of those statements reveal his attitude: his approach toward new situations and other people, and his approach toward life in general.

At the beginning of a novel, I think it's really important that your main character have either a positive attitude or an interesting negative attitude— or, to put it in more woo-woo but also more accurate terms, positive energy or interesting negative energy, where the character expresses his negativity with wit or verve. Someone with positive energy embraces life and what it might bring them; they're pursuing their desires, resourceful when faced with a challenge, looking outward at others, and DOING THINGS all around. That is the sort of person who you'd want to hang around with at a party, or be lost with in a forest, as they'll help you figure out what action to take next rather than freaking out over possible bears. (A person with interesting negative energy might worry about bears, but she'd also be knowledgeable or funny about it—listing fourteen ways a grizzly can kill you, for instance. That creativity creates a positive energy that counters the pessimism.)

A person with uninteresting negative energy, on the other hand . . . you've likely met this person at a party, too, the one who responds to a casual, "How are things going?" with a, "Well, you know . . ." and then stares off into space, giving you nothing to respond to and no reason why you'd want to dig deeper. Or worse: "Well, my girlfriend just broke up with me, and I'm never going to find anyone again, because the women here are all shallow and stupid, and my job sucks, and I make crap money, and . . ." (If I have ever talked to you at a party: I promise this is not you.) That person is worse than the first one because he's a whiner, unable to see anything of the world beyond his own needs and misery, and dumping all of that misery on you in turn. I'll even edit out "whine" as a speech tag when I see it in a manuscript, unless the whining is done by a character I'm not meant to like. If it's important that your protagonist display uninteresting negative energy at the beginning of the novel—because you need readers to dislike him initially for some reason, say, or he's locked in a deep depression—try to counteract that energy with a compelling desire, relatable vulnerability, or some strong plot hook at the outset, to carry your audience forward until we can see something more positive in him.

=== EXERCISES ===

How would you characterize the overall attitude or energy of your protagonist at the beginning of your book? What gave her that particular point of view? How does it serve your points or the role she plays in the novel? (A rambunctious attitude might cause the central plot trouble, for instance, or negative energy might point the way to her emotional growth.)

Try journaling a regular week in the life of a character. What topics would they think important enough to write down? How would they talk about them? What would they *not* write about, even if something significant in that situation occurred? What overall attitude and energy emerge here? (This is an especially good exercise for supporting characters, because it can be very easy to think only about your protagonist, and forget that the people around him or her need to be just as real.)

Action

Action is the choices your protagonist makes within the plot and his/her attendant physical movements. It might sound a bit odd to call action "choices," but every physical action begins with a decision, conscious or unconscious: the decision to stand up to that bully, and then the face-off; the decision that this secret cannot stand, and then revealing it. (Inaction can also be a form of action, like the choice to keep a secret the character really wants to tell, or to stay still and do nothing when someone nearby is being hurt.) Alone in all media, novels have the unique ability to show readers both the internal stew leading up to a decision, and then the external drama and consequences of it. The best novels exploit that duality in full.

Action is intimately related to attitude and desire. Attitude will set the emotional tone for your character's decisions, or even his ability to make them. If he has a pessimistic attitude and doesn't believe anything he does will truly make a difference, he'll probably avoid choices as often as he can, even if they point toward his desire. It might then be necessary to show him gaining some thread of hope before he can start to effect change within his life. And we do want to see him make change, because we readers expect characters to take action that will help them achieve their desire—to move toward it, once that intention is declared. If a character sets forth a desire he talks about throughout the book, but circumstances or his own lack of will keep him from DOING anything about it, readers can easily grow impatient with the character or this desire, because he needs to put up or shut up already. (Also, it will be a boring book.) So if your character has a defined desire, he also needs to have some follow-through.

As a rule of thumb, I expect to see a protagonist make at least three choices in the book with consequences that affect its central action. One of those should precipitate or happen in response to the inciting incident, and one should contribute to the climax in some way. If your protagonist isn't meeting this minimum standard for action (and you'd be surprised how often protagonists don't), then he will feel passive and incidental, the victim of or bystander to events rather than their instigator. This predicament often comes up when a protagonist is mostly observing the conflicts of other people, like his parents getting a divorce, or when his desire is impossible for him to accomplish—for instance, he wants his parents *not* to get a divorce, and no action of his will change the situation.

If these diagnoses apply to your novel, then I suggest giving your protagonist a second desire where he can take action. In other words, add a subplot where he is the prime mover . . . and then strongly consider making that your primary plot, and turning whatever situation he has no power to affect into a subplot. For instance, if your protagonist's parents *are* getting a divorce, the novel could easily settle down into his observations of everyone's behavior in this situation, which might be interesting as a character and emotional study but doesn't necessarily give him much to do. To make him a compelling character, invent a second plot where he wants to try out for the lead in the class play, or show him plotting how to run away from home. A strong desire like those would give you some action in the book while the larger emotional situation (the divorce) plays out in everyone's lives.

EXERCISE

Write the flap copy for your book. During the editorial process, I often ask writers to draft the flap copy for their own books, because whenever you have to write a compelling 250-word summary of a novel (as I frequently must do), it forces you to define its key characters, actions, and points of interest in a coherent vision of the book. Flaps usually include the opening situation; a little information to interest readers in the protagonist—his/her identity, desire, and/or key concerns; the inciting incident; at least one action your protagonist takes after the incident, setting up the novel's larger conflict, mystery, or lack; and the stakes (implicit or explicit). Finally, it should make the book's key narrative questions clear, and leave them unanswered, to make the reader want to buy the book. If you struggle to name these elements in writing the copy, or find the existing elements lacking, write the copy for the novel you *want* this to be. Later, you can revise the novel itself to match.

Degrees of Character

Of course, not all characters need to be developed in the same depth as your protagonist. The first time a new member of your cast appears on the page, readers expect to have that character's basic groundwork established, including their age (a quality especially important to children's and YA literature), gender identity, possibly their racial or ethnic identity, and their relationship to the protagonist. It's also useful to get a sense of their attitude, with perhaps a distinctive external pattern of speech or manner of behavior, to anchor this person in the reader's mind and distinguish them from other characters. After that, the depth in which the character must be developed depends upon what I'm calling the *degree* of the character within the novel.

First-Degree Characters. These are your protagonist, antagonist, and the two to four people who are most important in the protagonist's life and essential to the resolution of the action. In Harry Potter terms, Harry, Hermione, Ron, Dumbledore, Snape, and Voldemort are all first-degree characters. Beyond the facts about them listed above, we usually discover their postulates, identities, desires, and backstory in the course of the narrative, as their choices, actions, and consequences will frame the central action of the book. First-degree supporting characters often have their own emotional arcs within a book/series, changing and growing in multiple directions, not all of them in accordance with the protagonist's own growth.

Second-Degree Characters. These are people who play a specific role in the plot, but are not overly present in the narrative beyond that role in the plot. The list of second-degree characters in the Harry Potter books could fill up the rest of this page, but briefly, I'd name the Dursleys, Neville Longbottom, Mr. and Mrs. Weasley, Sirius Black, Peter Pettigrew, Luna Lovegood, Nymphadora Tonks, and Bellatrix Lestrange. These characters usually have one or two postulates, identities, and desires, each of which serves the plot.

Third-Degree Characters. These people have basically walk-on roles that do not substantially influence the action, but they help fill out the reality of the novel's world. They don't need much more than the groundwork qualities listed earlier. Ernie Macmillan is a classic third-degree character, a Hufflepuff in Harry's year who can reliably be counted on to say something stuffy. That gives him enough personality to seem real—an attitude and desire, perhaps: he wants to be important—but we don't need to know much more about him than those qualities.

Declaring a degree is not meant to limit a character in any way; it's always fascinating to see hints that your second- and third-degree characters are living lives as rich as your protagonist's. But it wouldn't have been the best use of J. K. Rowling's writing time, or our reading time, to go deep into the heart of Ernie Macmillan when he has so little to do with Harry's overall story. Degrees thus help writers prioritize the character work they need to do.

With that said, remember always that everyone is the hero of his own story. To the second- and third-degree characters and even the antagonist in your book, the protagonist of your book isn't the star. Instead, *they're* at the center of their own personal narratives, making choices and driving some action that just happens to include your protagonist as well.

══ *EXERCISE* ══

Write a synopsis of the novel or a few key scenes in the action from the point of view of someone besides your protagonist. (If your novel has an antagonist, try it with him.) What is that character doing when your protagonist isn't present? This should help you both get to know this character in more depth and see the plot events and your protagonist from a new angle.

Putting It Together

Here are all of these categories in one handy list. (You can download a Word version of it from my website at www.cherylklein.com.

GROUNDWORK

- Full name?
- How old is the character at the beginning of the book?
- Gender identity?
- Ethnic, racial, and socioeconomic background?
- Family situation?
- Where does the character live?

IDENTITY

- List three to ten roles the character fills, in descending order of priority for him or her.

INTERNAL QUALITIES

- What are some postulates of the character's personality:
- What is his/her compulsion for this book (if applicable):
- Name at least three resultant behaviors from the postulates or compulsion.
- What ethics/morals/values guide him or her?
- On a scale of 1–10, with 1 being a Neanderthal and 10 the Buddha, what's his/her degree of self-awareness?
- Name a few notable tastes that distinguish the character.

EXTERNAL QUALITIES

- What does the character look like?
- Identify several distinctive patterns of speech or behavior.

BACKSTORY

- List ten items from the character's backstory.

ACTION

- What does the character want? List all of his/her desires in descending order.
- What is his/her attitude and energy level?
- What action does the character take to get what he or she wants?

READER CONNECTION

- What degree of character is he or she within the novel?
- If the character is not the protagonist, what is the protagonist's relationship with him/her?
- What should the reader's relationship to him/her be? (We'll explore the ideas behind this last question in the next chapter.)

The more information you have here, the deeper and richer the character will feel. And, again, one easy way to add depth to any character is to ask the question, "Why?" Look at what you said about what he wants. Why does he want that? What experiences gave him the attitude you identified above? What is his guardian or culture like, that he has the ethical rules you named here? Write those answers out and connect them to other answers in other categories, and he will gain dimension at every turn.

Here are three more great questions for exploring a character:

- What keeps the character alive? (What is the character's joy?)
- What is the character's pain?
- How did the character get his or her name?

I adore the name question because a name says so much about a character's parents (that they would choose that name), family (that this name reflects a particular history and culture), and history (especially if the character has a nickname or chose a name for herself). And if we combine the character's joy and pain with the categories discussed earlier, the result will be the plot of a novel: how your protagonist overcomes her pain and gets her desire by means of the joy that keeps her alive.

Unless you're really starving for ideas, this checklist of character qualities will likely be most useful after you finish your first draft, when you can use it to cross-check your protagonist's roundedness, her full human self, against what is already on the page. Run through this checklist for each of the characters in your novel—the parents, the siblings, the antagonists, friends, and teachers—and you'll create a complex web of conflicting desires and actions: in other words, a novel.

CHAPTER 8

Interest and Change

Building Bonds Between Readers and Your Characters

The Great Relatability Debate

About every six months, regular as the seasons, we see an upsurge of an old argument in the literary community about whether protagonists need to be "relatable." Many adult literary novelists take offense at the very idea, saying that, as artists, their highest calling is fidelity to reality as they see it, and reality includes a large number of difficult people. (These people sometimes include adult literary novelists.) Some readers dismiss a protagonist as "unrelatable" if the character's groundwork differs from theirs—their gender, skin color, sexual orientation, or country of origin. Those people are bad readers. Other readers—perhaps the vast majority of the casual reading public—just look for protagonists to be "likable," which usually means the protagonist is a pleasant person who acts in a manner the reader regards as right. Such inoffensive characters allow readers to slip unobtrusively into their points of view and enjoy the action of the book.

I fall in the middle of this continuum, as I do feel strongly that if you're writing fiction, especially for children or young adults, your protagonist should be relatable. But what makes a character relatable, in my view, is that the person is a full and credible human being, with all the strengths and vulnerabilities that implies: a love for something that can be taken away; a body, prone to embarrassment, injury, pleasure, and lust; fear of loss, of failure, of death; goofiness, stubbornness, blind spots, private jokes; a mind and heart unique in all the world. As a human being, *I* have all of these traits, so if an author can show me these qualities (or hundreds of other possible traits) operating realistically within a character, I'll believe in and relate to that person. I might not *like* this person, particularly if she's whiny or mean, but if I recognize the humanity in her, I can relate to her. When I can't relate to a character, it's usually because her emotions or vulnerabilities feel hidden from me somehow; her qualities don't cohere in a credible manner; or she hasn't been drawn with enough dimension altogether.

Why does relatability matter in children's and young adult fiction? Well, pleasure can come from a number of factors in adult literary fiction—beautiful writing, a strong plot, an exploration of an idea or emotion, a connection to a character. But children's and YA fiction operates a little differently. Child readers might not always appreciate lyrical writing because they're struggling simply to decipher the words. Both child and YA readers like strong plots, but plots matter only *because* of characters—because we worry about our protagonist and we want to see her achieve her desire. We won't worry about someone we don't care about. Moreover, as children's and YA books usually focus on a character's emotional growth as he or she comes to a better understanding of the world, we readers need to be invested in the protagonist to want to see that growth happen. All of these factors point toward one conclusion: In children's and YA publishing, you need a protagonist who will capture the interest of readers—someone to whom they can relate.

I use a specific adjective for the characters who capture my interest: "compelling," because I feel compelled to read or know more about them. Maybe I like them, like Percy Jackson or Anne of Green Gables. Maybe I hate them, like Draco Malfoy, or Mrs. Coulter in *The Golden Compass*. But whatever my relationship to them, I want to know what they'll say or do next. Even more than an exciting story, compelling characters make the reader turn the pages, because they offer the intimacy of a relationship, the unpredictability of real human behavior, and the promise of a story and activity to come.

Creating Compelling Characters

In this chapter, I identify ten strategies to build relatability or compellingness into your people. As with everything else in this book, before you choose to implement any of these strategies, you should keep your points in mind—those things that you're designing your particular book to do. If you're writing a novel that's all about vicarious thrills for the reader, like sword fights or lots of kissing, then you'll probably want to create a protagonist whom readers like and invest in quickly, which will allow you to carry your readers right on to those thrills. If, on the other hand, you're writing a more literary novel that explores the complexity of reality, then your highest goal will be honesty about that reality, likability be damned. In that case, you might have a highly flawed protagonist with a mean streak or a drinking problem; but because you'll present those flaws honestly, the reader will still be able to recognize and relate to that reality in him or her. (For an excellent example of this in action, check out *The Spectacular Now* by Tim Tharp.)

Whatever your points, you'll also want to employ different characterization strategies, at different depths, for different members of your cast, depending upon where you're at in the plot, that character's role in the plot, and the characters' relationships to each other and the reader. Your hero, for instance, is likely going to be someone you'll want the reader to connect to emotionally, so you might try to make him as conventionally likable as possible. Moreover, you'll probably want that connection to happen up front, so you might place a lot of emphasis upon his more appealing qualities at the beginning, and show his deeper complexities and flaws later on. It's fine for readers to dislike your villain, though, so you might characterize her negatively early on and then deepen her with a secret or vulnerability later. Second- and third-degree characters should be as likable as their personalities dictate, but at a level of intensity where they don't distract from the journey of your protagonist. That is, every time Third-Degree Joe shows up, you don't want readers to think, *Oh, I hate this guy* (unless, of course, they should hate poor Joe at that moment). Keep the needs of your story in mind in selecting your cast and setting their likability levels.

Writers should employ the following strategies primarily in the first few chapters to establish the reader's initial relationship with the protagonist and other characters. Of course, those first few chapters are also what agents and editors review to determine their interest in a submission, so these methods should help you capture our interest as well. When I'm editing a manuscript, these techniques function almost as a checklist: I look for at least three of them to appear within the first two chapters (especially numbers 2, 3, 5, and 7), handled with some originality and subtlety. If I'm so involved with the text that I only notice their use after the fact, I know I'm reading a good book.

1. Think Differently.

To make your manuscript stand out, show us someone we haven't seen before, a voice we haven't heard, a story we don't already know:

> "Marcelo, are you ready?" I lift up my thumb. It means I am ready. "Okay, I'm going to wheel you in." Then he slides me inside the tunnel of the machine. I like the feeling of being closed in. The lights are not bright enough to hurt my eyes but I close them anyway.
>
> —*Marcelo in the Real World* by Francisco X. Stork (first lines)

We can discern a couple of things about Marcelo from these few lines: His narrative voice is somewhat stiff and formal. He likes the feeling of being closed in, and more than that, he will take the time to remark on that feeling, to tell us about it, while another character might take it entirely for granted. The same goes for his describing the brightness of the lights. Because of this precision and sensitivity, I sense there is something *differ-*

ent about this guy, something I don't see in most YA protagonists, and I will read on just to find out what's going on with him.

This is an example of the most basic form of reader-writer bond: *interest*, where we readers find something in this person worthy of our attention, and we'll watch the character until they stop being worthy of it. That worthiness can come from any of the techniques that follow here, but newness is especially attractive, where the character does something fresh, says something I've never read before, that shows me the uniqueness of his mind or actions. Interest is really a level all your characters should achieve, because it means that the character is a distinct individual, not a generic type. I also think of it as the level your *antagonist* should achieve, as all the other levels here involve some warm feelings between the protagonist and the reader. You may not want readers to like your villain, but if he's going to have an involving conflict with the hero, he has to be interesting enough to qualify as a worthy opponent.

The best kinds of interesting characters are complete and specific human beings, as Marcelo is shown to be within his book. One easy way to create an interesting character is to upend a cliché. Take a writing prompt—say, "kid + pet"—and write down the most obvious answer to it—say, "boy + dog." Then write ten variations on it:

- A boy who wants a cat when all the other kids in his class want dogs.
- A boy who wants a kangaroo.
- A boy who wants to *kill* a dog.
- A girl who accidentally killed her dog, so she is deathly afraid of getting a new one.
- A boy who is terrified of cats (and his uncle has six).
- A transgender kid fascinated by moray eels, which can shift between genders.
- A young scientist who wants a guinea pig . . . to use as, um, a guinea pig.

And you could go on from there. All of these situations promise me interesting protagonists whom I haven't seen before, and interesting premises with them, so I'd want to read on to find out *why* this boy wants to kill a dog, or what the nature of the scientist's experiments will be.

2. If the Character is Someone You Want Readers to Like, Give Them a Solid Reason to Do So.

Affection comprises the second form of reader-character bond. It happens when readers simply like the character, when we would want to be the character's friend in real life. We like characters for pretty much the same reasons we like people in our nonfictional lives: warmth, entertainment, companionship, stimulation, pleasure in their presence. These pleasures might come from the characters' voices, if they're first-person narrators, or through their action, dialogue, and internal monologue, if we see them through a third-person lens.

A few specific reasons we like people, which are easy to show in a first chapter:

✎ Kindness, moral goodness, or empathy

> Harry moved in front of the tank and looked intently at the snake. He wouldn't have been surprised if it had died of boredom itself—no company except stupid people drumming their fingers on the glass, trying to disturb it all day long. It was worse than having a cupboard as a bedroom, where the only visitor was Aunt Petunia hammering on the door to wake you up; at least he got to visit the rest of the house.
>
> —*Harry Potter and the Sorcerer's Stone* by J. K. Rowling

This is one of the first things we see Harry do in the entire series: look at a snake on a trip to the zoo. But look at *how* he looks at it. He doesn't feel sorry for himself because he's an underfed orphan, who the Dursleys use as a servant. Instead, he puts himself in the snake's place, identifying with it, and feeling more sorry for *it* than he does for himself. That shows us Harry has a kind and empathetic heart, and that makes it easy to like him and be invested in him for all the action that follows.

If you want to make a reader *not* like a character, then have them act like Dudley Dursley in this same scene. He pounds on the glass of the snake's enclosure, and when it doesn't move, he whines, "I'm bored!" and walks away. Readers immediately know he's selfish, demanding, and impatient—not a particularly likable person.

✒ Good energy: warmth, optimism, and imagination

> "I suppose you are Mr. Matthew Cuthbert of Green Gables?" she said in a peculiarly clear, sweet voice. "I'm very glad to see you. I was beginning to be afraid you weren't coming for me and I was imagining all the things that might have happened to prevent you. I had made up my mind that if you didn't come for me tonight I'd go down the track to that big wild cherry tree at the bend and climb up and stay all night. I wouldn't be a bit afraid, and it would be lovely to sleep in a wild cherry tree all white with bloom in the moonshine, don't you think? You could imagine you were dwelling in marble halls, couldn't you?"
>
> —*Anne of Green Gables* by L. M. Montgomery

Imagine you're at a party, and a redheaded girl starts talking to you. She is delighted to meet you, as she's excited by everything she encounters, and she tells you that if she hadn't met you tonight, she might have climbed up and slept in a cherry tree. I admit you might find her a bit grating, especially if you are of a more cynical bent, but are you going to be bored hanging out with her? No way. You want to see what she'll say next.

What I love about Anne is she has good energy, which came up under "attitude" in the previous chapter. She is interested in the world around her; she expects good things to happen; she will *make* good things happen. She also gives off emotional warmth, so other people in the story feel accepted by her, and we readers get drawn into her circle as well. (Protagonists who act holier, cooler, more popular, or smarter than thou can be difficult to connect with, because such paragons might judge and reject us. Anne is the polar opposite of that model.) She also demonstrates confidence, imagination, fearlessness, and resourcefulness here—all very attractive qualities in people or characters.

As I said earlier, people who have negative energy can be really hard to invest in—people who are bored, bitter, or pessimistic, without being interesting or doing anything to change their circumstances. Compare, however:

> It is my first morning of high school. I have seven new notebooks, a skirt I hate, and a stomachache.
>
> The school bus wheezes to my corner.... Where to sit? I've never been a backseat wastecase. If I sit in the middle, a stranger could sit next to me. If I sit in the front, it will make me look like a little kid, but I figure it's the best chance I have to make eye contact with one of my friends, if any of them have decided to talk to me yet.
>
> —*Speak* by Laurie Halse Anderson (opening paragraphs)

I think *Speak* works where many negative narrators fail because Melinda's voice is so self-contained and strong. She isn't super-positive, but she isn't asking for our sympathy, either, and the mystery of why she is so upset, why her friends won't talk to her, keeps us reading on. It also helps enormously that Melinda offers such a spot-on assessment of the school bus-seat situation, listing truths readers might recognize, and showing a lot of:

✎ Humor or wit

Sometimes we laugh with the character, as in Melinda's "Ten Lies They Tell You About High School" later in *Speak*, or in this next example:

> See those girls sitting cross-legged and singing the theme song from *Friends*? They wouldn't be doing that right now if it wasn't for me. See that guy over there taking the shoelace out of one of his sneakers? Same thing. That girl picking her nose? SHE WOULD BE DEAD AND HER NOSE WOULD BE FULLY UNPICKED IF IT WAS NOT FOR ME.
>
> —Charlie in *The Year of Secret Assignments* by Jaclyn Moriarty

Or we laugh *at* the character, enjoying their humor, whether they intend to be funny or not. I think Anne of Green Gables falls into this category, as we might laugh at her for being so nutty, but that laughter also endears her to us; we want to hear more of her unique point of view.

✐ Enthusiasm, curiosity, or engagement with the world

Enthusiasm in this context means being passionate about one particular subject. People who love something passionately are usually interesting people (in at least the fact of their passion, if not its practice), and that good energy will often extend to other people or action later in the plot.

> Dear Lydia, You are as beautiful as the Irish equalizer by Robbie Keane in injury time in the Ireland v. Germany game, World Cup, 2002, Korea.
>
> —Seb in *The Year of Secret Assignments*

This guy not only loves soccer so much that he will compare a girl's beauty to a goal, but he can be very specific about *which* goal, right down to the minute. That specificity and passion is funny and endearing, and it makes me like Seb very much.

✐ Expertise, intelligence, or skill

Seb's letter also demonstrates his expertise in soccer history—another attractive quality, as readers admire people who have some notable talent, intelligence, or ability.

> Lydia was in a melancholy mood so we didn't do anything illegal. We just invented recipes using the strangest ingredients in the kitchen plus some different kinds of old wine. Also, Lydia set off the smoke alarm seventeen times. She's been analyzing how smoke alarms work.
>
> —Cassie in *The Year of Secret Assignments*

Aren't you interested in Lydia now? Don't you want to see what she'll do when she's cheerful?

✑ Insight or honesty

I have the kind of skin that is not allowed in the sun for more than fifteen minutes before turning into an overcooked lobster. Sunburn for sure each time I visit the beach. My skin is there for all the world to see and point at and judge. Guerra. Casper. Ghost. Freckle Face. Ugly. Whitey. White girl. Gringa. I've been called all of those names. Skin that doesn't make me Mexican enough. Skin that always makes people say, "You're not what a Mexican's supposed to look like."

—Gabi, *A Girl in Pieces* by Isabel Quintero

When Mary Lennox was sent to Misselthwaite Manor to live with her uncle everybody said she was the most disagreeable-looking child ever seen. It was true, too.

—*The Secret Garden* by Frances Hodgson Burnett (first lines)

Readers love seeing truths expressed in a text, when something in a book chimes with what they know about the world and promises to reveal more of its secrets. When a character makes an observation that feels true or insightful, or is up front about his or her own vulnerabilities, we trust them, because we know they aren't sugarcoating anything for us. In the first example, Gabi is painfully honest about not just the physical consequences of her skin tone but the cultural ones, demonstrating that she won't soft-pedal anything in her story. With *The Secret Garden*, it's not just the bluntness about Mary's unpleasantness that draws us in, but the surprise that the author isn't doing anything to make her less disagreeable: If this story dares to throw its main character under the bus right upfront, what else might it do? You'll read on to find out, won't you?

And speaking of disagreeable characters, I'll point out here, you can render characters less attractive, or even repellent or evil, simply by reversing any of these qualities—making them nasty, or unimaginative, or relentlessly negative, or unable to take independent action.

3. Match the Character's Emotions and Internal Conflicts to Those of the Age of Your Likely Reader.

Close your eyes and picture the young reader for whom you're writing this book. It could be a real person you know, or yourself at a younger age; it could be a child or teenager whom you've made up entirely. How old is he or she? What are their biggest concerns in life right now? Their dominant emotions? Show us those concerns and feelings in the character early on, and the odds are good that you'll connect with your readers' feelings as well.

> At thirteen I was tall and large boned, with delusions of beauty and romance.
>
> *—Jacob Have I Loved* by Katherine Paterson

When I read *Jacob Have I Loved*, I was ten years old, in thick glasses and a back brace for scoliosis. I longed to be pretty and popular, but I was failing miserably at those goals, and my extreme self-consciousness made it hard to imagine a time when I might feel okay in my own skin. The circumstances of Louise's life in coastal Maryland were vastly different from mine in suburban Missouri, but her awkwardness and vulnerability felt so naked on the page, and spoke so deeply and uncomfortably to my own, that it seemed as if Katherine Paterson were writing about *me*. Thus I read the book desperately to see how the story would come out, to be reassured that I might someday find some clarity and a place of my own.

I think of this as the third type of bond that readers can form with characters: *identification*, where readers connect emotionally with a character based on some similarity of circumstance, emotion, or psychology. Readers can identify with a character without even liking them very much; in my opinion, people responded to *Twilight* as strongly as they did not because Bella Swan was a fascinating, lively person, but because the way she loved and was loved by Edward spoke so deeply to the universal desire to be adored in spite of your flaws—to be loved passionately just for who you are. Identification drives the kind of desperate reading I described above because the book feels like a promise: If this character can find her way through confusion and difficulty—can attract the attention of the gorgeous vampire despite her clumsiness or can carve out her own identity as Louise does—then so might we.

Identification is a bond that lies somewhat out of the writer's control, because you can't know exactly which readers will find your book, nor what they'll connect to within it. But the more you can cue your character's development and desires to the emotional truths of their age, or the more universal you can make those desires as expressed through their very specific circumstances—Louise's longing for beauty and romance being universal, her role as a crab fisher in Maryland specific—then the more likely it will be that your intended reader might identify with them.

At the opposite end of the identification scale:

4. Give the Character Wildly Different External Circumstances than Your Likely Reader.

While we are interested in people like ourselves, we also *know* many people like ourselves, and frankly, the lives of people like ourselves can be pretty boring. That makes it exciting to read about people whose outward lives are very different from our own. Sometimes this difference lies in their country or culture, as in this example from a book set in Afghanistan:

> I traced the letters in the dust with my finger, spelling out my name: *Zulaikha*. Squinting my eyes in the middle time between night and morning, I checked to make sure my brothers and sister were still sleeping. Then I began to write the alphabet. *Alif, be, pe, te.* . . .
>
> —*Words in the Dust* by Trent Reedy (‡; first lines)

Sometimes the difference lies in the protagonist's situation, as she might lead an outwardly more awesome life than the reader.

> Massie Block hated herself for looking so beautiful. She angled a silver soup spoon toward her face and quickly glanced at her reflection. The new caramel-colored highlights in her dark hair brought out the amber

flecks in her eyes and made them sparkle, just like her stylist, Jakkob, had promised.

—*Best Friends for Never*, a Clique novel, by Lisi Harrison (first lines)

This latter example demonstrates our final form of reader-character bonding: *aspiration*, where readers get to take on the skills of our protagonist or the thrills of his life for a brief period of time. We enjoy reading about Massie and her life of backstabbing luxury; or Katniss Everdeen, who can shoot the eye out of a rabbit with a bow and arrow; or James Bond, who combines spying with seduction. We may not connect as directly with aspirational characters as we do with people with whom we identify, because the extreme circumstances of their lives create the kind of emotions most of us (thankfully) don't have to deal with: guilt over causing someone's death, or fury at a world-shaking betrayal. But reading novels about these characters' adventures is like being their best friend—we get to come along on their journeys, participate in the action and hear their feelings about it, and then close the book and walk away if events turn dark or painful. And so we're grateful they're going through these events and we're not: We get all of the excitement, none of the tracker jackers.

If you're creating an aspirational protagonist with some kind of superpower, be it flying or fashion sense, try to build in #3 in this list as well, to create a point of relatability for the reader. Without that, there aren't any chinks in the characters' armor, any ways in which they're weak and everyday like us, and such invulnerability can get boring. (Superman's creators had to invent Kryptonite to keep him compelling.)

5. Give the Character a Compelling Desire.
We talked a lot about desire in the previous chapter, but we'll take it from a different angle here. Suppose you're writing a YA novel, and you decide that your character's desire is to get a job with the IRS so he can pull off a gigantic tax fraud five years from now. I have some bad news for you: That is not compelling. To make it compelling, his desire should be:

✎ Interesting to the intended reader

> Sometimes I set stuff up in my mind like it's going to be true, even though in my heart I know it's not true. It's when I want something so bad it gets real to me before it even happens. I could see me doing this with the basketball tryouts. I mean, like, I knew that nothing I did on the basketball court was going to get my grades up and everything, but somehow I still had this vision of me busting out on the court and then everything being all right. It didn't make sense, but there it was.
>
> —*Slam!* by Walter Dean Myers

Greg "Slam" Harris wants to make his high school basketball team, and he also wants everything to be "all right"—a vague wish, perhaps, but an immensely sympathetic one for anyone in troubled circumstances. Many teenage readers might recognize their own desires in his longings, so this qualifies as "interesting to the intended reader." In contrast, the IRS example collapses because the IRS isn't interesting to most teenagers. (Or adults, for that matter.)

✎ Morally right (unless your character with the desire is meant to be a villain, of course, or morally questionable in general)

> My chest was tight, but I looked at the blue sky, clear and pale above the tree line, and said out loud, "Fine. I'll do it." *I* would speak for Patrick. I'd look straight into the ugliness and find out who hurt him, and when I did, I'd yell it from the mountaintop.
>
> —*Shine* by Lauren Myracle

Not only is this a textbook example of setting up a character's desire explicitly, this narrator has a morally great cause—finding out who assaulted her friend. By rooting for it, we readers will also be on the right side, doing the right thing, which feels good to us.

✎ Has high stakes and immediacy

> I've confessed to everything and I'd like to be hanged. Now, if you please.
>
> —*Chime* by Franny Billingsley (first line)

Clearly, what this character wants is literally a matter of life or death. And life-or-death situations generate action and excitement, so, boom: This character is compelling to me. This also demonstrates technique #1 in this list, "Think Differently," because how often do you hear people both demand to be hanged and then add "Now, if you please"? That intriguing contrast draws me in. And going back to the IRS example again—tax fraud is not a matter of life or death, and the plan would unfold over a number of years, which lacks immediacy. Again, it's a fail.

6. Put Character in Pain, Danger, or Jeopardy.

> They took me in my nightgown.
>
> —*Between Shades of Gray* by Ruta Sepetys (first lines)

> [The letter] began, "Sir, I must explain my actions," and then stopped. Costis couldn't explain his actions. He rubbed his face with his hands and tried again to compose his anguished thoughts into cold words and orderly sentences.
>
> —*The King of Attolia* by Megan Whalen Turner

Characters who are in trouble automatically draw our interest because their situation activates our sympathy and creates narrative questions: Are they going to be safe? How will they escape? What will we learn about them in that escape? This technique only works for characters you want the reader to feel warmly toward; if you create a nasty character and put him in jeopardy, the reader might be perfectly happy to leave him there. I also think that if you're going to use pain and jeopardy, you need to employ them in combination with at least one other technique from this list, so our sympathy can deepen into affection and not just remain shallow pity.

Some writers love their characters so much that they hesitate to cause them pain. I can sympathize with that difficulty, but it's important to remember here that you are not your characters' parent, in charge of keeping them out of danger. Instead, it's your job as a narrative artist to *put* them in danger, to let them run around and be stupid, to make awful things happen to them, even to have them do awful things themselves. You then must show readers how the characters feel when those awful things happen to them, or when the consequences of their actions rebound upon them, because that is the way they will change and grow.

I *love* suffering in a novel. I am a total pain junkie for bad things happening to good characters. That is, in fact, the way some writers plot their novels: Come up with a character, think of the worst thing that could possibly happen to him (within the bounds of good taste and the world of the novel), and make it happen. We then get to see both highly dramatic action and how the protagonist will respond to this challenge and develop as a person, and that pairing makes for good novels.

Speaking of responses:

7. Have the Character Take Action and Show Energy.

Nothing kicks off a novel more excitingly than discovering a character who will DO THINGS—or has already done them and is dealing with the consequences, or is planning on doing them shortly, like Lydia above, and Anne of Green Gables, and Costis struggling with his confession, and the heroines of *Shine* and *Chime*. If a character has a desire, then they'll need some doing to back it up. If a character is in pain or jeopardy, they'll need to DO THINGS to escape or protect themselves. Give us a character who makes decisions, who acts, who DOES THINGS, and readers will follow him anywhere.

Editor Andrew Harwell once pointed out a terrific rule of thumb: The first major dramatized action that your protagonist performs in the novel establishes his character for the reader. We readers will listen to what the protagonist has to say, certainly, especially if she's a first-person narrator. But we pay more attention to the action she takes and the reasons she takes it, because "anything we do reveals us"—emphasis on the DO. If your character's first action is complaining to his mother about homework, he's instantly a whiner in the reader's eyes. If he helps an old lady across the street, he's a kind and thoughtful person. If he helps the old lady across the street only because the old lady's hot granddaughter is nearby, he loses all the kindness points and reads as conniving instead. And if he stays still the whole first chapter, doing nothing but sitting and thinking, then we'll judge him on the quality of those thoughts and what he does with them next. Choose your protagonist's first action carefully, and be sure it makes the right impression on the reader.

8. Use Other People as a Lens on the Character.

According to the Transitive Property of Reader-Character Relations, readers will echo the reactions of characters they already know and like and/or trust, and oppose the reactions of characters they don't like or trust. Consider the opening of *Harry Potter and the Sorcerer's Stone*. The Dursley family is shown to be amusingly small-minded and aggressively normal, so we readers enjoy feeling superior to them. But we also learn the Dursleys hate the Potter family for being so different, and since we dislike the Dursleys, we automatically like the Potters—a useful first step in making readers sympathize with Harry. Think about how this kind of character math works as you introduce new figures into your book.

You can also use supporting characters to add more dimension to a character who thus far has had only one identity.

> In the woods waits the only person with whom I can be myself. Gale. I feel the muscles in my face relaxing, my pace quickening. . . . The sight of him waiting there brings on a smile. . . .
> "Hey, Catnip," says Gale.
>
> —*The Hunger Games* by Suzanne Collins

In the first six pages of *The Hunger Games*, we see that Katniss loves her family, but she's not a particularly kind, enthusiastic, or pleasant person. Then she goes to meet Gale in the woods, and *this* happens: She relaxes. She smiles. She experiences heretofore-unseen pleasure, and Gale likes her as well, which confirms Katniss must have some warmth we haven't seen yet. That affirms our own interest in her and maybe even warms it up to affection, and that makes us extremely invested in her when she volunteers for the Hunger Games at the beginning of the next chapter.

A corollary to the Transitive Property: Readers like characters who are liked by other people. They are suspicious of characters who aren't liked by other people. If you're writing premise-driven fiction, consider giving your protagonist friends right away, because the friends provide an instant affirmation of the worthiness of the reader's interest in the protagonist. With that interest confirmed, you can get right on with the plot.

9. Invest the Character with Secrets or Mysteries.

Like Chekhov's gun, a secret or a mystery in fiction always carries the implicit promise of its explosion. As a result, secrets guarantee activity, which in turn will attract readers. Later in the first chapter of *Harry Potter and the Sorcerer's Stone*, Professors McGonagall and Dumbledore spend *half a page* in their brief scene together discussing the fact that Voldemort couldn't kill baby Harry, which instantly grants Harry a mystery and mystique that is hard to resist. Or:

> He caught me. Dragged me behind the garage. Took Joe Pepitone's baseball cap. Pummeled me in places where the bruises didn't show. A strategy that my . . . is none of your business.
>
> —*Okay for Now* by Gary D. Schmidt

What isn't our narrator telling us? We readers want to know.

Establishing a mystery is another technique that is best used in combination with another strategy here, because a mystery about someone whom you don't care about is not that involving. Mysteries are also easy to overdo: If someone spends more time boasting that he knows a secret than offering us a chance to learn that information, we might get annoyed with him. But if you can show us that the character is withholding information for a good reason, or hint at depths that lurk under a calm surface, we'll be genuinely intrigued.

Finally:

10. Give the Character Internal Tensions or Contradictions.

One of my favorite quotations regarding character comes from Samuel Johnson: "Inconsistencies cannot both be right; but imputed to man, they may both be true." Interesting characters often have two conflicting elements to their personality. A young man might declare publicly that he is a vegan Buddhist, but sneak a cheeseburger when he feels lost; a girl could be a wallflower in class, but a diva on the dance floor. Severus Snape is probably the most fascinating character in the Harry Potter series, because he treats Harry with cruelty and contempt, but Dumbledore assures Harry (and readers) that he remains on the side of right. How can we reconcile these oppositions? We read on to find answers.

Unlike many of the other techniques, you don't necessarily need to introduce character complications in Chapter 1. Show us your protagonist's kindness or her terrific imagination to gain the reader's affections early on. Then, as you write the rest of the book, look for places where you can bring out new contradictions and depths in her—places where someone causes her pain or challenges her certainties, which will strip away some of her niceness. We readers will accept these contradictions so long as you establish the internal postulates, backstory, or conflicting identities that hold these elements in tension together. The more complications and dimensions they have, the more complications and dimensions your plot can have in turn, and the richer and more real your book will feel as a whole.

=== *EXERCISES* ===

Make a list of the first ten things your protagonist or another important character in the manuscript says or does (beyond factual statements in first person, like, "I walked across the room"). Look at that list objectively, trying to forget your knowledge of the context or what happens next.

- **What do you think of that person as seen in this list?** Is he or she interesting? Someone the reader would want to hang out with? Someone *you* would want to hang out with? How does your protagonist relate to others around him? Is she kind or nasty? Does she offer good energy or bad vibes?

- **What kind of bond would a reader have with this character?** (What kind of bond *should* a reader have with this character?) How many of the connecting techniques or qualities above appear in your list? If it's important for the character to give off negative energy: What could you do to make what she says still have some humor, insight, or truth? How can you bring out her vulnerability within the negativity?

Give this list to someone who hasn't read the manuscript and ask for their impressions of the character.

Character Change and Growth

Once we are hooked into a protagonist, we want to see evidence of their development. That is, we want to see how they change emotionally or morally over the course of the novel, through what happens to them, or what they cause to happen, and the events that result—all of which should get the character, and reader, to the emotional and thematic points of the book. I especially encourage you to pay attention to the protagonist's flaws here, the postulates and behavior that might result in bad decisions and terrible mistakes, because what do those cause? PAIN! And pain forces characters to change, which creates growth.

As an example, I'll talk a little about *Marcelo in the Real World*, which we will discuss in depth in the plot section. A quick summary: Marcelo Sandoval is a young man on the autistic spectrum who attends a special school called Paterson, where he believes he belongs (a postulate: He needs to stay in a protected space). His father, Arturo, believes Marcelo could challenge himself further, particularly by attending a public school. He asks Marcelo to spend a summer working in the mailroom of his law firm, Sandoval & Holmes, with the promise that if Marcelo completes the summer successfully, he will get to spend his senior year at Paterson. At the law firm, Marcelo's coworker Jasmine expects him to perform at a professional level, and somewhat to his own surprise, Marcelo discovers he can do it. Another lawyer's son, Wendell Holmes, introduces him to new ideas about power and sex, which challenge Marcelo's innocence on several fronts.

Most crucially, Marcelo discovers a picture of a girl with "half a face." He feels great empathy with the girl, and sets off on a quest to find out who she is and what happened to her. He learns from the girl's lawyer (a man named Jerry Garcia) that her name is Ixtel, she was in a car accident where a supposedly shatterproof windshield exploded, and Sandoval & Holmes represents the manufacturer of the windshield. Marcelo then has to decide whether he will help Ixtel get the restitution she needs from the law firm, even though that means he will effectively "fail" the summer in his father's eyes and have to go to public school. Jasmine assists him with his quest throughout, and Marcelo tries to make sense of feelings he's never experienced before as their friendship deepens into love.

Marcelo grows in the novel because one event after another pushes him out of his comfort zone and forces him to find new depths or skills. His encounters with Wendell, Ixtel, and his shifting image of his father all cause him considerable pain, but he also realizes he can absorb that pain, see the ugliness of the world, and decide to fight against it rather than be part of it. He also shows that he can function in nonprotected spaces quite effectively, which means that Marcelo's own postulate was false, and Arturo was actually right at the beginning. Marcelo's transformation from a naïve innocent to a capable young man feels authentic and powerful because we readers are so invested in his goodness and safety (via numbers 2, 5, and 7 in the list above), and we experience every step of that world-opening journey alongside him.

As an editor, I expect characters to acquire more dimension and depth like this as I read along. If I know everything about a protagonist from the beginning, and nothing happens to open her up and push her toward an emotional point, the action will likely feel inconsequential and thus dissatisfying. Characters changing is also important because we all change and become more complex every day—change is *real*. Thus it should be reflected in the reality of your novel.

The most important elements of creating a character are truthfulness and time. Be truthful in your writing about what you've observed of the world and people's behavior in it, as readers respond to characters and feelings they recognize. That doesn't mean the characters and events have to be people readers have met or incidents they've experienced themselves, but that the characters and events feel consistent with the rules of both this fictional world and the real world readers know. And the best way of creating recognition is to be true to life, anchoring your characters in your knowledge of yourself, other people, and how we all change and grow, combined with your own marvelous imagination and perspective on the world.

And all these things take time. You *could* start a novel with a checklist like the one in the previous chapter: Your protagonist is named Abby, she's twelve and biracial in Memphis, Tennessee, her primary identity is as a big sister, one internal quality is impatience, one external quality is tapping her finger on her lips when she thinks, her pain is her parents are divorced, and so forth. But it's far more likely you'll find out all of her nuances as you write her, especially as you see her take action and react to other people. It doesn't matter whether you can create the character in a checklist if you can't bring her to life on the page, and you need to give that time to develop. That happens the same way you get to know a good friend: multiple experiences together, multiple conversations— multiple drafts, usually.

Saul Bellow said, "The main reason for rewriting is not to achieve a smooth surface, but to discover the inner truth of your characters." Keep digging down until that inner truth is revealed.

CHAPTER 9

Power and Attention

Writing Outside Your Own Groundwork

We wake up. We eat. We work or play or study. We laugh. We mourn. We move toward what we want. We lose loved ones. We worship. We fight against a "them." We gather together. We comfort one another. And we tell each other stories. Every day in history, all around the world, this is what we humans do.

But this is also too simple. Because we wake up on tatamis in Kyoto, or down-filled mattresses on Park Avenue. We eat paella in Barcelona, or bibimbap in Seoul. We worship by bowing toward Mecca, or in a church on Sunday. We fight as child soldiers in Sudan, or against standardized tests in Brooklyn, or for clean water in Rio de Janeiro. We are brown and gay, cis and Asian, rich and neurodivergent, trans and white, abled and poor, straight and black. We are very different from one another, and often we love each other. But often we hurt each other; often, we are the "them."

These differences in who we are and what we do can matter as much as our commonalities, especially in telling stories. Fiction has the incredible power to put readers into the lives and minds of characters whose backgrounds and natures are nothing like theirs, and create an empathy and understanding that readers can take into the real world. But that power also creates a tremendous responsibility for the writers facilitating that connection, as they must recognize the privilege of their roles as facilitators and represent these unfamiliar characters and backgrounds credibly. That privilege can also be misused if those characters are misrepresented or stereotyped, or if the stories reinforce unjust power dynamics in our real world. These negative effects get even more magnified in books for children and young adults, where these stories may provide young readers' first encounters with another culture or history, and can help shape the views of the adults they will become.

In this chapter, we'll consider two forms of writing that can be especially charged with question of power, and thus require writers to pay particular attention to their relationship to their material. The first is writing across cultures—"culture" being the admittedly loaded and imperfect word I am using to signify race, ethnicity, religion, class, gender identity, sexuality, physical ability, neurotypology, and all the other categories we list under "diversity." The second is writing historical fiction, unpacking the baggage of the past to bring it to life in the present. In addressing these forms, I will say right off that I am white, straight, cisgender, able-bodied, and upper-middle-class, and my voice and the voices of people like me get heard a lot in American media. (Put another way: I have privilege up the wazoo.) What I know about these subjects, I have learned from the writers and critics mentioned throughout this chapter and in the list of additional resources you can find at my website, and by editing novels by authors of many cultures writing about many different time periods and people. Please check out the full articles or books referenced in this chapter and the online resources, as those writers have lived these diverse cultural experiences and studied their fictional representations in depth.

Before we get to those two forms, however, I believe six principles apply to all writing outside our own experience.

Six Basic Principles

1. The goal for writers: Create complex characters whose lives, thoughts, feelings, and actions reflect both the groundwork they exist within and their own unique essences.

In other words: Create real people, no matter what age they are, what culture they come out of, or when they lived. The reality of a character is rooted in her essence, as we discussed in "Identity and Choice." But a great deal of her essence will come from her *groundwork*—my term for the place, time, and cultures she lives in, and the power relationships among those cultures. Her groundwork will shape her postulates, behaviors, ethics, outward appearance, desires, and actions—indeed, every other aspect of her character—as it interacts with the essential qualities she was born with. It will also help determine her entire life philosophy, by giving her a sense of what is true, important, and possible for her within her time and cultures. To make your character real, you need to understand her groundwork as well as you know her essence.

This is important because, from an aesthetic perspective, it's simply bad art to make characters who don't seem real. This falsity can appear when a character's essences or actions show no signs of the groundwork they come from: an eight-year-old who talks like a forty-year-old, or a Latino boy whose only indication of his heritage is what the text calls "skin the color of *café con leche*." But it can also happen when you create characters who are *only* that groundwork, whose essences and actions are lost entirely in clichés of it: gay boys who mince and preen, or Victorian characters who are either poor but jolly strivers or overdressed sticks-in-the-mud. Either of these directions shows that you haven't observed, imagined, researched, or thought enough about your characters and their reality yet, and you'll need to go deeper and do better in revision.

2. Your fictional work can contribute to real-world consequences, so imagine responsibly.

I believe every reader should be able to relate to a well-written character, as I said earlier. I also believe readers feel a special spark in reading about a protagonist who reflects their groundwork or experience back to them. When that spark lights, the book has accomplished the most important social work that children's and YA literature can do: portraying the experiences of children and teenagers authentically, letting them know they have been seen, affirming the importance of what they're feeling and going through, and thus providing connection and even hope. But only about 10 percent of all children's and YA books published in the United States are by or about characters of color (the total across all races/ethnicities), which means young readers of color have significantly fewer opportunities to experience this spark via a protagonist who looks like them. We desperately need more books to offer that opportunity.

At the same time, presence in literature isn't all that matters, as consistently seeing false, clichéd, simplistic, negative, or subservient portrayals of yourself can be worse than seeing no images at all. If characters from marginalized groundworks are always relegated to second- or third-degree roles, never written with full complexity or the honor of their own story lines, that not only informs readers with those groundworks that they are "less than" it assures readers from mainstream groundworks that they deserve to be at the center of nearly every story.

It's also important to recognize that the narratives we tell young readers about our history can enormously influence how they understand and value it. A white teenager might read *Gone with the Wind* and mourn the loss of antebellum plantation life; give her *To Be a Slave* and *Day of Tears* by Julius Lester, and that transforms the Confederacy into the dystopia it was. We need to supply all young readers with the most historically complete stories we can, to help them form a nuanced understanding of themselves and the complex world in which they are growing up.

As a writer, you are one voice in a complicated, contentious, tendentious literary ecosystem with very old roots, and you may feel your voice is too insignificant to matter. I assure you that your choices as a writer and reader make a difference. The YA novelist Justine Larbalestier wrote, "We white writers often ask the wrong questions. Instead of 'What am I allowed to write?' how about 'What effects could my writing have on others?'" No matter their subject or groundwork, that is a question all responsible children's and young adult authors should keep in mind.

3. While emotions are universal, what evokes them and how they are experienced and expressed are not. Put another way, you should certainly feel with your characters, but their emotions must come from who they are, not who you are.

I'm going to tell a personal story here. In 2013, I published a novel called *If I Ever Get Out of Here* by Eric Gansworth, a writer who is enrolled in the Onondaga Nation and grew up in the Tuscarora Nation. From the first time I read the manuscript, I loved Eric's textured prose, distinctive characters, backbeat sense of humor, and sensitive portrayal of a cross-cultural friendship between a Tuscarora boy named Lewis Blake and a white kid. At the same time, I was puzzled by some of the book's intrapersonal dynamics. Everyone on Lewis's reservation made fun of him all the time, insulting his hair, his family's poverty, his love of the Beatles, and his academic achievements. This constant barrage of insults felt rather hurtful, so it made sense to me that Lewis wanted to leave the reservation, which was what the title seemed to imply. The white middle school Lewis attended in the book was even lonelier than the reservation, but perhaps he wanted to go to college down the line, I thought, or attend a boarding school. Thus, in the course of our editorial work, I asked Eric if he might want to build a desire to go to a boarding school into the manuscript, to give Lewis something to work toward.

If you're familiar with Native American history, you are probably (quite rightly) laughing at me at this moment, or else horrified by my ignorance. For, beginning in the late 1870s, thousands of Native children were taken from their families and sent to boarding schools hundreds of miles away, where the accepted aim was to "kill the Indian and save the man." These children were punished for any sign of their native languages or practices, and quite often beaten, starved, and emotionally or sexually abused. When Eric and I talked about my idea, he told me his grandparents had spent time at one of these schools, and the schools play a significant role in Native Americans' collective memory. Given that, my suggestion was wildly out of tune with the manuscript.

Eric also explained to me that teasing is a form of affection on the Tuscarora reservation, as *everyone* trades nicknames and insults in a manner that's taken as standard within the community. Individuals never take the digs personally, he said, because they also recognize that very few people will leave the reservation for good, so everyone needs to find ways to live together. The "Here" in *If I Ever Get Out of Here* thus referred not to the reservation, but to Lewis's mostly white middle school, and the exclusion and mistreatment he faced there.

So Eric and I discussed my misunderstanding, I apologized for being so very off base, and we went on to publish the novel happily on both sides, in part because we were able to talk frankly about cross-cultural issues like this. Still, my obtuseness unsettles me as an editor, especially one who wants to publish a diverse mix of authors and stories. I had projected my own values as a "nice" white person and a children's book professional—both cultures in which teasing is automatically bad—onto a cultural situation I assumed I understood, and then suggested the character respond as a person of *my* cultures and privileges would. If Eric had gone along with the suggestion simply for the opportunity to be published (as some authors feel they must), then the ultimate book would not have been as credible or enjoyable to the many Native American kids who have now read it, because it wouldn't have represented the truth of their experience. (And whenever you publish a book about another culture, as a primary goal, it should be credible to the people you're writing about.)

All of this is to say: As human beings, we all feel fear, joy, grief, anger, affection, etc., and you can and should build on your own experience of those emotions to create those feelings within your characters and for your readers. But if you are writing outside of your own groundwork—or when you create any character, really—never assume that where those emotions come from for *you* is also where they will come from for your characters. It's your responsibility to figure out what evokes those emotions for your characters within their groundworks, and how they express them accordingly. This leads to my next principle:

4. Good writing is not about you. Be humble and get out of the way of your characters.

Again, this is true when you create any character, especially one speaking in first person: You need to decenter yourself and forget your own postulates and personality so you can enter the worldview and experience of this totally made-up person. But forgetting your own postulates and personality requires having some awareness of them in the first place! As an example, let's suppose you grew up in a household where your parents talked with you about sexuality from an early age, gave you condoms and a lecture on responsibility and pleasure at fourteen, and let you stay overnight with your girlfriend at seventeen. Now you want to write a book in which two teenagers from a conservative religious community fall in love and face temptation like never before. Given your background, you may instinctively want to portray the community's precepts as repressive and unnatural, which could be what you actually believe, and which is also an attractive position for a novelist, as it provides you with an easy villain and an obvious conflict. But this would not do justice to your characters in all their dimensions, as they would likely find meaning in following their religious traditions, and see real honor and romance in the idea of waiting until their wedding night. You serve your characters most and write them best when you understand their thinking and treat their choices as valid.

In an excellent blog post entitled "Writing Past Your Shit 101,"* the novelist Justina Ireland sets forth a practical method for negotiating the distance between you and your characters:

> **1. Who is your character? Make a list. . . .** This is a pretty easy exercise that we usually do in our heads whenever we start a story. We think about our character, what she wants, who she is, and who the people around her are. . . .

---

* http://justinaireland.com/dammit-this-is-a-blog/2015/8/20/writing-past-your-shit-101-getting-out-of-your-own-way-and-writing-people-not-like-you

For this exercise I'm going to use a character from a book I'm working on. Ophie is an eleven-year-old black girl from 1930s Mississippi who can throw fire. At the beginning of the story her mother sells her to a circus sideshow. So Ophie's list would look like this:

- Young
- Throws fire
- Sold by her mother
- Circus
- 1930s (black and poor)

Your list can be longer, but I think it's best to start with a relatively short one and grow from there.

2. Compare yourself to the character you're writing. At this point we're going to identify our shit. Your shit is any of the traits on that list that you do not share with your character. . . . Write your shit next to that of your main character's:

- Young—Not young
- Throws Fire—Doesn't throw fire
- Sold by her mother—Mom hasn't sold me yet
- Circus—No circus
- 1930s—2015!

Simple, right?

3. Identify your shit. Now get over it. For every trait where you identified a huge difference between you and your character, these are potential hurdles to nailing your character's perspective. To get over your shit you need to realize how it colors your worldview. For example, even though I'm black, being black in the 1930s was way different. So this is a place where my expectations of how the world works could really get me all twisted up.

This "identifying your shit and getting over it" can be a tremendously difficult thing to do, because, again, it requires being able to recognize your "shit" in the first place—the postulates you live and likely were raised with, which might be as natural and invisible to you as breathing. If you have not thought about these issues before, then I'd add one more step to this process:

═ EXERCISE ═

Make a list of all of your personal cultures, including your race/ethnicity, religion, sexuality, gender identity, dis/ability, and socioeconomic class. (Feel free to add your own categories or other identities here.) How did you become a member of that culture? Did you inherit it from your parents (what the writer Andrew Solomon calls a "vertical identity"), or did you grow into it on your own or with a peer group (a "horizontal identity")? Think about the feelings, acts, or experiences that define this culture for you—its mental, emotional, or physical realities. What are a few postulates of it? Name four things that people of your culture do or refuse to do that outsiders might not understand. How did you learn them? What are your feelings toward this culture now?

If you want to write outside your own cultures, externalizing them like this should help you see them more clearly and start to be able to stand outside them. That said, this "getting over it" is not something you do once and then you're fine forever; it will be an ongoing process of discovery, learning, and self-correction throughout your research, writing, and revision, and even for the rest of your life. You will need to be quiet, listen deeply to others, and avoid jumping in to offer judgment or your own perspective; you will need to accept both how much you have to learn and what others have to teach you. Part of this acceptance may involve recognizing how you and your cultures have acted or continue to act badly toward others in the past or present, and how you may have benefited from that oppression. None of this is easy, but ideally it will widen your range of understanding and empathy, and make you a better writer in the process.

Getting out of the way of your protagonist is only half the battle; you also have to create a character who will fill that space authentically. And that means you need to:

5. Learn the reality of the groundwork you're writing about.

Creating a reality for your characters encompasses two major constructs. First, you need to know the physical reality they move through every day: where they live, the food they eat, the clothes they wear, how they get home from school, what games they'd play. This allows you to create a believable setting for the action, and it also determines much of your protagonist's groundwork, in the way any kid who grows up in rural New Mexico, say, will think and act differently than one born and raised in New York City.

Their groundwork will also shape their internal realities, from the things they do and don't think about, to the explicit lessons that the parents teach their children, to the implicit messages that suffuse their environments. As an example, many African-American boys in the United States get "the Talk" from their elders at a certain point in their lives—an explanation of how to behave if they get stopped by the police—and they live with the expectation that the police *will* stop them, the knowledge of an immediate presumption of guilt. The mental realities of a groundwork can also resonate down generations, even when the family's circumstances change. A child in the Great Depression might learn to eat every morsel on his plate, no matter how terrible the food, because he doesn't know when he will get another meal. If, in the 1960s, he required his children to follow that same rule, it might result in weight issues or familial resentment, creating a new conflict from an old struggle. Do the very best you can to absorb all your character's external and internal realities into their essence.

How do you learn about a reality that isn't your own? Justina Ireland identifies the first step:

RESEARCH! For each of those categories I identified I need to get my happy ass out there and research. I need to read as close to authentic, primary source documents as possible. That means I need to see if I can find pieces written by circus performers from the 1930s, and if not, then circus performers from the early 20th century.... THE GOAL SHOULD BE TO GET AS CLOSE TO YOUR CHARACTER'S TRAIT AS HUMANLY POSSIBLE. I need to read pieces written about neglectful mothers, and I need to either hang out with younger kids (in a noncreepy way) or try to remember what being eleven was like, since I once actually experienced that.

As Ireland says, prioritize materials *by* the people of the culture and time you're writing about—news articles, journals, archival documents, fiction, etc.—over resources *about* them written by outsiders. Talk (or rather, listen) to people from that culture or who grew up at that time about their experiences. Learn the history and historiography of the culture, as well as how people live in it today. Read contextual material to understand the sociology and economics of the situation you're writing about. Go to the place where your novel is set, if at all possible, to observe the rhythms of the days, how the history lives in the present, even the color of the light. Don't think of research as a burden: It's a terrific opportunity to learn more about your protagonist, draw connections among her multiple identities, and ultimately go deeper into her life and the story you'll tell about her.

I'll make a plea here as an editor: When you sit down to write, please do not put all of that research into your story! Authors often do this either out of a genuine love for the subject and desire to share cool information—"The ancient Egyptians adored board games! Isn't that crazy awesome?"—or because they're trying to prove they *have* done their research and ward off criticism. As with all writing, the information you include should be strictly what is relevant to your protagonist's experience or the novel's points, and, with a first-person narrator, what she would realistically notice and remark on in the course of the action.

6. Understand the general; write the specific.

The reason you need to know as much as you can about your protagonist's groundwork is to avoid "the danger of a single story," as the brilliant Chimamanda Ngozi Adichie calls it in her wise TED talk by that title.* When a writer knows only one story of a culture—having only one image of its people, or letting one image blot out all of the diversity thriving within it—the resulting characters will often turn out to be stereotypical and clichéd. Seeing more, knowing more, understanding more, gives you the opportunity to think more widely and write more interestingly.

Still, in writing a novel, you are not writing the story of all children or teenagers in an entire culture or historical moment; you're writing about one set of fictional characters at one particular place and time. Thus you need to craft specific characters out of that wide-angle view, using their many diverse groundworks and essences to create the kind of complex multidimensionality we discussed in point #1 above. Daniel José Older's heroine in *Shadowshaper*, Sierra Santiago, is sixteen, an artist, an Afro-Latina of Puerto Rican descent, a resident of the Bed-Stuy neighborhood in Brooklyn, a good granddaughter to her abuelo Lázaro, a good friend to her group of girlfriends, a watchful person who picks her battles, and a fierce fighter once she's in them. She doesn't alternate among these qualities and identities; her character is the sum of all of them, and they all play a role in her action within the book. That is the kind of richness you should be aiming for in all your first-degree fictional people.

With these six principles as a baseline, we'll look at the two specific forms I mentioned earlier.

---

* http://www.ted.com/talks/chimamanda_adichie_the_danger_of_a_single _story/transcript?language=en

Writing Across Cultures

As noted earlier, when the topic of writing across cultures or groundworks comes up on panels or online, it often devolves into the question of "Who is allowed to write about whom"—whether a man can create a female protagonist, or a white person can create a protagonist of color. The answer is, everyone is allowed to write everything: There are no Writing Police who will break down your door and take you to Writer Jail the moment you daydream a story starring someone different from you. Moreover, if you're writing a novel set in the ever more diverse contemporary United States, it *ought* to incorporate people with a wide range of groundworks, as otherwise it won't reflect the reality your young readers see every day.

But while you can do whatever you want, you will not receive a Get Out of (Writer) Jail Free card for the end result. Writing a novel based in a cultural groundwork that's not your own can necessitate a lot of work, over and above the work writing fiction already requires. You will likely be held to a higher standard of credibility than authors with that groundwork have to meet, and if you can't achieve that standard, you may well get critiqued for it. If this seems unfair to you, and/or you aren't up for doing the work, meeting that standard, or facing that possible critique, then it might be better not to try it at all.

That may sound harsh, but it's the truth of the present climate in children's and YA publishing, where we see intense demand both for more books that centralize marginalized cultures and people, and for more authority, empathy, and humility within those books when they are published. "Authority" means that the writer has either grown up in or demonstrated a long-term engagement with the culture portrayed in the book. (Research is a basic beginning here, but lived experience is vastly preferable.) "Empathy" means that the writer understands the realities, joys, and pain of that culture deeply, portrays its nuances within the book and the characters (so it's more than a single story), and is on the side of the people of that culture in the face of the dominant powers—an alliance demonstrated through both the overt plot dynamics and the subtler intricacies of the writing. And "humility" means that the writer is aware of her power and responsibility in writing about this culture (especially if few portrayals of it exist), and she writes with honesty, thoughtfulness, and respect for that culture's voices. Every writer, editor, critic, and reader sets their own standards for authority, empathy, and humility, which are often determined in part by their relationships to the culture shown in the book, and there is no method that will prove definitively to everyone that you possess these qualities. The best you can do is actually have them, and demonstrate them thoroughly in your writing.

Indeed, in terms of humility, you should think seriously before you begin about what kind of novel you want to write and your motives for telling a story cross-culturally. What is your connection to the community you're writing about? Why *do* you want to tell this story? If you want to show more of the reality of our world, which is incredibly diverse, that makes sense. If you're "doing diversity" because it's trendy, that's questionable, because you're taking other people's cultural experiences solely for your own publishing benefit. If you hope to reveal either the awesomeness of a particular culture or the complexities of some issue within it, consider finding writers from that culture and signal-boosting *their* stories, rather than sharing their stories for them. Daniel José Older calls this check of your motives "the Why and the No" in a commanding essay first published in BuzzFeed, "12 Fundamentals of Writing 'the Other' (and the Self)"*:

> Sometimes, folks skip over the most basic questions: Why do you feel it falls to you to write someone else's story? Why do you have the right to take on another's voice? And should you do this? The answer isn't always no—as writers, we are constantly entering other people's heads. But too often we don't stop to consider whether it's the right thing to do. Sometimes, the answer is no.

If you decide to proceed, do so with care for the sensitive cultural ground you're treading. In her excellent essay "Appropriate Cultural

---

* http://www.buzzfeed.com/danieljoséolder/fundamentals-of-writing-the-other

Appropriation,"* Nisi Shawl describes three categories of people who write about other cultures. (She credits Diantha Sprouse for originating this formulation.) The first category is Invaders, who "take whatever they want for use in whatever way they see fit. They destroy without thinking anything that appears to them to be valueless. . . . Theirs is a position of entitlement without allegiance." The second is Tourists: "They can be accommodated. Tourists may be ignorant, but they can be intelligent as well, and are therefore educable." Finally, "Guests are invited. Their relationships with their hosts can become long-term commitments and are often reciprocal." (Writers do not get to decide whether they're Guests.) Shawl continues:

> When first learning about and incorporating aspects of another's culture, then, we ought to act like the best of all possible Tourists: to stay alert and to be observant, watch for the ways our own background influences how we interpret our surroundings. We ought to remember that we have baggage. We ought to be prepared to pay for what we receive. . . . We ought to be honest about the fact that we're outsiders. And since we're in an unfamiliar setting, we shouldn't be ashamed of occasionally feeling lost. We ought to swallow our pride at such times and ask for help, ask for directions.

In touring a new world, you'll inevitably be confronted with the power relationships between cultures, and the history of dominant cultures invading and pillaging nondominant ones. Invaders assume all cultural material—historical experiences, artistic creations, religious and mythological systems—belongs to anyone who becomes aware of it, and it is all fair game for their own work. This attitude leads to cultural appropriation—the act of taking cultural property that belongs to a group

---

* http://www.irosf.com/q/zine/article/10087. Shawl is also the cowriter (with Cynthia Ward) of an entire book on this topic, *Writing the Other*, which I highly recommend.

with less power and using it for an Invader's own ends. (It's analogous to stealing a culture's copyright.) When an Invader appropriates that property, it often gets stripped of the layers of meaning, ritual, pain, emotional effect, and accumulated experience that an insider would see in it; or worse, the Invader steals that effect and meaning as well, to lend to their own work a depth it otherwise would not achieve. Writers should tread carefully here, and consider the idea that some things don't belong to them or are not for them to write about.

As a tourist, you should pay attention to "the danger of the single story," and the importance of specificity on both the cultural and individual levels. If you were writing a book about a Native American girl, for instance, it would not be acceptable to use the experience or practices of the Lakota nation to represent those of the Cherokee (nor to mix the two), as that would imply their stories were identical. The same goes for generalizing from one region of a country to another: Imagine what would happen if a well-meaning Ukrainian writer tried to set a story in South Dakota, but his only image of American people was the cast of *Friends*. The result would likely not be credible to any American reader.

The single story can be just as pernicious on the individual level, as no two people from the same culture ever act and feel in the exact same fashion on every matter, and that individual diversity should come through in your book. In 2011, I published Trent Reedy's first novel, *Words in the Dust*. The book was narrated by a thirteen-year-old girl in Afghanistan—a groundwork that was very far from Trent's personal experience as a white man from Iowa (albeit one who had served with the National Guard in Afghanistan). Because of that disjunction, I believe I snorted audibly when I received the pitch from Trent's agent. But the novel won me over completely (and has since won praise from Afghan and Muslim readers as well), in part because Trent deliberately set up points of view and counterpoints of view within both his characters and their cultures. If the white medic from the United States seemed like a positive character because of her desire to help Afghans, Trent also showed readers her obliviousness to Afghan cultural practices, which hurt her cause. While the protagonist,

Zulaikha, wanted to go to school, her sister Zeynab was eager to marry and have children of her own. This doubling strategy created both complex characters who were more than one single "good" or "bad" identity, and realistically diverse viewpoints within the two cultures that come in contact in the book.

This same complexity can be present in any situation in which a character juggles multiple cultural or other identities. If you create a Hasidic boy who loves playing *Minecraft*, for instance, there may not be anything particularly Jewish about his online experience except that he can't play on Saturdays. A Chinese American girl attending an exclusive prep school in Silicon Valley might have more in common with her classmates there than with her cousins newly arrived from Guangzhou. A gay teenager in Los Angeles in 2016 will have a vastly different experience of gay life than a boy in Los Angeles in 1991, when AIDS was raging within the community and gay culture was much more hidden and concentrated. In each of these cases, you need to know as much about the culture as the characters themselves know by the end of the book, and then balance the representation of the culture on the page with their individual essences and experiences in the story.

You also must look at how the character would be influenced by their culture's interaction with the dominant culture in both positive and negative ways. The gay boy in Los Angeles may experience homophobia within American culture at large, but he might then appreciate his high school's GSA as a safe space all the more. While race does not play a major role in the plot of *The Great Greene Heist* by Varian Johnson (‡)—a hugely fun middle-school caper novel starring the ultrasmooth Jackson Greene—we see a chilling moment in the school office that demonstrates its presence:

Ms. Caroline Appleton—officially the school's senior administrative assistant, but old enough to remember when it was okay to be called a secretary—peered at Jackson over the rim of her glasses. "Are you here for your weekly meeting, or are you in trouble?" she asked. "Boys like you are always up to one thing or another."

Jackson looked at his skinny brown hands. He never quite knew what Ms. Appleton meant when she said "boys like you." He hoped she meant something like "boys named Jackson" or "boys who are tall," but he suspected her generalizations implied something else.

Ms. Appleton's microaggression anchors the romp of the novel in the power dynamics of the real world. Later, Jackson and his team will use Ms. Appleton's racism against her, as they convert her confusion over the identities of two Asian students into an opportunity to procure a key item for their heist. Showing specific representations of cultural experience on the page ensures that your characters' groundworks run more than skin-deep.

To learn about such experiences large and small, you need to do research using all the methods described earlier. At the same time, be aware of the limits of research, and of your sources in general. Who wrote your primary sources? What are the power dynamics involved in *their* creation? If you're writing about a Kikuyu girl in Kenya, say, a male elder of her clan may be the person who gets to "speak" in media, but he would probably have a very different view of her life than she would. Daniel José Older suggests researching how the culture has previously been represented in media by outsiders, and how people of that culture responded to that representation. Being aware of those depictions will help you write more original stories that don't repeat tired or false ideas.

All of this has been looking at the culture from the outside. When you sit down to write, you must imagine it from the inside, where all of these dynamics, issues, and details will be subsumed into your protagonist's everyday existence and the book's story. In some books, like *The Great Greene Heist*, that story will not engage with cultural issues directly, but simply be enacted by a diverse group of characters. In others, like *Shadowshaper*, cultural questions will be central to the plot. Try to know your protagonist's groundwork and external reality well enough by this point that you can concentrate on writing the story as best you can.

If your novel dramatizes multiple cultures in contact, be very aware of who has agency in the book—who makes decisions and creates change in the action. If a protagonist from a dominant culture instantly becomes the leader of a group of diverse characters or a nondominant people, and then solves all of their problems (also known as the "White Savior" complex), that shows clichéd thinking. Likewise, if characters from a nondominant culture exist solely to help the dominant protagonist on her way to heroism or emotional growth, through her witness of their suffering or her activism on their behalf, that is centering her experience at the expense of theirs. On the flip side, Older points out that people from a dominant culture can contribute to the diversity conversation by writing their own experience of cultural complications:

> There is no shortage of books by white people about people of color; what we don't see a lot is white people writing about the emotional, political, social experience of being white, the challenges and complexities of whiteness. We don't see many men writing about patriarchy, how it has damaged us, how we dance in and out of these impossible gender binaries in our daily lives. Yes, these sound like essay topics, but really, these are exactly the kinds of inner conflicts that breathe life into a character.

In all your writing, keep in mind the diversity of the audience your book might reach. It's extremely easy to think of your intended audience as readers who are just like you, meaning they might look and think like you as well. People of every groundwork will be reading your novel, however, and stereotypical plot events, anecdotes, and even individual words and phrases (like "gyp" or "low man on the totem pole") can be offensive to members of a particular culture reading the book. Even if you don't feel concerned about causing offense here, many people would be jarred out of their reading experience by the inclusion of such references, and it's good to break the waking dream of your novel as little as you can.

Finally, you should have the manuscript read by several insiders of that culture—ideally people who are as close to this particular subculture as possible. (Getting multiple vetters helps you avoid the single-story problem.) If you don't have friends from that culture, then you may be able to find experts in academic departments, cultural centers, or a willing librarian; but your vetters must be people of that culture, not an outsider who studies it. Ask them to watch for particular things you're worried about. Listen well to what they have to say, and incorporate their critiques. You should pay these people for their time and work.

No matter how much research you do, you are pretty much guaranteed to get some things wrong, and you may need to revise some portion of your original conception of your characters or action in order to be accurate or respectful to the culture in question. Be grateful when you discover you must make such revisions, because you've just been saved from publishing something really dumb. You should always be a little nervous when writing cross-culturally; if you aren't, or if you find yourself prioritizing your own creations over portraying a cultural reality as rightly as possible, you may be acting like one of those thoughtless Invaders. Be a Tourist, stay humble, and write better.

Writing Historical Fiction

Cleopatra was the glittering queen of Egypt, murderer of her sister, consort to Julius Caesar, wife to Mark Antony: How did it feel to be her daughter? What was it like to fight for Napoleon at Marengo, or witness Captain Cook "discovering" your island home of Kauai, or live in the Agra Fort with Shah Jahan? The power of historical fiction lies in its ability to put readers inside those extraordinary experiences and offer an interpretation of those events—a perspective made especially persuasive by its narrative form. To write responsibly here, authors need to make thoughtful choices regarding the facts they choose to include, the possible interpretations of those facts, and the implications of the book as a whole.

The first choice a writer makes is the historical situation to explore, which often grows out of a personal fascination with a time period and the questions it raises. Your choice needs to be compelling to people besides you, however. Why would a child or young adult reader (or the adults who buy books for them) want to know about this topic or pick up a book about it? Look for a situation with appeal in at least two of these four categories:

- **Personality:** Writing a novel involving Cleopatra or Napoleon gives readers the opportunity to "see" those figures in all their genius and ruthlessness. They are people who DO THINGS, and the novel will offer us an opportunity to get to know them beyond the historical facts.
- **Situation/conflict:** Look at the qualities of a good premise on p. 42, and try to find historical situations that allow for those dynamics, particularly in pairing compelling external action with character development. The first contact between native Hawai'ians and James Cook would be full of drama for both sides.
- **Setting:** Take us to a time and place that's interesting to picture in our heads and holds the possibility of many stories, like the incredible Agra Fort in northern India.
- **Relevance to curriculum:** Beyond trade sales, historical fiction can have a secondary market in schools, as teachers might use it as supplemental material for history classes. Knowing when a particular subject is taught in schools might help you determine where to position the age level of the book.

In making your choices, be very aware of the power dynamics involved, especially if you're choosing to write cross-culturally. Again, what you write here might offer a young reader their first view of a historical situation; give them one that honors the richness of people who have not always been represented complexly.

Once a situation is in place, you must create a protagonist. If your protagonist is a real person, like Cleopatra, your plot should follow the known historical events. You then construct your protagonist's essence and additional backstory so she enacts those events in a psychologically coherent fashion. If your protagonist is an invented character in a compelling situation or setting, or in proximity to one of these great personalities, then you'll need to invent a personal plot for this protagonist to run alongside the historical events. (As an example, in *Cleopatra's Moon* by Vicky Alvear Shecter (‡), Cleopatra Selene, the queen's daughter, struggles to come into her own in the shadow of her dazzling mother.) Either way, the novel must remain reasonably true to the facts, while incorporating stakes, rising action, subplots, a climax, and all other elements of a strong plot, to make these historical events (whose endings are never in doubt) newly fresh, suspenseful, and compelling.

What does "reasonably true" mean? Opinions vary here, depending upon how a writer weighs the value of accuracy to historical fact against the emotion of the reader's experience. As a rule of thumb, the more accurate you can be to the history, the better. Major historical actors, events, and outcomes should remain the same, but your invented protagonist could be present or even take over minor duties at those events. You can introduce new characters or events to fill out your character's emotional development or gaps in the historical record, so long as they do not otherwise contradict that record. Combining or eliminating less significant or repetitive events, or eliding dates in service of a timeline, are also generally considered acceptable. (You should generally include an author's note acknowledging any large changes; see Laurie Halse Anderson's *Chains* for a marvelous example.) On the other hand, when Eric Gansworth and I were working on *If I Ever Get Out of Here*, I suggested that we could shift the month of a real Paul McCartney concert that his protagonist attended in order to tighten up the timeline of the book as a whole. Eric replied that the history of Native Americans has been so badly misrepresented in literature, he wanted the history in *his* novel to reflect strictly the facts. Be aware of who it affects if you alter or soften history.

Before you can change the historical record, you have to know what it is. That requires research—reading as much material as you can about that time to absorb the facts of the events and the feeling of the period. Once again, primary sources from multiple points of view should be paramount. Depending upon the time period and subject matter, it can be difficult to find primary sources written by women or people from a nondominant culture; you may need to read between the lines of other documents, or extrapolate from the few accounts that do exist. For events within living memory, consider interviewing people who were present at them. Look at photographs and paintings to get a sense of the visual culture of the time; study the media your protagonist might have consumed (including newspapers, novels and poetry, and theater) to learn the dramas and daydreams of the day. Take notes about your personal reactions to your material as well: What excites you? What disgusts you? What details stand out? What utterly blows your mind? Your fellow modern readers might well share those reactions, so they can be great pointers toward your ultimate story.

From your research, you should be able to gather enough material to create your protagonist's groundwork, which would encompass everything we've talked about on the subject up to this point, plus an appropriate general mind-set for the character at that time. You need to be wary of the dangers of a single story here as well. For instance, given the Crusades, it's easy to theorize that all medieval Christians hated and feared Muslims; but in fact many Christian and Islamic people lived peaceably together in the Holy Land as traders, tourist guides, or simply fellow citizens. If a character's mind-set would render him offensive to modern sensibilities—if the protagonist's father is a Crusader who believes Muslims should be slaughtered, and says so—that requires careful handling, as many people in your book's audience would find his statements reprehensible. You could contextualize the father's opinions by showing the background they come out of; you could elide them by creating a plot that doesn't evoke their expression; you could show him as ridiculous, thus rendering his prejudices likewise laughable; or his feelings could change over time, and he could come to regret his earlier bombast. At least one Muslim character, positively portrayed, could counter his crudeness with complexity. History is full of unenlightened opinions and behavior, nuance and contradiction; the historical novelist must bring a wider understanding to these old problems.

As you write, the historical events should emerge from your characters' lives the same way the action develops in contemporary novels—that is, through their emotions and actions, dramatized on the page. The events that are about to unfold are not inevitable and fixed facts to your characters; they're the living, present results of their own passions, choices, or work, and with one small change, the action could go in an entirely different direction. Try to make that action as living and present as possible, and avoid historical portentousness about the long-term results. (That is, don't write, "What ho, Robert! It's a beautiful day at the Globe Theatre in London." "Yes, Will. Your *Hamlet* will be a smashing success!"). Create the excitement and significance of events at that time, in that moment, for those characters, and let the history take care of itself.

Similarly, try to minimize your explanations of the historical background, and instead work the information readers must know into the protagonist's point of view or daily life. Some contextual explanation almost certainly will be necessary, especially at the beginning of the novel, when readers are getting oriented to the characters, their relationships, and the time period. But try to keep that explanation plot- and character-relevant and realistic by tying it back to your protagonist's personal concerns, and making the source of the information protagonist-appropriate. In *One Crazy Summer* by Rita Williams-Garcia, ten-year-old Delphine observes her mother, Cecile, meeting with three strangers in 1968 Oakland:

> I was sure they were Black Panthers. They were on the news a lot lately. The Panthers on TV said they were in communities to protect poor black people from the powerful; to provide things like food, clothing, and medical help; and to fight racism. Even so, most people were afraid of Black Panthers because they carried rifles and shouted "Black Power." From what I could see, these three didn't have rifles, and Cecile didn't seem afraid. Just annoyed because they wanted her things but she didn't want to give them. Big Ma said God could not have made a being more selfish than Cecile. At least she was like that with everyone, not just us.

Williams-Garcia expertly sets up both the historical purpose of the Panthers and the fear they created here, but because the passage begins with a believable source for Delphine's knowledge—the TV—and concludes by tying back to her emotional quest in the book—understanding her intense, enigmatic mother—this feels like character information rather than infodump. Eric Gansworth achieves a similar feat in Chapter 1 of *If I Ever Get Out of Here*, in a passage he added partly in response to my misinterpretation of the teasing: "I didn't grasp that the way we talk to one another on the reservation was definitely not the way kids talked in this largely white junior high. On the rez, you start getting teased a little bit right after you learn to talk, and either you learn to tease back or you get eaten alive." Those few lines contextualized the teasing for non-Native readers while also setting up the novel's conflict between Lewis's white middle school and the reservation world.

The goal for all historical fiction is always to write great fiction: to make those conflicts, quests, documented events, authorial inventions, and interpretations reveal complicated, living people of the kind described at the beginning of this chapter. In all your fiction, strive for that honesty and complexity foremost. Recognize the power dynamics both of and within your writing. Get yourself out of the way. Pay attention—the most basic writerly skill. Create the most complex characters you can, living lives as rich and textured as your own; and keep listening and learning.

CHAPTER 10

Structure and Sensibility

The Power of Plot

I've been teaching writing workshops for over a decade now, and I've discovered that more than any other aspect of fiction, plot stresses writers out. They're told plots must be BIG and FAST-PACED and SEXY and SALEABLE to even get close to being published; plotting seems to have some hidden, byzantine standards that are impossible to fulfill. As a result of all this pressure, the subject can feel tremendously difficult, because it's so easy for a plot to seem too quiet, or boring, or just wrong.

Well, the writers are right, to some extent: There *are* actual standards for plotting, and writers *are* expected to fulfill them or be judged negatively. The good news is that these standards are neither obscure nor complicated, and they can be bent to suit almost any kind of novel you want to write, from a sprawling political fantasy to a quieter, more domestic coming-of-age novel. In every case, you just need to know the elements of plot, and how to use them to maximize the emotional impact of your book.

Before we delve deeper into this topic, it's worth thinking about what plot does within a novel, and why we bother with it at all. I see plotting as intimately linked to the entire purpose of art, which I define as follows:

Art is the successful creation of an intentional emotion or thought in another person, through a work of imagination and insight.

One of the key lessons I've learned as an editor is that a good work of art has an idea or feeling it intends to convey, and it does that successfully for the vast majority of its audience. (I don't say "every person in its audience," as readers and their reactions are too wildly diverse to ever achieve 100 percent success; but a "vast majority" is nothing to sneeze at.) But how to make that emotion or idea come across? That leads to my next tenet:

To express or create emotion in narrative art, you must invent the right imaginary characters and events for your purpose and make their actions real and meaningful enough that they evoke the feeling you want to establish in the reader.

(Narrative theorists call this invention the "objective correlative.") This means you must choose the *right* imaginary characters and events for your purpose—the ones that will pull forth the *right* reactions and thoughts from readers, based upon their relationship to your characters and their experiences. From this point of view, plot is simply the selection of events and the structure in which those events unfold to create the desired emotional effect. The whole goal of plotting is to maximize those right reactions, those right emotional effects.

That raises an obvious question: What are the "right" reactions and effects?

This is entirely up to you. What do you, as an author, intend the reader to feel and think about with this story? We already investigated this question at some length in discussing points, so look back at your answers there. Basically, your protagonist will start the novel unconscious of your emotional and thematic points, or even have postulates opposed to those ideas. The plot then shows him the way toward those points, or the falsity of those postulates, as he faces new challenges and discovers new abilities and relationships in the course of the novel. By the end, those postulates will have been faced, and he and his world will be irrevocably changed. In sum, a plot should get your character to the emotional point, while leading the reader to the thematic point, all while giving the reader the experiences in the experiential point.

This likely sounds more daunting than it actually is. As a matter of fact, you are probably already incorporating points, structure, stakes, and all the other aspects of plotting we'll discuss here into your novel just as it is now. I'm simply putting names to these things, breaking them down into component parts, so we can see how each part works, and how you might be able to refine those parts within your individual book to make its machinery run even more smoothly. So please don't feel intimidated by any of this—or by plotting in general! Plot is just storytelling with a little more form to it, as you'll see.

Eight Principles of Plotting

Let's begin with some basic principles about plotting. (I'll be introducing a lot of terms throughout this chapter that come together in the Plot Checklist on p. 200, so you might wish to copy it out and keep it handy.)

1. A story is a sequence of events. A plot is the deep structure formed by those events, which give the action shape and lead to the book's meaning. In *Harry Potter and the Sorcerer's Stone*, the *story* is about an orphaned boy—an outcast even in his own family—being chosen to go to a magical school, where he makes friends, takes classes in magic, learns to play Quidditch, discovers that an evil overlord wants to kill him, and has a first encounter with the overlord. The *plot* is about a boy who is unloved and abused, finding a place where he is valued and receives emotional support, and discovering a challenge that threatens his new place of stability.

2. We can identify the plot by a change: Your protagonist's circumstances change over the course of the novel, and so might he. If the protagonist himself changes, that change is usually the emotional point. You can have a story with three hundred pages of events—characters fighting, falling in love, journeying to distant lands—but if the characters end up in the same place where they began, emotionally and physically, you don't have a plot. That story might still be fabulous just as an entertainment, but without some meaningful change in the characters or their lives, it's not reaching the depths it could achieve. (If you ever have a manuscript rejected as "slice of life," that means the editor or agent couldn't perceive a change coming about through the book's events.)

3. The two dimensions of a plot are the action plot and the emotional plot.

- **The action plot is the change in the character's circumstances.** For instance, Harry Potter is plucked from obscurity and hardship, informed he has a great history and destiny, and sent off to Hogwarts, where he becomes a hero.
- **The emotional plot is the change within your protagonist.** At Hogwarts, Harry makes friends and finds courage within himself.

Another way of thinking about this: The action plot is the challenges imposed upon your protagonist from the outside by his circumstances or other characters. The emotional plot is the challenges that arise from within the character. (Some writers use "external plot" and "internal plot" for these accordingly.)

While books often have multiple action plots and emotional plots, as a rule of thumb, it is extremely useful to have one central action plot that launches the action at the beginning and is resolved at the climax. That arc will determine the length of the book, and all of your subplots will support it.

4. Your plots will begin when a change occurs. Your protagonist moves to a new town; she loses an old friend; she meets a new enemy. Only once some clearly identifiable external change like this has taken place, pointing the way to the novel's overarching action, can we say the plot has begun. As a rule of thumb, you should start your novel as close to the occurrence of this change as possible, while still establishing your characters and context.

5. Your protagonist's choices and actions must advance the plot. In the ideal novel, action and character development function like the double helix of DNA: Our protagonist wants her desire (part of her character), so she does something in order to get it (action). This gets her in trouble, which makes her feel badly (character), and escaping that negative feeling inspires her to try a different approach to her desire (action). Then the consequences of *that* action rebound on her, challenging an internal postulate (character) as she reacts yet again (action). As this cycle repeats over and over, our heroine learns more and more about herself and her circumstances, until the novel arrives at its climax.

6. Your plot is over when the changes have been completed, and/or when all of the points have been achieved. If you haven't gotten to these points, or the changes are not fully accomplished, then the book will feel either meaningless or incomplete.

7. Not all books have both kinds of plots, or balance both kinds of plots equally. And that's fine! If you're writing a rip-roaring fantasy adventure, you will need more action plot than emotional plot. If you're writing a novel about a boy dealing with his grandfather's death, that will likely be heavier on the emotional side than on action. (If you're writing an ongoing series, the protagonist's emotional plot and some larger action plots can stretch across several books, though each volume should have its own independent action plot.) In all cases, try to have enough of each kind of plot to keep the story moving forward, while simultaneously developing the reader's connection to the protagonist and consequent response to what happens to him.

8. A plot matters only if readers are interested in the characters. To revisit our earlier discussion of relatability, you have to construct a protagonist whom readers want to follow. If they don't believe in or aren't interested in your characters, the action won't carry any emotional charge for them, and they may not finish the book.

═══ *EXERCISES* ═══

Make a list of all of the story lines in your book, and classify them as action or emotional plots. Which one is your central action plot? Put a star next to it, and then, in a sentence, define your protagonist's change in circumstances from the beginning to the end of the novel. Which one is your central emotional plot? Put a heart next to it, and then, in another sentence, define how the character changes. (Hint: This last will likely be a restatement of the emotional point of the book.)

Create a bookmap for your novel.

Bookmaps

A bookmap, in its simplest form, is a scene-by-scene or chapter-by-chapter outline of a novel. I am agnostic on whether writers should outline their books before they write the first draft; that depends entirely on you and your working style. But I absolutely recommend a bookmap once you've completed a first draft, because it allows you to see the entire plot in compact form and think through its development scene by scene. (My author Trent Reedy compiles his bookmap as he writes his drafts, because it gives him a running account of what scenes he's already written and where he is in the book.) I make a bookmap for every novel I edit, organized by chapter and scene.

You can create a bookmap using a Word document, a spreadsheet, Scrivener, a blank calendar, index cards, a giant piece of posterboard—whatever method best suits your novel, the way you think, and the way you like to look at information. (Some visually oriented writers even storyboard each scene in their novels.) If you're making a written bookmap as a revision tool, you could start with the rubric below, but feel free to add or subtract categories depending on what you need to track in your novel. (I confess I usually just note numbers 1, 2, 4 and 5 from the following list in my own editorial bookmaps, and zoom in on 3, 6, and 7 only if something about the scene isn't working for me.) Anita Nolan's article "The End Is Only the Beginning"* offers further useful suggestions. You can see a (much simpler) bookmap for the entire text of *Marcelo in the Real World* on the Resources page at www.cherylklein.com.

1. **Scene number, chapter number, and starting page number.** I define a scene as "a dramatized action, in a certain limited time frame, during which something changes." The boundaries of a scene are usually set by its narrative arc, which we'll explore in more detail in the next chapter. If you

---

* http://www.anitanolan.com/theend.html

have a long passage of narration that doesn't quite count as a scene, with no specific action or definite end, just include the information from it with the next dramatized scene.

2. **When and where does the action of this scene take place?** This can be either a specific day/date, if you know it, or just a time relative to the previous scene.

3. **What characters are major players here? What do they each want at the beginning of the scene?**

4. **What is the action of this scene?** If you have time, I suggest writing this as both a longer paragraph and a one-sentence summary.

5. **What new information do we learn from this scene? What is the change that takes place by the end of it?**

6. **What is the point of this scene—what is it meant to do, show, or accomplish?**

7. **Note anything you either did well or would like to address in revision.** In particular, think about whether the scene achieves the point from #6, and, if not, what changes might help it get there.

Here's a sample based on the first chapter of *Harry Potter and the Sorcerer's Stone*:

1. Scene 1, Chapter 1, Page 2. (Page 1 describes the Dursleys; page 2 is the first dramatized action.)

2. A Tuesday at the end of October, at Number 4, Privet Drive, and the nearby town where Mr. Dursley works, all somewhere in England.

3. Vernon and Petunia Dursley, who want to keep the Potters' existence secret and continue with their perfectly normal lives; an unfamiliar man in a violet cloak, who is celebrating the disappearance of a You-Know-Who.

4. Long version: As Mr. Dursley goes about his day, he sees a cat

reading a map and strange people in cloaks. Some of them talk about "the Potters" and their son, Harry. Another man in a cloak embraces him and mentions "You-Know-Who" and "Muggles." The news says owls have been flying about all day, and Petunia becomes tense when Vernon mentions her sister. Short version: Mr. Dursley goes about his day, experiencing a series of strange events that seem to be linked to the Potter family in some way.

5. We learn a great deal about the Dursleys and their fear of difference or strangeness, especially in relation to the Potters, who have a son named Harry. People in cloaks are celebrating the disappearance of a "You-Know-Who." Vernon is enjoying his day at the beginning, but is nervous and on edge from these unusual events by the end.

6. In my opinion, this scene is meant to contrast the Dursleys' aggressively petty "normalcy" with the apparent fun the cloaked people are having; make Vernon Dursley ill at ease (which readers enjoy seeing); and intrigue readers with the cloaks, owls, and shooting stars, and the references to the Potters and You-Know-Who.

1. Scene 2, Chapter 1, Page 8.

2. The evening of the same day on Number 4, Privet Drive.

3. Minerva McGonagall wants information; she, Albus Dumbledore, and Hagrid all want to see Harry Potter safely delivered to the Dursleys.

4. Long version: Professor Dumbledore arrives and puts out all of the lights on the street. He greets Professor McGonagall (the cat reading the map earlier), and they discuss the day's celebrations, Voldemort's defeat, the deaths of Lily and James Potter, and what's to become of Harry. Hagrid arrives on a flying motorbike with baby Harry, whom they leave on the

Dursleys' doorstep, and the wizards depart. Short version: Professors McGonagall and Dumbledore discuss the day's events and Harry's future; Hagrid arrives with baby Harry, and they leave him with the Dursleys.

5. We learn about Voldemort's defeat, which is the reason for all the celebrations, and the Potters' deaths. By the end, Harry has been left with the Dursleys.

6. I think this scene is meant to provide a lot of backstory; establish the mystery of why Voldemort couldn't kill baby Harry; create sympathy and a sense of destiny around Harry; and prove that witches and wizards are much cooler, more sympathetic, and more fun than the Dursleys.

Once you've bookmapped the entire text, pull out the short-version summaries and put them in their own document with the scene numbers for a quick reference guide to the action of the novel.

I'll suggest exercises you can run on your novel using your bookmap throughout the next few chapters, along with some commentary about what those exercises might show you. There are no right or wrong answers here, as a bookmap isn't a test; rather, it's a tool you can use to highlight structural patterns, strengths, and weaknesses in your manuscript, discovering information that might be useful to you in a revision.

Plot Types

I believe all stories in essence represent one of these three types of plot:

Conflict: a story where one character's desire opposes another entity's desire. Conflict plots often get expressed as "Human vs. Human" or "Human vs. Nature" or "Man vs. Himself." On the thematic level, a conflict plot is a story about two or more competing ideas about ways of being in the world, like greed vs. generosity, or power vs. love, as they're battled out through two or more representative entities—one of whom is our protagonist. Notable examples include Katniss (representing hardworking everyday citizens) vs. the Capitol (spoiled elites) in *The Hunger Games* by Suzanne Collins, and Piddy Sanchez (innocence) vs. Yaqui Delgado (violence) in *Yaqui Delgado Wants to Kick Your Ass* by Meg Medina. Conflict plots usually provide the most straightforward satisfaction for readers because the players and stakes are clear and the climax and resolution decisive.

Mystery: a story where the protagonist seeks a piece of information. On the thematic level, a mystery is usually a quest for an object representing an idea or ideal: A detective searches for a thief because she wants to restore justice, or a child searches for his mother because he wants the stability and love parents represent. Classic examples include *The Westing Game* by Ellen Raskin; *Harry Potter and the Chamber of Secrets*; and *When You Reach Me* by Rebecca Stead.

Lack: a story where the protagonist seeks some kind of emotional fulfillment. I sometimes think about renaming this the love type, because the protagonist almost always lacks and then develops some form of love for himself or someone else. Most emotional plots are lacks. Notable examples include *Eleanor & Park* by Rainbow Rowell; *Hush* by Eishes Chayil; and *8th Grade Superzero* by Olugbemisola Rhuday-Perkovich (‡).

Of course, nearly all novels use more than one of these types and/or combine them in complicated ways. *Marcelo in the Real World* is framed first as a conflict plot with Marcelo vs. Arturo, his father. (I'll be talking about *Marcelo* a lot through this chapter; if you need a refresher on its plot, it was summarized on p. 123.) After Marcelo goes to work in Arturo's law firm, it turns into a mystery accompanied by a lack, as Marcelo tracks down the disfigured girl in the photo and experiences feelings he's never had before in getting to know Jasmine. The initial drive is a conflict; the bulk of the action is a mystery; the emotional richness comes from the lack. . . . What's the right way to classify this book?

And never mind having multiple plots in one book; it is totally possible to define a single plot in more than one way. Suppose you have a story where a boy and a girl are both looking for a missing amulet, and whichever one finds it first gets to rule the country. You could call that a conflict plot of boy vs. girl; or a mystery plot, because they're seeking information about the amulet; or, supposing they become friends in the course of the search, a lack plot, as they find new support in each other. Nearly all conventional mystery plots could also be called conflict plots, as they're the detective vs. the wrongdoer, or lack plots, as the character lacks information. Nearly all lack plots could likewise be conflicts, as the protagonist must overcome some internal barrier or external antagonist to achieve wholeness. Any story seen from another angle can become a different story entirely.

Still, I believe identifying the type of plot you have is useful, because the type can help define both your protagonist's drive and obstacles at the outset, and then provide a form in which each of your key structural events must happen. If you realize you're writing a conflict novel, for instance, you then know that you'll have to have a scene establishing the antagonistic sides at some point (likely early on); the bulk of the action will involve each side building up its strength and testing its opponent; and the climax will be the final confrontation, which will bring the conflict to some kind of resolution. Gaining that sort of clarity about a book can help guide your choices at every turn. (I would ultimately call *Marcelo* a conflict plot, as the conflict arc provides the book's narrative spine, and thematically, it's a story about the Marcelos vs. the Arturos of the world.)

So which type seems most appropriate for the central plots of your novel? If you have a choice among competing story dynamics, as in the boy/girl/amulet example above, then think about your character's drive in the novel, and what kind of story you're most interested in telling. Does your character want to defeat an enemy? To find a piece of information? To fulfill an emotional need? Which sort of plot do you most enjoy as a reader? Which one excites you most as a writer? From a thematic perspective, what types of ideas do you most want your book to explore? If you enjoy an internal or relationship focus most, you might want to make it a lack plot. If you're interested in two competing philosophies, try a conflict plot. If the character needs to gain knowledge, it's a mystery.

=== **EXERCISE** ===

Go through your list of story lines from earlier and categorize each one as a conflict, mystery, or lack. If it's a conflict, define the combatants and the goals or principles they stand for. If it's a mystery or lack, identify what the protagonist is looking for or lacking.

Plot Structure

A plot structure is a pattern that provides rhythm and shape to a narrative work—a set form in which both the story's action and the reader's emotion can unfold. While the rest of this chapter will focus on the Freytag's pyramid structure, you are by no means required to use it in this single-minded configuration. For example, the Anne of Green Gables books by L. M. Montgomery, Elizabeth Enright's Melendy Quartet, and the delightful Penderwicks novels by Jeanne Birdsall all offer discrete stories in each chapter that together chronicle a particular period of growth for their characters. In *Goodbye Stranger* by Rebecca Stead and *Criss Cross* by Lynne Rae Perkins, the authors select and arrange a series of everyday crystalline moments—none of them very significant or compelling from the outside—to construct perfect glass castles of character, language, and theme. (All of these examples do follow Freytag's pyramid in building to a climactic change or epiphany for their characters, you might note; they simply use it at a softer volume than, say, *The Lightning Thief.*) Altogether, the only requirements for a plot structure are that your book should have a recognizable sequence of changes and consequences, and maintain some kind of both forward motion and narrative and emotional equilibrium in dramatizing that sequence.

Freytag's Pyramid

Pick up a picture book. Go to the opera. Listen to a Top 40 song. Sit down with a sitcom. As diverse as these media are, the same story structure underlies every one: Freytag's pyramid. The nineteenth-century German novelist and playwright Gustav Freytag would likely be forgotten but for his handy little pyramid, which is in turn based upon one of the oldest extant works of literary criticism, the *Poetics* of Aristotle. Freytag created it to describe the five-act dramatic structure of classical plays, but its model of rising action building to a cathartic climax and a denouement that resolves the work's themes can be applied to the vast majority of works in Western dramatic art. It is certainly not the only way to tell a satisfying story, as noted above, and narratives in many other cultures open up in a more cyclical or serial style. However, as the dominant model of Western narrative, the pyramid has set Western consumers' expectations of how a story will be told. As a result, you either need to follow the pyramid in order to satisfy readers' expectations for a story, or signal to readers early on in the work that you're *not* using this model, so they'll be able to recalibrate their assumptions accordingly.

I use a modified version of the pyramid with four key structural events that must be dramatized for the reader:

- The inciting incident
- The escalating and complicating action
- The climax
- The resolution

We'll think through each of these events one by one.

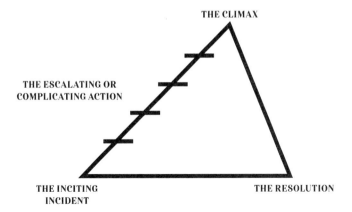

THE CLIMAX

THE ESCALATING OR
COMPLICATING ACTION

THE INCITING
INCIDENT

THE RESOLUTION

The Inciting Incident

Your inciting incident is an event that

A. introduces the conflict, mystery, or lack, or
B. makes that conflict/mystery/lack personal for your protagonist, or
C. gives it new urgency, or
D. all of the above.

It is the moment your action plot and your protagonist meet for the first time, either because an element of the plot comes to claim him, or because he does something that jump-starts the action. It is the beginning of the change, and as such, it signals to readers that the novel is truly beginning too.

- **In a conflict plot,** the inciting incident will be the event that establishes the antagonistic sides. Voldemort has been wreaking havoc in the wizarding world for decades before Harry Potter's birth, but the inciting incident for the novels happens when he kills Harry's parents, making that ongoing conflict urgent and personal to Harry (and, because we are interested in Harry, us readers).
- **In a mystery,** the inciting incident is twofold. First, there's the mysterious event itself, which will often take place before the book begins: A

man is killed; a necklace is stolen; an older sister goes missing. Then a second event makes your protagonist aware of the mystery's existence: The beautiful blonde enters the gumshoe's office with a story about her husband; a girl checks her jewelry box and finds that her favorite necklace is gone; the boy discovers a recent letter from the sister he believed to be dead.

- **Lack plots** usually feature two kinds of inciting incidents: Either the protagonist encounters the person who will fulfill the lack, or some event shows us the lack in the protagonist's life—the negative space— whether the protagonist is aware of it or not. In *Speak*, during Melinda's miserable first day at school in Chapter 1, we see the lack of friends and other connections in her life, which in turn points to the mystery of what happened to her before the book began.

As a practical matter in a reading experience, the inciting incident should ideally be an event that:

1. **Happens in the first two chapters.** You can push it to the third, if those early chapters are intriguing and short; but beyond that, readers will wonder when if ever the action will be starting. In general, the sooner the better.

2. **Is interesting and noteworthy all on its own**—something that makes the reader sit up and say, "Huh, *that's* fascinating," or "Cool!" One of my favorite inciting incidents happens in *Stealing Air* by Trent Reedy (‡), where our protagonist is rescued from a fight by a kid on a rocketbike, who then takes him speeding through the streets of their small Iowa town. The rocketbike is awesome and unexpected, and the ride is exciting and exhilarating, so the book gets the reader's heart racing right from the beginning.

3. **Is suitable to the nature of your story.** Not every book should begin with such a literal bang. Within the confined worlds of Jane Austen novels, an unfamiliar person coming to visit is enough of a major event to get a story started.

4. **Disrupts the status quo.** The event should drop a pebble into the pool of the protagonist's life, so to speak (if she doesn't cause the splash herself).

5. **Reveals the protagonist's character at the outset of the book.** We should learn something about who she is through either her causing that wave or her reaction to it. When Katniss's sister Prim is chosen for the Hunger Games, not only does that make the simmering conflict with the Capitol deeply personal and high-stakes to Katniss, it gives us an opportunity to see how brave Katniss is and how much she loves her sister, as she immediately volunteers to take Prim's place.

6. **Sets up clear lines of action and/or questions that will follow out of this event.** It's called an "inciting incident" because it should incite questions and more action, and inspire the reader to want to know what happens next.

Piece of cake, right? Overall, I'd urge you to concentrate most on 3 and 6—that is, creating an inciting incident in tune with your story whose consequences will create more action. Keep it simple—a choice made by your protagonist, a challenge presented to him—and see how he and his world react from there.

 Exposition. The exposition is the setup for your novel, in which the characters and context are established, and often we see status quo that will be disrupted by the inciting incident. In particular, as your protagonist does not know the emotional point of your novel, the exposition should subtly show us that status-quo unconsciousness.

In Freytag's original five-act pyramid for plays, the exposition came before the inciting incident, which meant, in practical terms, a chorus or two minor characters would come onstage and explain the entire setup that the play would then carry forth. (If you've ever been bored by the opening scene of a Shakespeare play, you've been a victim of this model.) In modern drama, we expect exposition and the inciting incident to be much more closely intertwined. The inciting incident can happen before the book even starts, so the exposition shows the characters reacting to the change unfolding in their lives. In *Harry Potter and the Sorcerer's Stone*, James and Lily Potter are killed offstage on page 2, and the effects of their deaths ripple outward through the lives of the Dursleys, Professors Dumbledore and McGonagall, Hagrid, and at last Harry—the warmest, most charming announcement of a double murder in fiction. You can also place the inciting incident in Chapter 1, then set up the backstory (exposition) for it in Chapter 2. In *Graceling* by Kristin Cashore, Katsa meets her match in the first chapter while escaping from a king's dungeons. Only in the second chapter do we learn exactly why she was there and what motivated her mission. Both of these structures plunge us immediately into the books' action plots, and show us the characters' natures as they're confronted with unexpected events that change their world.

The final and most common structure for an exposition/inciting incident combination is to have Chapter 1 and even possibly 2 show us the exposition, planting the seeds for the inciting incident, and then have the following chapter reveal the incident itself. *The Hunger Games* starts with Katniss rising from the bed she shares with Prim, walking through her starving village, and hunting with her friend Gale. From a character perspective, we're seeing her strength, resourcefulness, and expertise with a bow and arrow; from a plot perspective, we witness what the Capitol has done to its districts, and how Katniss will sacrifice to provide for and protect her sister. Katniss and Gale also talk about the Reaping, with narration introducing the rules of the random draw, and thus, when Prim's name is pulled at the very end of Chapter 1, we have all the information we need to understand why Katniss volunteers in her place.

Marcelo in the Real World offers two rather quiet opening chapters: Marcelo in a doctor's office, having his brain scanned as he listens to his "internal music," and then visiting his special school with his mother. Because that music will be greatly disturbed by the end of the book, and his father will threaten to make him leave his school, these scenes set the stakes for the overall novel, while allowing readers time to adjust to

Marcelo's unique voice and worldview. When the inciting incident arrives in Chapter 3, with his father's proposal for his summer, we're invested enough in Marcelo's goodness and hopes that we feel this invitation as a real danger. The pacing in both of these examples works because the exposition clearly establishes the specificity and peace of the world that the inciting incident will blow up, as well as the protagonists' unique abilities to respond to that incident.

The first chapter is often the hardest chapter in the book to write, precisely because it must balance character and backstory, forward action and depth. If you're struggling with it, especially in a first draft, you might try just writing straight exposition ("Jhumki Patel lives in Santa Monica with her parents, an actor and a pediatrician"), then plunge into the story proper with your inciting incident. Once you've completed a first draft, you can figure out what information your reader really needs to know, then go back and rewrite that first chapter to set the story up. Many writers like to have the first chapter reflect the last chapter in some way—but that's hard to do before you've written the last! So don't be afraid to write the whole book first.

EXERCISES

What is the inciting incident of your central action plot? What event marks the beginning of that larger change?

- Look at what you wrote down and measure it against the lists of A–D and 1–6 above. How much does your incident meet those criteria? Is it appropriate to the type of your central action plot? Is it an interesting event that disrupts the status quo and reveals your protagonist's character? What questions does it leave the reader with once it's over?

- If you don't find it satisfactory: Which criteria is it not fulfilling? Try to brainstorm five other possible incidents that might better satisfy the criteria.

Get your plot backstory in order.–If your novel's world has a lot of backstory—a complicated sequence of events leading up to the inciting incident, or an intricate political and social history that your protagonist will uncover in the course of the action—make up a timeline or an encyclopedia entry covering all the important dates and events. That will help you keep track of your invented facts as you build a novel on top of them.

If you've made a bookmap:
Find the inciting incident of both your central action and emotional plots on your bookmap, and draw boxes around them. Does the action inciting incident happen in the first three chapters?

↪ **The Stakes.** We've established that an inciting incident must be a compelling event that changes the world of our protagonist and shows us a little of who she is. In many situations, it will also define the stakes—that is, the thing the protagonist will win or lose in the course of the action, and thus the thing she must work or fight for to ensure the outcome she desires. The stakes provide a structuring arc for the book as a whole: When your protagonist gets them, or doesn't, the story will be over. There should be stakes for both your action and emotional plots.

The stakes can take many different forms:

- **What the protagonist wants—her desire.** If she says at the beginning, "I want to win the blue ribbon at the state fair," that ribbon is what's at stake.
- **What the protagonist needs (whether she knows it or not).** This might be something that's obvious to us from the beginning—like Harry Potter's need for a loving family and home, which Hogwarts will become for him—or it might be more implicit: If a character declares at the outset that her life is perfect and nothing is missing, that's a sure sign she needs something else.

- **What the protagonist might lose.** In this case, the protagonist already has something, like a pet or a friend, and it might be taken away. In *Marcelo in the Real World*, the opening stakes are Marcelo's choice of school: If Marcelo doesn't work in the law firm to Arturo's satisfaction, he won't get to attend Paterson.
- **Emotional growth/wholeness.** This is usually the stakes of the emotional plot: If the character doesn't go through X experiences that change her for the better, she will remain at her stunted level of growth or emotional incompleteness for the rest of her life. These stakes are often most clearly seen in retrospect, admittedly, especially if your novel involves the protagonist learning that she must change. But if some lack in the protagonist is obvious to us from the beginning, then the cost of her not changing will be as well.

Your stakes need to be proportional to the size of the action that follows. *The Hunger Games* is filled with gore, hunger, and fights to the death: If Katniss went through all that just to win fifty bucks, we'd have no respect for her or for the plot. Since she's fighting for her life, however, the stakes are big enough to justify our investment.

The stakes also need to be understandable to the reader given who the character is and the circumstances in which she lives. Suppose your protagonist is a twelve-year-old African American girl in Ankeny, Iowa, in the present day, and what she wants most in all the world is to attend a *Dragnet* fan convention. This is obviously a pretty random desire for a modern twelve-year-old, so you as the writer would have to create enough background to make it *not* random—showing us *why* she's a *Dragnet* fan, where that desire originated, what about the convention is important to her—and thus make that desire, and those stakes, understandable and even sympathetic.

As with the inciting incident, as a rule of thumb, you should try to establish the stakes within the first three chapters. Readers like having reasons to be invested in the plot as well as the characters, and to know why the action they're reading matters. That said, the stakes will very likely change in the course of the novel, as your protagonist goes through new experi-

172 | The Magic Words

ences, makes new connections, and has her vision of the world widened. Marcelo starts out wanting to attend Paterson, but once he sees the picture of the disfigured girl, he wants justice for her even at the cost of his choice of school. Katniss starts out wanting to survive the Hunger Games herself, but by the end of the novel, she's been through enough torture at the hands of the Capitol that she's willing to give up her life to make a larger statement. These are both examples of the incredibly useful "Wants vs. Needs" plotting technique: Give your character a strong desire that will get the action started and launch all the novel's changes (Wants). Then introduce elements that will open out her world and reveal the deeper thing truly required for her growth (Needs).

=== **EXERCISES** ===

At the beginning of your book, what is at stake for the protagonist in the action plot? And the emotional plot? What would happen to him if the change we see in the action didn't come about? What are the stakes in the action plot by the end? And the emotional plot? What is the protagonist finally fighting for?

If you've made a bookmap:
Draw a star by the place where your action plot stakes first appear, and write the nature of the stakes in three words or fewer. Go through the bookmap and draw another star wherever you see a change in either the stakes or the protagonist's desire. At each point, write in the nature of the new stakes or desire. Repeat this exercise for your emotional plot, using a smiley face in place of a star.

ଚ **When you look through the various names you assigned to the stakes, do the concepts they embody grow progressively more intense or meaningful?** They don't *have* to follow this arc, but if they carry less emotional charge, that's often a sign of diminishing drama.

The Escalating or Complicating Action

When I teach picture-book writing, I define the three stages in every story as "Problem, Process, Solution." Those same stages often apply to novels as well, if not usually so neatly. The exposition, inciting incident, and stakes set up the novel's problem. Once they're established, we move into the *escalating and complicating action*, as I call it—the protagonist's process of considering, deepening, worsening, working through, collaborating on, and fighting against the problem, and ultimately finding a solution to it.

The escalating or complicating action consists of events within the book that raise the stakes, change the course of the story, or change the rules of engagement. They can be happy events as well as difficult ones, and they should comprise the vast majority of the narrative time spent in your novel—roughly 75 percent. The goal is to create a smooth narrative driven in part by your protagonist, where interesting events unfold organically out of the consequences of previous events, and readers steadily grow more involved in the action as they learn more about the protagonist and his world. Some examples of interesting events:

✑ In a conflict plot:

- The antagonist hurting your protagonist in some way.
- The news that the antagonist has acquired a new weapon or ally.
- The protagonist's discovery of a new weapon or ally.
- The protagonist's committing an act of extreme stupidity.
- A battle between the two sides.

✑ In a mystery plot:

- The discovery of new clues (information) in the mystery. Well over half the plot of a traditional mystery involves finding out what caused the first inciting incident in the novel—the crime that got the detective involved.
- An event that raises the stakes, like the discovery of another dead body.

↪ In a lack plot:

- If the usual thing lacked is love, then the escalating events should show the protagonist taking steps toward developing the connection established in the inciting incident: thinking about the other person, a conversation, a first date, some activity together.
- Or they will be events that imperil that developing connection: a betrayal, a missed call, a bit of gossip.
- If a character lacks something internal, the escalating events could be steps toward or away from that internal growth: a mistake that helps her to see more rightly, or practicing a new skill, or accomplishing a task she hasn't been able to complete before.

Given the whole range of events that *could* happen within your novel and its plot type, how do you decide *which* events should happen? In what order should they happen? And then how do you join them together?

Well, this is entirely dependent upon you, your characters, and the story and points of your book, so I can't give you specific advice. But I can suggest six strategies for choosing and arranging your events, which might help you find a path through the possibilities. Each one offers both useful principles for plotting overall and a slightly different angle on the problems of creating reader interest, maintaining narrative tension, and developing your characters over the course of the novel. Because they *are* somewhat redundant, I recommend using just the one or two strategies that resonate with you most in writing your initial draft, and then considering the principles of the others as you firm up the book in revision.

Satisfy audience expectations—surprisingly, if possible. If you're writing a novel where your protagonist will discover that she has magical powers, then we readers expect the scene where she first realizes this to be full of action and surprise—she stops a car with her mind, say, or unwittingly transforms a chair into a chimpanzee. If you instead choose to have her discover her power by getting a letter in the mail announcing it, and she doesn't believe the letter and then ignores it for two weeks, you're going to have a disappointed reader. Ditto if you're writing a romance: It's inherent in the genre that the first encounter, the first touch, the first kiss will be big events in the lives of these characters, and readers will come to the book precisely to experience the intensity and pleasure of those events. Build up steadily to those big moments, and don't stint on the emotion or drama when you get there.

It's useful to remember that *you* are part of the audience here as well. If you think about your book as something you'd read for pleasure, what would the big moments be? What set pieces are you excited to experience? What characters do you want to see in combat or conversation? How will those encounters play out? Write the scenes that satisfy your own readerly expectations for the book (like you're writing fan fiction for your own novel), and you'll satisfy your readers as well.

═══ *EXERCISES* ═══

Think about your favorite moments in narrative media (TV, film, theater, and comics as well as books)—incidents that surprised you, stirred your heart, or made you say, "Oh, *dear!*" Can you see any commonalities or patterns in those moments? What made them so great? How might you build incidents like those into your work?

The flip side: What are your pet peeves as a reader? What plot devices or narrative rhythms annoy you, especially in your chosen genre? What clichés do you want to avoid?

Using the twenty-things method, brainstorm a list of at least twenty events that could happen in your novel, based on the characters, setting, and premise. (If you started from "Ouch!" on page 49, you've already done this.) Choose five or more favorites and put them in some kind of order, with the event that would generate the most emotion as the climax. Writing your first draft then becomes a matter of getting your characters from one event to another.

Have characters make choices and DO THINGS, and then follow your protagonist's desires and compulsions to their natural conclusions. We established it as a principle earlier that interesting characters DO THINGS. If your protagonist just lets everything happen to him, then he comes across as passive and boring. In particular, if he doesn't make some decision or help resolve the plot in some way at the climax, then we don't have any way to know whether the changes wrought in him through the plots have truly been effective.

There is in fact an entire alternate plot structure you can follow here, which was first outlined by Laurie Halse Anderson in a brilliant 2008 talk at the Kindling Words conference, and which I've refined further here:

1. The book establishes a protagonist who has:
   - Something to gain or lose (often a desire).
   - A compulsion of which he may not be aware. Again, a "compulsion" is some internal driver or postulate that influences all of his behavior. It could be a character flaw; it could be a great virtue; but whatever it is, it underlies everything the character does.
   - Or both.

If both are present, that immediately sets up both an action plot, as the character will want to pursue his desire, and an emotional plot, as the character will have to address his compulsion. The "something to gain or lose" will likely be a reflection of whatever compulsion you have in mind, or the character may ultimately have to choose between the compulsion and that desire.

It's worth remembering that a compulsion can also be a good thing. In *The Hunger Games*, Katniss lives in an imperfect world—one that explicitly wants to kill her once she enters the games. Her compulsion to fight and survive then helps her navigate the obstacles she faces there. In every novel, something is broken: the protagonist, the world, or both. And while neither will ever become perfect, both can be made better in at least one small degree. Your novel should dramatize that degree. (Unless, of course, you're more interested in chronicling brokenness, in which case your novel should dramatize the world deteriorating that much more.)

2. The story presents the protagonist with a situation:

- That will evoke the compulsion—again, possibly unbeknownst to the character.
- In which something important can be gained or lost (again, often a desire).
- Or both.

This situation could be something the character gets into all by himself, or something that comes for her, like Katniss being selected for the Hunger Games. Either way, it is the arrival of a change that will profoundly influence the character's life—the Inciting Incident, in Freytag's pyramid terms.

3. The situation then forces the character to make a choice or take action.

John Gardner wrote, "Real suspense comes with moral dilemma and the courage to make and act upon choices. False suspense comes from the accidental and meaningless occurrence of one damned thing after another." Moral dilemma happens when your protagonist faces multiple possible responses to a situation and must make a decision among them. It's especially compelling if the options are equally good or equally bad—for example, if Ron and Hermione were both in danger and Harry could only save one of them. If the reader is interested in the character, such a high-stakes choice creates pain, and pain creates further interest: we want to see how the character will get out of the situation.

4. In the new situation engendered by the results of #3, the plot repeats steps #2 and #3.

These are the escalating and complicating events, and they cycle around again and again in the double-helix form described on page 155, until . . .

5. At the climax:

- The compulsion in the character is recognized and understood.
  - "Understood" does not necessarily mean "corrected"—the character can and probably will be driven by that compulsion again, as it's likely part of his or her essential makeup. But it does mean that the compulsion no longer wreaks havoc unconsciously; the character knows enough now, and has grown enough now, to recognize its mischief and restrain some of its negative effects.
- Or the important thing is lost or won.
- Or both.

That is, the changes of the action or emotional plot have been accomplished, and the book is over.

Looking at *Marcelo in the Real World* through this lens, Marcelo's compulsion is his desire to have order in his world, and his belief that people will behave according to orderly standards. In Step #2, he is confronted by a situation in which his father, Arturo, is not behaving up to that standard; Marcelo finds a picture of the disfigured girl, Ixtel, and learns Arturo represents the manufacturer of these terrible windshields. In Step #3, Marcelo makes the choice to visit Ixtel's lawyer and find out what happened to her. In Step #4, the lawyer presents him with the truth of his father's character, and thus another choice about what Marcelo could do to help Ixtel. Simultaneously, back in Step #2 again, Marcelo is confronted by the request Wendell makes of to him—to try to help him seduce Jasmine—which Marcelo does not fully comprehend. In Step #3, as his relationship with Jasmine develops, he makes the choice that he will not help Wendell. In Step #4, this eventually comes back to bite him. And thus the plot of the novel keeps unfolding on several fronts, in the multiple areas where Marcelo has to make choices.

This entire method can be summarized as "Plotting Is Compulsion vs. Obstacles": what your character, by his very nature, is compelled to do, versus the things that keep him from doing it.

=== EXERCISES ===

The following exercises all involve a bookmap, if you've chosen to make one, but the reflections on them could be useful with or without that tool.

Find the place in your bookmap where your protagonist's compulsion, desire, or thing to be gained or lost is first established in the manuscript. Write COMPULSION, DESIRE, or THING next to it.

- How is this established for the reader? Is it shown to the reader (if not necessarily to the protagonist) through interaction with another character or an obstacle? Is it simply stated in the narration? (There is no one right way to do this; it's just worth knowing the degree to which it is spelled out for the reader.)

- If a compulsion exists, how much is the protagonist consciously aware of it at this point in time? *Should* he be aware of it, or would the manuscript work better if he gradually became aware of it over the course of the manuscript?

- A compulsion or desire often resonates in multiple areas of a character's life. Think about ways the general choices he makes might reflect the compulsion and help pull together the novel's emotional and action plots.

- Often when a character's compulsion comes under pressure, the actions resulting from that compulsion get more intense, because the character will cling to the safety of that compulsion even if it proves unreliable. Do you see that pattern in the choices your protagonist is making here? Alternatively, if she's learning more about her compulsion as the novel unfolds, might she make choices less under its influence?

Put an asterisk in the margin every time your character makes a significant choice—one that has consequences beyond the individual scene where it occurs. What patterns might you see in these asterisks?

Double-underline the point at which the compulsion is sat-isfied or the thing to be lost or won is lost or won. (These could be two different points if you have both a compulsion and a thing that's at stake.) Look at the events that happen after this scene. Are there conse-quences here as well? If a compulsion has been addressed, how can a reader tell the protagonist has grown?

Set up and knock down obstacles. To define a narrative concept we've been invoking already here, "obstacles" are the things that get in the way of your protagonist achieving her desire. They can be internal factors, like a character's deepest beliefs or narratives about herself; if she won't tell her crush how much she likes him because she's been rejected before and she's afraid of it happening again, that fear (and the emotional pat-tern it creates) is an obstacle that she must overcome. They can also be external factors, like antagonists or the character's circumstances. If your protagonist wants to be a professional basketball player, but he also needs to work two jobs to pay for his grandfather's heart medicine, that lack of time to practice is an obstacle. They might even be basic facts of your character's world, but they won't become real obstacles until they touch your protagonist on a personal level. The Capitol is the ultimate obstacle to Katniss's compulsion to survive in *The Hunger Games*—a fact that's useful to know for the big picture of the trilogy. But the more relevant obstacles in Book 1 are the other tributes, the fire and illness that over-take her in the arena, and the tracker-jacker nest she must negotiate to get out of the games alive.

If you don't have obstacles, or the obstacles aren't significant enough, your character's journey will seem too easy. To avoid this, as a rule of thumb, you should have at least one decent-sized obstacle for every plotline. If the protagonist can overcome the obstacle through one obvious conversation or one day of research or other work, that obstacle is not significant enough. At the same time, obstacles need to be proportional to the type of story you're telling. If you're trying to write a light romantic comedy about a girl's quest for popularity, and the obstacle is that her father is in jail for a triple murder, that will feel out of tune with the experiential point of the book.

Obstacles can also be used to increase the tension in your manuscript. If you don't have enough action, you don't necessarily have to make more events happen; you can just make the events that happen more difficult.

- **Set limits on your protagonist by taking a strength away from him.** Perhaps the plot presently hands him a piece of information or some good luck that he should have to work for instead. Or what if he wasn't rich? What if he didn't have friends?
- **Create an antagonist.** The most interesting antagonists will block your protagonist's desire while being allied to her in some manner. Perhaps both characters want the same thing, but take opposite means to get it. Or they have the same history, but understand their experiences differently and thus act differently in the present. The protagonist might even care for this person who's keeping her from her dream. A connection like that adds an emotional dimension to the plot obstacle the antagonist presents.
- **Add a ticking clock.** If the character must accomplish some task within a set period of time, then time itself becomes a powerful obstacle that can greatly increase the tension, as readers will read faster as that deadline approaches.

Of course, you don't want to make the action *impossible* for your protagonist, or make the book feel like a video game with endless levels to navigate. That can happen when the obstacles stop having any emotional challenge for the character or resonance for the reader—when they're merely obstacles for obstacles' sake. But if you can keep that resonance going, then as a general rule: The more obstacles exist, the more your protagonist must overcome, and the more action, interest, and tension your book can have as a result.

=== *EXERCISES* ===

**Off the top of your head, list all of the obstacles your pro-
tagonist must face in the action plot. Then do the same for
the emotional plot,** listing all of the things she must get past to achieve
some internal growth.

If you've made a bookmap:
For every scene, write out the obstacle your character must overcome in
it. If you can't identify the obstacle in the scene, consider what that scene
is really about, and also whether that scene is truly necessary. Jennifer Crusie says that every dramatized scene should show a conflict of some kind.
I would revise that to say it should show a character negotiating an obstacle—whether human (an antagonist, or an ally who may have a different
agenda), internal (wrestling with a wrong belief, say, or trying to work out a
right course of action), or external (climbing a mountain, trying to get food
for the day).

- Scenes without obstacles—characters sitting around shooting the breeze,
  say, with nothing to be worked out or accomplished—can be useful
  in a manuscript, as they offer a little breathing space in the action and
  a chance for us to get to know the characters in more depth. Still, you
  should look for ways to make these scenes plot-relevant, and try to keep
  them fairly rare and tight.

- Are there multiple scenes in which the protagonist faces the same obstacle? If so, that's not necessarily a bad thing—indeed, if we're saying that
  plot is "Compulsion vs. Obstacles," it's almost the entire point, as the
  character must throw herself at the obstacle until it falls or she changes.
  To keep those repeated confrontations from feeling repetitive, however,
  show us that the character has grown enough between each encounter
  that every incident has a slightly different cast, so the character asks different questions or takes away different answers each time.

Always choose action over mere events. I'm going to talk about this one using *Twilight* by Stephenie Meyer—a novel that often gets a bad rap from a literary perspective. This happens in part because its dramatic action can be defined as follows: Bella meets Edward. They are attracted to each other. They fight their attraction for about two hundred pages. They admit and revel in the attraction for about one hundred pages. The evil vampires try to kill Bella for two hundred pages. Then Edward saves her at the climax, and it's over.

Now, the problem with that plot is not a lack of events, as a lot of stuff happens in each of those sections: They study cell division at school, he rescues her from thugs, they go out to dinner, he sparkles for her, they play vampire baseball. . . . (If you haven't read this novel: I am not making any of this up.) But all of these little events serve only to reconfirm the dynamics we already know, and as a result, the novel doesn't feel like it's advancing emotionally, even as the pages pile up. Readers feel like "nothing happens" in a book when any of the following conditions are true:

1. The reader doesn't care about the characters: Then "nothing is happening" because the reader isn't invested in the people to whom the events happen.
2. The reader doesn't care about the stakes, *or* the stakes are too low: Then "nothing is happening" because what *is* happening doesn't matter to the reader.
3. It takes too long to move from one phase of the plot to the next.
4. And/or events within that plot phase feel repetitious.

Yet *Twilight* succeeds as a novel nonetheless because the events create pleasure for readers. When I read the book, it gave me all the wonderfully vertiginous feelings of falling in love: the excitement, the wonder, the sense that the world had reorganized and was prioritized around this one other person. Creating those feelings in readers is a true literary accomplishment, just as important (or even more so) as having a well-structured plot, just as Bella's emotions are as important as any ginormous battle or explosion. And where pleasurable feelings exist, we readers often don't mind repetition for a while, because it means we get to dwell in those feelings that much longer. Still, I eventually got impatient with the book, waiting for some real change to happen already. If the same kind of events occur over and over again in your novel and they give *you* intense pleasure, that's a good beginning! You just need to be sure that pleasure extends to readers, and/or that you show some kind of change proceeding out of each event.

Indeed, *Twilight* usefully illustrates the difference between events and action. An event can be any movement shown within a narrative work, like the characters going out to dinner, or traveling cross-country, or playing baseball. In contrast, true dramatic action is an event that:

- Meaningfully changes the character or her circumstances.
- Challenges the character's existing modes of being.
- Advances her understanding.
- Creates conflict.
- Requires choices or more action.
- Or just kicks the emotional level up a notch.

In general, action shows the character facing decisions and making choices that have consequences, while events might just be "one damned thing after another," to quote John Gardner again. As often as you can, choose action over mere events.

Likewise, choose consequences over continuations—"therefores" and "buts" over "and thens." This is a concept I first learned about from Trey Parker and Matt Stone, who use it to plot their TV show *South Park*. Once you have some action going—like, say, in scene A, a girl has intimate eye contact with a beautiful male vampire—three kinds of scenes can follow it:

- **AND THEN: A continuation of the preceding scene.** Scene B shows something happening at the same emotional level: The girl continues to stare into the vampire's eyes, or maybe just touches his hand.

- **THEREFORE: A consequence of the preceding scene.** Scene B dramatizes the consequences of Scene A: The eye contact becomes incredibly intense, *therefore* the girl kisses him.
- **BUT: A complication of the preceding scene.** Scene B introduces an obstacle to the consequences of scene A: Here the eye contact might grow more intense, *but* the girl remembers she is a Slayer, so she drives a stake through the vampire's heart.

To create a tight plot, try this rule of thumb: Every scene should be followed by a scene that dramatizes a *therefore* or a *but*, not an *and then*. *And thens* are pariahs here because they neither deepen the emotion nor move the story forward; they are merely events, not dramatic action. *Therefores* and *buts*, on the other hand, create continuous chains of action and reaction, where every event makes a difference in either the protagonist's emotional development or the drama of the book. The more of those you have, the more compelling your novel will feel.

There is one other category here, which is *meanwhile*. If, while Scene A was taking place, the girl's werewolf best friend was running shirtless through the woods, it's fine to show us that as a follow-up scene to A (assuming his running will have some importance to the plot). Or if, after staring into the vampire's eyes, the girl went home to talk to her father, that would be a *meanwhile* as well, as the girl/daddy subplot is separate from the girl/vampire one. But those best friend or daddy scenes then need their own *buts* or *therefores* the next time those subplotlines come back to the fore. And the next time the girl meets up with the vampire, I'd expect to see a *but* or *therefore* to their staring earlier on.

This is a very hard rule of thumb to hold to absolutely, and one that perhaps applies more stringently to the tight time frame of a screenplay than the baggy world of a novel. Still, as a rough guide, try to have at least half of your scenes serve as *buts* or *therefores* to the preceding action. The higher your percentage, the tighter your novel will be.

=== EXERCISES ===

If you've made a bookmap:

When you're looking at two consecutive scenes that focus on the same action plot:

- If the action of Scene A directly causes Scene B, write *Therefore* in between them.

- If the action of Scene A does not directly cause Scene B, write in *And then.*

- If Scene B introduces an obstacle of some kind to what was decided in Scene A: *But.*

- Or if Scene B dramatizes a different plot or subplot: *Meanwhile.*

- Repeat this process for your whole bookmap, using Scenes C, D, E, etc.

Total up your *Therefores, And thens, Buts,* and *Meanwhiles.*
Divide each quantity by the number of scenes you analyzed here and calculate the percentages. If you have at least 50 percent *Buts* and *Therefores*: Well done! If you have a higher percentage of *And then* scenes: Look at each *And then* scene. Do you remember why you wrote it? What were you trying to accomplish? Do you need to keep that scene, or could it be cut, or perhaps transformed into a *But* or *Therefore* scene?

Have at least one narrative question in play at all times. In "A Simple Way to Create Suspense," a funny and smart essay you can find online, the adult suspense writer Lee Child identified an irrational readerly habit that writers should use to their advantage: Once a question—pretty much any question at all—is set up for readers, they'll generally hang around to find out the answer. As a result, novelists can create suspense simply by posing a question at the beginning of the book, then delaying the resolution as long as possible. Your inciting incident and/or stakes already set up the primary questions of your novel: Who will triumph? What is the solution? How can this person become complete? Each escalating or complicating event can then set up or answer lower-level questions that play into those primary questions: Can your protagonist gain the weapon she needs to face her enemy? What will it take to gather the clues? How will this first conversation with the crush unfold?

These questions can and do change throughout the course of the novel; as one gets answered, another takes its place, and the book will likely accumulate *more* questions as it goes. The first plot-level question in *The Hunger Games* is: Will Katniss survive the games? Then, right at the end of the first third, Peeta declares his love for her. Instantly we have additional questions: How will Katniss respond to this declaration? Will she still be able to kill him in the games, as she must to survive them? What happens if she falls in love with him, too? Set up an event that creates a high-stakes narrative question like these, and then another event (several scenes later) that answers, changes, or deepens it. Do that again and again, and you'll create a series of hooks that will pull readers through the whole book.

EXERCISES

If your novel feels boring at a certain point or its pace is flagging, make a list of all of the narrative questions you have in play at that moment. Do you have too few questions? It may be time to introduce new elements. Too many questions? The reader may not know what's most important to the character or story. What are the stakes for each of the questions? Do you need to increase them? Is it time to answer one question and replace it with another?

If you've made a bookmap:
Each time an important new narrative question is introduced, write that question in the margin. When one of those questions gets answered in the manu-

script, put a checkmark next to it with the scene number where it's answered. Do you have any unchecked questions by the end? It's okay to leave a couple of plot questions open, especially if you're illustrating the messiness of life or writing an ongoing series, but in general, the more you can tie up all the threads, the more well-woven and satisfying your novel will feel.

Subplots

Subplots are any ongoing action that involves a change and is not your central action or emotional plot. Every novel, even a chapter book, should have at least one subplot. I state this as a necessity because a good novel has the same richness as real life, and real life is full of plots and subplots: As an adult, you have your family, your romantic partner, your job, each of your friends, your spiritual and creative lives.... Any one of those can be a subplot (or the main plot) in the ongoing novel of your life, and the same is true for your protagonist in *her* life. Thus you need to honor that multidimensionality in real lives by including subplots in your book. Each additional subplot creates an additional layer of interest and complication, and every relationship in a book can be its own plot as it contributes to the protagonist's growth. But all of these plots should ultimately add something to the points—showing us more of what the protagonist learns and how he learns it, if you've got an emotional point going; contributing to the thematic point; or offering some contrasting or intensifying action to involve the reader more deeply in your experiential point.

Subplots need to be constructed with the same fullness as your central action or emotional plots. As such, they can also usually be categorized as conflicts/mysteries/lacks, and they will often have their own plot arcs (inciting incident, escalating and complicating events, a climax, etc.), which show us the action developing over time. These structural events must be layered onto and braided in with the larger action or emotional plot events in a sequence that will be unique to every novel.

If subplot development flummoxes you, here's a basic formula you can try: Establish your central action and emotional plots first, with the inciting incident in Chapters 1 through 3 as discussed. Then, in every immediate subsequent chapter, include one event that furthers those action or emotional plots, layered alongside at least one event that introduces or develops one of your subplots. For instance, in *Marcelo in the Real World*, the three central subplots are: (1) Marcelo's relationship with Jasmine; (2) his relationship with Wendell; and (3) the mystery involving Ixtel's identity. If you read through the bookmap of the novel on my website, you'll see that both Jasmine and Wendell are introduced formally in Chapter 6. (Those introductions are not full inciting incidents of the kind described above—neither character enters on a rocketbike—but they're both perfectly appropriate to the action of the novel, which is more important.) Chapter 7 shows Marcelo in conversation with Wendell, which deepens their relationship; Chapter 8 shows him working alongside Jasmine, which develops their connection in turn. Chapter 9 focuses on Wendell again, 10 on Arturo (where the conflict with him is the central action plot), and 11 on Jasmine; 12 is a reflection on everything Marcelo has been experiencing so far, 13 on Wendell, 14 on Jasmine; and in 15, Marcelo finds the picture of Ixtel (via Wendell), which launches the mystery subplot. You can doubtless see the pattern emerging here—how the novel toggles among the central action plot and the two subplots to establish Marcelo's relationships with all the characters and set up their actions in the second, Ixtel-focused, half of the novel.

I'll add that this is an especially useful method if you're writing a book where the action is entirely realistic and friends- and family-centered, like any of Hilary McKay's or Lisa Yee's brilliant middle-grade novels (‡). Because there isn't so much of a loud, bang-bang central action plot to these kinds of books, the main interest of these novels arises from the development of the relationships and getting to know our characters over time, which this pattern facilitates.

When I acquired *Marcelo in the Real World*, the manuscript didn't include Chapters 8 or 11—two scenes that show the development of Marcelo's relationship with Jasmine (a lack subplot). To explain why they were added, let's take two characters named Joe and Janelle. It is incredibly easy for an author just to say, not long after they meet, "Joe and Janelle spent a lot of time together, and pretty soon, they became friends." That's especially tempting if you have a larger, more exciting action plot you want to get on to—that Joe and Janelle are going to time-travel together, say. But for that friendship to matter to me as a reader—for me to be a third party in the relationship, which is essentially what I want to be—I need to see *how* Joe and Janelle become friends. What does he say that captures her (and my) interest? What does she say that keeps the conversation going? What do they like to do together? How do they connect, and why should I connect with them? Those things need to be dramatized for the reader as fully as the first time they step through that time-travel portal. (Indeed, those demonstrations could also happen *as* they step through that portal; it's totally possible to work your central action plot and a lack subplot at the same time.) In order to make this happen with the Jasmine subplot in *Marcelo*, Francisco wrote Chapters 8 and 11, which focus solely on the two characters as Marcelo learns to navigate his first "real-world" friendship. Even within a big, exciting conflict or mystery action plot, relationships are often the most important story lines in a children's or YA novel, because they show most directly the emotional content and growth in the book.

With that said, you don't want to clutter up a novel with too many subplots. Part of the pleasure of reading novels is that they have more organization and structure than real life, and you get to choose the number and types of relationships and problems you want to have. To determine which ones are necessary, as a rule of thumb, all subplots should supply either support or complication to the central action and emotional plots. By "support," I mean that the events that happen in Subplot X help the main character accomplish something in, or discover something she needs to know for, those central plots. If the central action plot is a conflict where our heroine needs to defeat the evil antagonist, and a romantic subplot helps her gain confidence because she knows someone loves her and is supporting her, then said subplot qualifies as a supporting subplot.

By "complication," I mean that the events that happen in Subplot X make the central action or emotional plots more difficult or painful for the protagonist to accomplish. If the central action plot features the same conflict with the evil antagonist that I've just mentioned, but this time her lover is gathering information on her *for* the antagonist, then this romantic subplot becomes a complication, because both the lover himself and her feelings for him are obstacles to the heroine's goal. Still, in both cases, what happens in the subplot clearly connects and contributes to the central plot in a substantive way, and, as a result the existence of both subplots is justified.

This leads me to another illustrative anecdote about subplots in general and those of *Marcelo in the Real World* in particular: When I acquired the book, there was no mystery subplot. In the first draft, when Marcelo found a picture of a girl with only half a face, that photo was attached to a letter from her lawyer spelling out what had happened to her: She was in a car accident, the windshield exploded, they would like $50,000 for surgery. The rest of the novel consisted of Marcelo making a decision about what to do, figuring out how to do it (how to get the money), and carrying that purpose out.

This was a great moral dilemma, which I really appreciated, as it forced Marcelo to choose between helping this girl and attending his beloved school. But because so much of the action was concentrated solely on his internal decision-making, Marcelo himself didn't have much to DO in the text. And if one of the qualities of interesting characters is that they DO THINGS, I wanted to see him be involved in more actual events.

So I talked with Francisco about this, and he decided to get rid of that overly informative letter. Suddenly we had a mystery subplot: Who is this girl? Why is her picture at the law firm? What does she want? Marcelo had to use clues within the picture to find her, so we saw him DOING THINGS to solve the mystery, before he got to the point where he had to make a decision. He also worked with Jasmine on the photo, which furthered their lack subplot by deepening the relationship between them. And because he took action, the search, and the finding of the girl, meant more to Marcelo and to readers. Each of those subplots also exerted a strong influence on the conflict plot with Arturo, as they changed Marcelo's view of the law firm and strengthened his confidence. As a result, they served that central action plot in just the way subplots should. If you need to get your protagonist more involved in the action, consider taking something away from him in a subplot (inventing an obstacle for him, as mentioned earlier), or creating a subplot in which he might be more challenged.

══ EXERCISES ══

Make a list of all of the subplots in your novel and categorize each one by type. conflicts, mysteries, or lacks. (You'll likely be able to adapt your earlier list of story lines to do this.)

Write out what each subplot contributes to your central action and emotional plots.

- ✑ Is writing these contributions easy or tortured? If one of your justifications feels particularly tortured—if you had a really hard time making the connection between a subplot and the main plots—it might be worth taking another look at that subplot. I worked with a writer once whose central action plot focused on the relationship between a girl named Lucy and her mother. As a result of her interest in military families, the author introduced a subplot with a boy in Lucy's class whose mom was serving in Iraq. The subplot was meant to contrast the relationship, between Lucy and her mom and the boy and *his* mom. However, Lucy mostly observed the boy's difficulties, felt sorry for him, and took away lessons for her own relationship with her mother. Because there was no action or connection between Lucy and the boy, the subplot felt extraneous, especially given the other, more character-centered action going on in the novel. The author ultimately cut it.

- ✑ Is everything necessary and unique? Are there any redundancies? Sometimes a romantic subplot will give your main character a little more self-confidence—but so does the speech-contest plot. Do you need both, or can you drop one? (Look at what else each subplot contributes to the book in deciding which one to cut, if necessary.)

- At the other end of the scale: What more dimensions do your characters or action or emotional plots need? Could a new subplot bring out those dimensions?

If you've made a bookmap:

Get out a set of highlighters or colored pencils, and assign each subplot its own color. Highlight all the events of that subplot in the appropriate color. (This is an especially useful exercise if you're juggling a lot of story lines.) If a subplot has an inciting incident or a climax, identify those by drawing a wavy line underneath them. Note that multiple plotlines can share events.

- What patterns can you see in looking at all the colors? Do any colors disappear for a long period of time, or clump up when they should be more evenly distributed?

- Read through each subplot color in turn. Does that subplot develop naturally over time? Are there any jumps in logic or emotion that you might need to expand upon or revise? Where is the subplot's climax?

The Climax

The climax is the point in your action plot at which the major elements of the action are brought to a crisis and then resolved. It will often involve a decision or serve as the ultimate consequence of all the decisions made up to that point. The qualities of a climax should be something of a mirror image to the qualities of the inciting incident, namely:

A. It should also be an actual event—not something settled in dialogue in passing, for example.

B. It should be at least partly driven by the protagonist, as the result or culmination of the changes in his character. Ideally it is the place where the emotional plot that has been developing throughout finally connects within the character or pays off in the action, bringing about the climax of the action plot as well. Remember the climax of the character-driven plot structure discussed in point #2 of escalating and complicating events above: "The compulsion in the character is recognized and understood, or the important thing is lost or won, or both." If the character's compulsion has been that she will run away from trouble, at the climax she should *not* run or even want to run: She has to face her fear. If he's been too scared to talk to his dad about their family secrets, he has to show the courage to raise the subject himself. If his dad says, "Son, we need to have a talk," then the dad is driving that climax, and it doesn't work, because we don't see a change in the son's character.

C. It should resolve the major lines of action and/or major questions that were set up by the inciting incident. In that way, it will also often demonstrate the thematic point, by offering the story's most definitive answer to the thematic questions that have been raised throughout the book.

D. It should be suitable to the nature of the building action.

You can have multiple small climaxes within the book as your emotional plot and various subplots come to a head, but as a rule of thumb, the climax for your central action plot should come *last*. Readers expect the climax to the central plot to be the *biggest* event in the book, and any major action after the biggest event might feel like an anticlimax. As a corollary of thumb, once you've reached the climax of both kinds of plot, the book should end within three chapters. The action is effectively over, so the text should close itself out as well.

Earlier we said that one easy way to determine what kind of plot you have is to look at the climax: What is settled there or gained there, and how? An equally important question is whether the climax is in line with the rest of the book's action (point D above). Has all of the action been building up to the resolution of that particular change? If you have a central conflict plot, your climax should be the culminating face-off between the two antagonists—not, say, your hero kissing his new boyfriend, which would be the climax of a lack. If it's a mystery climax, you need to reveal the information your protagonist sought. And for a lack, the lack must be fulfilled.

One last *Marcelo in the Real World* development story: In the original draft, the disfigured girl, Ixtel, lived in Cancún, Mexico, so Marcelo and Jasmine traveled there from Boston to see her. They gave her a check to compensate her for her injuries, and later that night, they kissed on the beach, at which point Francisco discreetly cut away from the action. The trip to Mexico comprised the last fifth of the book, but something about it felt off to me. In order to determine what it was, I asked Francisco to tell me what he wanted his book to be about (defining his thematic point, really). He wrote me a wonderful letter stating that he was exploring a question Marcelo articulates in the text: "How do we go about living when there is so much suffering?" He saw the novel as a story about a young man awakening to the world's pain and becoming a warrior in the fight against that suffering.

This answer *thrilled* me as an editor, because it's always exciting to see authors with big ambitions and the literary chops to achieve them. But it also forced me to say, "Okay, then, I think you need to cut the trip to Mexico." Marcelo and Jasmine traveling to Cancún together and kissing on the beach made the story more about their romance than about justice and suffering—a case where the climax did not serve the thematic point. Moreover, Ixtel didn't *have* to live in Mexico. She could be in New York, or even Boston, which would remove the emotions associated with "a trip to Mexico" for readers while still allowing Marcelo and Jasmine to visit her. Francisco understood the point immediately, and revised accordingly, for a much more satisfying climax all around.

EXERCISES

If you've made a bookmap:
Find the climaxes for both your action plot and your emotional plot and circle them.

Now that we've gone through all the major structural events, go back through the entire bookmap and underline each event that advances your central action plot, including its inciting incident and climax.—Put a heart by each event that advances your central emotional plot, including *its* inciting incident and climax. (These could very well be the same events you just underlined.)

Read through the underlined events (your central action plot events).

- **Are all of the events in the right order?** If you're writing a mystery novel, for instance, you can't build a case on a particular piece of information until that information has been revealed.

- **Are any events missing?** Make sure you have all your big scenes and necessary steps in the logical development of your story.

- **Are any events redundant?** As an example, if a detective has multiple informants in a novel, you could easily waste half your narrative time on her discussing each new clue with each informant in turn. Don't give your protagonist six conversations going over the same material unless each of those conversations somehow advances the plot.

Read through the events marked with a heart, and ask the same questions.

The Resolution

The resolution of your novel shows how your character now acts differently and how her circumstances have changed as a result of everything she's been through. If the climax is the mirror of the inciting incident, the resolution is the mirror of the exposition, because it reveals the new status quo. In a conflict resolution, we want to know: What happens to the winner and loser? In a mystery: Who has benefitted from this information, and how? Is the wrongdoer punished, and the quester rewarded? For a lack: Will the characters live happily ever after—or at least contentedly together? What can the protagonist do now that she couldn't before? And in every case: How have everyone's lives changed?

Beyond this, a satisfying resolution for a children's or YA novel will usually include at least two of these three dynamics from narrative theory, which I learned from the work of scholar Michael Cadden:

- **Closure:** The story dynamics move the action toward a clear ending point—for instance, a return to the starting place of a quest, or the school year coming to a close. Marcelo's novel ends at the same time as his summer at the law firm, offering natural closure. (The opposite of closure might be the action abruptly ending in the middle of a scene, like *The Sopranos* series finale.)
- **Completion:** The conflicts, mysteries, or lacks of the action plot feel fully resolved. By the end of *Marcelo*, the questions posed by all of the plots and subplots (Jasmine, Wendell, Ixtel) have been answered, and thus have achieved completion.
- **Aperture:** The protagonist's emotional journey/plot has likewise been resolved; we feel he has changed and grown. If Marcelo never accepted his role as a warrior in the fight against suffering, or if he felt like he needed to return to Paterson at the end of the summer rather than embracing his new abilities, the novel would not have aperture.

Most resolutions in children's and YA literature include all three dynamics, at least for stand-alone novels. Writers can achieve interesting and memorable effects by denying readers one or more of them, as *The Chocolate War* by Robert Cormier does, for instance. However, this denial often makes readers uncomfortable, so make sure that decision would be in tune with the points of the book. If you're writing an ongoing series with a definite endpoint, then for each individual volume in that series, you should likely choose to have completion for the action plots of that particular book, and perhaps a measure of aperture or closure to go with it; but any outstanding questions about the larger arc of the series will keep it from achieving all three dynamics until the very last book.

═══ EXERCISES ═══

In the resolution of your action plot, what shows readers that the status quo is different now?

Do you want your ending to have closure, completion, and aperture? If so, how are those elements shown in the story?

∼

How do you plot a novel? I suggest you first write a story: Create a character with a desire and a compulsion, and then see what she does. Force her to make choices, follow the consequences, and repeat that process until you come to a natural endpoint. Then go back and look at the structure of that story to craft the plot. Does its nature fall into a particular plot type? What is your inciting incident? Does the plot build consistently over time? Does the protagonist bring about the climax of your central action plot? How does the resolution show that our protagonist has changed and established a new status quo? Revise and keep revising until you reach your points.

Finally, remember that the overall goal of a plot is to make readers *feel*—to provide a structure for the action to develop, for surprises to unfold, and for readers to react. All of the terms and exercises we've discussed here are only tools in creating those feelings, not ends in themselves. If you and your beta readers experience the feelings you intended at every stage of the book, then don't worry about specific obstacles or plot types and so forth: You're accomplishing what you set out to do, and doing just fine.

═══ *EXERCISE* ═══════════════════════════════

As a summary exercise here, fill out the Plot Checklist. I use this worksheet with every novel I edit to gain perspective on the manuscript after I finish reading it and consider its plot elements separate from its language. It forces me to define all of these elements within the novel; indeed, it makes me confirm that these elements are present, period. If I feel uncomfortable or uncertain about any of my answers, that points me in a direction I need to think about editorially, to ask the author to raise the stakes or strengthen the inciting incident or flesh out a desire.

Please feel free to personalize this checklist for your narrative needs. If your book has multiple protagonists, then you may want to use multiple copies of the checklist, one for each protagonist, to track their separate development. There are also many lovely novels that resemble real life—including the aforementioned *Goodbye Stranger* and *Criss Cross*—that have less of a central action plot through-line than multiple plot threads that weave together to create a shimmering whole, and the checklist as laid out here does not serve these books very well. (When I edit books like these, I still use the checklist, but I might list several threads under the central action plot, and trace them each through the Freytag's pyramid-related questions.) As with any tool, the most important thing is that it should help you get your job done. You can download a Word version of this checklist from my website.

PLOT CHECKLIST

Title: _____ Draft #: ____

Date: _____

Central Action Plot: Conflict   Mystery   Lack

    Stakes (beginning and end):

Central Emotional Plot: Conflict   Mystery   Lack

    Stakes (beginning and end):

Desire/Compulsion: What does the protagonist want?

Overarching Obstacles: What keeps him/her from getting it?

Exposition: The situation at the beginning:

Inciting Incident: The status quo changes when:

Escalating or Complicating Events *or* Phases:

Subplots / Relationships:

Climax: Everything comes together when:

Resolution: The reader can tell things have changed because:

Experiential Point:

Emotional Point:

Thematic Point:

CHAPTER 11

Obstacles and Negotiation

Seven Ways of Looking at a Scene

T he basic building block of any narrative work is the scene, which we defined earlier as "a dramatized action, in a certain limited time frame, during which something changes." This encompasses a vital element of plot, you'll note—a change—and every scene should have its own small plot, which will also usually follow the rhythms of Freytag's pyramid. When I'm editing a scene that doesn't feel satisfying to me, I test it against a series of questions and exercises that help me determine what it should be doing and work through any points of confusion in it. We'll complete these here using one of my favorite chapters from *Marcelo in the Real World*.

Chapter 3

I get out of the car and head for the back door. I see Arturo in the backyard grilling steaks. I hoped to enter the house without him seeing me. I am not ready for the discussion that I know will take place and I need more time to anticipate his questions and memorize my replies. But Aurora yells at him from the back door.

"Sorry we're late. We got stuck in traffic."

He answers her without turning around. "I didn't see any dinner cooking, so I thought I'd grill something."

"I'll make the salad," Aurora tells him, and goes in the house.

I am about to go in when Arturo speaks. "Marcelo, can I talk to you?"

I walk as slowly as I can. Arturo is stabbing the red meat with a giant fork.

"Not done yet," he says. He closes the black lid to the grill and sits on one of the white iron chairs. "Sit down for a minute." He pulls out a chair. "How was Dr. Malone?"

"He was well." I'm still standing. I'm looking at the red needle of the thermometer attached to the grill. It is moving past three hundred degrees.

"Marcelo," I hear him call. He is holding a goblet half-filled with ruby-colored wine. I know Arturo is not fond of my visits to Dr. Malone's office. He believes the tests imply there is something wrong with me, which he does not think is the case. "So, what did the good doctor do to you this time?"

"The brain was scanned while Marcelo listened to music."

"Try saying that again."

"My brain was scanned while I listened to music." I remind myself not to refer to myself in the third person. Also, I must remember not to call him Arturo.

"Thank you. Is that right? Real music or the kind you alone can hear?" Talking about the Internal Music, I have learned, makes Arturo nervous. I attempt to change the subject.

"After Dr. Malone we went to see the newborn pony at Paterson."

"That's good. But you didn't answer my question."

There is no chance of ever changing the subject with Arturo. "Real music," I answer. It is not a lie. The IM is as real as any other kind.

"How long will these visits go for?"

"They last about an hour."

"No, that's not what I meant. I mean, how much longer are these experiments or observations going to go on?" Before I can answer, he says, "I have a proposition that I want to discuss with you."

I feel my chest begin to tighten. "I am not going to Oak Ridge High." I can hear my voice tremble as I say this.

Arturo's face turns serious. I brace myself. I know how Arturo can switch from father to lawyer in an instant. The face of Arturo the father does not come out as often for me as it does for my sister, Yolanda. I get more of Arturo the lawyer: his eyes unblinking and fixed on my face, the volume of his voice modulated with complete control. He becomes a person who will lose his composure only if he wishes to.

"Here's what I would like to propose." I expect him to pause because he is speaking faster than he usually does. But he goes on speaking as fast as he speaks to Yolanda. "I want you to work at the law firm this summer."

This is a total surprise. It takes me a while to find words, any words. When I do, I say: "I have a summer job at Paterson."

"You'll help in the mailroom." He doesn't hear or chooses not to hear what I say.

"I have a job already," I repeat.

"Sit down, please." He points to the chair. I sit.

He moves forward on his chair so that our knees are almost touching. He lowers his voice. He is a father now. "Son, I want you to have a job where you interact with people, where you have to figure out new things by yourself. What do you do at Paterson that teaches you what you don't already know?"

"I will be learning to train the ponies."

"But this is the stage of your life when you need to be working with people."

"Why?"

"It is an experience you haven't had, really. At Paterson you are in a protected environment. The kids who go there are not . . . normal. Most of them will be the way they are all their lives. You, on the other hand, have the ability to grow and adapt. Even your Dr. Malone thinks this is the case. He's said so since the very first time we saw him. All these years, it wasn't really necessary for you to go to Paterson. You don't really belong there. I know you realize this yourself. There's nothing wrong with you. You just move at a different speed than other kids your age. But in order for you to grow and not get stuck, you need to be in a normal environment. It is time. Here is what I propose: If you work at the law firm this summer, then at the end of the summer, you decide whether you want to spend your senior year at Paterson or at Oak Ridge High."

Now he pauses. He knows I will need time to sort this out. One summer at the law firm versus a whole year at Paterson. I miss out on Fritzy's early months, but I still get to train him next year. Arturo interrupts my thoughts.

"There's just one thing." I see him pick up the glass of wine and raise to his lips. This time his words come out very slow. "You can do what you want in the fall . . ." He waits for my eyes to meet his eyes and then he continues. "But this summer you must follow all the rules of the . . . real world."

"The real world," I say out loud. It is one of Arturo's favorite phrases.

"Yes, that's right. The real world."

As vague and broad as this term is, I have a sense of what it means and of the difficulties that it entails. Following the rules of the real world means, for example, engaging in small talk with other people. It means refraining from talking about my special interest. It means looking people in the eye and shaking hands. It means doing things "on the hoof," as we say at Paterson, which means doing things that have not been scheduled in advance. It may mean walking or going to places I am not familiar with, city streets full of noise and confusion. Even though I am trying to look calm, a wave of terror comes over me as I imagine walking the streets of Boston by myself.

Arturo smiles as if he knows what is going through my mind. "Don't worry," he says soothingly, "we'll go slow at first. The real world is not going to hurt you."

There is a question floating inside of me but I can't find the words for it just yet. I open and clench my fists as I wait for the question to formulate itself. Finally, it arrives. I say to Arturo, "At the end of the summer, will Marcelo, will I decide where I want to spend my senior year . . . regardless?"

"Regardless? I don't follow you."

"You said that if I follow the rules of the real world this summer, I will get to decide where I go next year. Who will decide whether I followed the rules? I am not aware of all the rules of the real world. They are innumerable, as far as I have been able to determine."

"Ahh." It is Arturo the father who is speaking now. "Well, look. The corporate world has its rules. The law firm has its rules. The mailroom has its rules. The legal system has its rules. The real world as a whole has its rules. The rules deal with behaviors and the way to do things in order to be successful. To be successful is to accomplish the task that has been assigned to us or which we have assigned to ourselves. You will need to adapt to the environment governed by these rules as best you can. At Paterson, the environment adapts to you. If you need more time to finish a test, you get it. In the mailroom, a package will need to go out by a certain time or else. As to who will determine what, it seems to me that for this exercise to have any meaning, there must be something at stake. If you go through the motions and just show up every day and not try, then no, you will not have the ability to decide where you spend next year because you will not have followed the rules of the real world. It seems to me that at the end of the summer, we will both know with absolute certainty whether you succeeded or not. But, if for some reason we disagree, it seems to me that the ultimate decision should be mine. I am the father and you are the son. I will be your boss and you will be the employee. Does that make sense?"

I nod that it does. I never lie. But I do now. There is something about what Arturo just said that does not make sense.

Arturo is waiting to see if there are further questions. He knows it takes me a while to process information. I do have one final question.

"How will Marcelo be successful in the mailroom?" I would like to have a diagram or picture of what this means so that I can prepare for it.

"Each assignment given to you will have its built-in definition of success. You have a right to ask for instructions from anyone in the law firm who gives you an assignment. Success will be based on your ability to follow those instructions. I know this is very vague and you would like more clarity. You have to trust me. You are not going to be asked to perform tasks that are beyond your abilities. Do you trust me? I have always been fair, haven't I?"

This time I don't know how the word "trust" is being used. But "fair" I understand. "Yes," I say. It is true. Arturo has always been fair.

"Good," he says. "I will be honest with you. I am hoping that after this summer, you will choose to go to Oak Ridge High. There is a life out there that is healthy and normal that you need to be a part of. So, is it a deal?"

"There are some things I cannot do even if I wanted to," I say.

"Like what?"

"There are so many things Marcelo still has difficulties with. I cannot walk by myself in a strange place without a map. I get flustered when I am asked to do more than one thing at once. People say words I do not understand or their facial expressions are incomprehensible. They expect responses from me I cannot give."

"Maybe the reason you can't do those things is not because you are not able to, but because you have not been in an environment that challenges you to do them. Jasmine, the girl who runs the mailroom, will show you the ropes. I've talked to her about you. She'll go easy on you at first. But going slow doesn't mean you won't need to expand beyond your comfort zone."

I am thinking that next fall, I will be able to work full-time at Paterson training Fritzy and the other ponies. I can visit the ponies on the weekends this summer. Arturo is basically asking me to pretend that I am normal, according to his definition, for three months. This is an impossible task, as far as I can tell, especially since it is very difficult for me to feel that I am not normal. Why can't others think and see the world the way I see it? But after three months, it will be over, and I can be who I am.

"Think about it. Let me know first thing in the morning."

"All right," I say. "I will think about it." I start to walk towards my tree house. Namu, who has been lying at my feet all the time, walks by my side.

"You are getting too old to live in a tree house," I hear Arturo say behind me.

I pretend his words do not reach me.

The seven questions and exercises I might put this scene through:

1. What is the action or informational point to this scene? What change does it show us in the book's plots or subplots?

We ask these questions first so we know what we should be working toward within this scene—the overall purpose that justifies its existence. This scene sets up the deal between the two men, and shows us how and why the change in Marcelo's summer plans comes about. If there were no deal and no change here, the scene would feel pointless or incomplete— an "And then" rather than a necessary "But" or "Therefore." As it is, the scene's existence is definitely justified, as Arturo introduces both the stakes and the central action plot for the entire novel.

2. What do we learn about the characters through this scene? How do they change thanks to it? What is its emotional point?

As a rule of thumb, every scene should advance the central plots or a subplot in some way, *and* contribute to our knowledge of the characters and/or their ultimate emotional challenges or growth. Characterwise, here we meet Arturo for the first time; see how Marcelo relates to him, with a combination of respect and distrust; and witness the overall strength and tension of their father-son bond. The emotional change in the scene parallels the action change: Marcelo starts the scene nervous about the conversation to come, but determined to hold out for Paterson. By its conclusion, Marcelo is uneasy but resigned to the idea of working in the law firm, and we share his foreboding.

3. What is the experiential point of this scene? What do we want the reader to feel here? How is that feeling evoked?

In most children's and YA novels, the reader generally shares whatever emotion the protagonist is feeling, and the writer must get the protagonist and reader in sync. This one-to-one correlation can be complicated by the reader's relationship to the protagonist—if we dislike him, for instance, we might feel satisfaction when he gets hurt—and by the amount of information the reader has relative to the protagonist: If we can see or understand more about the novel's situation than he does, then our reactions will be rooted in our feelings toward him, combined with the additional perspective we gain from our greater information. (If we have less information than he does, then we might cling to him more closely, as he's our only guide in navigating this situation.) Here Marcelo feels tense and uncomfortable, and as we identify with him, that's the primary emotion we readers experience as well. But it's a good kind of tension and discomfort for fiction, because it comes out of the presentation of a new challenge, which promises more action and keeps us reading.

4. What is being negotiated?

Every scene should be a negotiation: A character is wrestling with an idea; a child is trying to understand why her sister is leaving the family; two people on a date have to figure out what the other person is like, how to please them, and whether they can have a good time together. To define the terms of the negotiation, try these questions (some of which appeared in the bookmap rubric):

- **Who are the characters involved in the scene?** Marcelo and Arturo.
- **What do they *both* want in this scene?** If the characters share a desire, that sets up the possibility of common ground. Here, they both want to determine where Marcelo will go to school.

- **What do they *each* want in this scene?** However, that common ground could easily be lost to their individual desires, or their differing visions of what that ground looks like. Marcelo wants to go to Paterson. Arturo wants him to go to Oak Ridge High, and he also wants to introduce the law firm idea to Marcelo for the first time.
- **What is the obstacle to each character getting what he or she wants?** The obstacle for Marcelo is Arturo's resistance to Marcelo's difference from others. The obstacle for Arturo is Marcelo's resistance to being "normal." Since their desires are each directly blocked by the other, they're in what Jennifer Crusie calls a "conflict lock," which creates the strongest scenes, because good drama happens when characters are forced to confront their differences.

As noted earlier, as a rule of thumb, every scene should have an obstacle of some kind. It could be another character whom our protagonist opposes, or something he's turning over in his head and just can't see yet, or a secret that a friend is keeping that will come to light in the action. The scene should then involve the protagonist coming to terms with that obstacle in some way, and end once victory, defeat, or détente has been achieved.

- **What is the overall plot dynamic here—a conflict, a mystery, or a lack?** As the two characters directly oppose each other, this scene is clearly a conflict. In a mystery scene, the obstacle will often be ignorance of a fact that the character wishes to find out: Where are the jewels, who is the father. In a lack scene, the obstacle will often be an overriding emotion: the character cannot achieve his desire because he lacks the bravery or some other quality necessary to do so.
- **What is the emotional or philosophical subtext to this conversation?** "Subtext" is a layer of emotion that underlies the action in a scene and deepens or complicates the surface level of what is being said. Not every scene or incident needs to have a subtext, and the lack of one does not make a scene bad. As Freud is said to have said, sometimes a cigar is just a cigar, and sometimes one character is just asking another to help him with his homework, with no real implications beyond math class the next day.

On the other hand, the presence of subtext can be a great way to highlight the depth and complexity of a character or a relationship, and to enrich a plot beyond its surface dynamics. Suppose Ali and Benny have been best friends since childhood, and they're now sophomores in high school. Ali slacks off on all his homework, while Benny gets every assignment done on time. If Ali then asks Benny to "help" him with a quiz he desperately needs to pass, Benny might suspect that Ali is asking because he hasn't studied at all, and he now wants a free ride based on Benny's hard work. If grades have been a source of tension between them in the past, then the scene could have a subtext involving friendship (would Benny be resentful? Or happy to help?), the future (Benny is presumably planning for one, Ali might be enjoying the moment), fear (does Ali feel confident asking, or does Ali himself worry that Benny will resent it?), and all the other dynamics that can play out in a relationship.

The subtext relates to the larger action plot insofar as Ali and Benny's relationship forms part of the plot or its own subplot. Maybe Ali makes this kind of request of Benny all the time and never reciprocates, and Benny's affection for Ali is slowly transforming into resentment. In that case, even if they only talk explicitly about the quiz within this scene, the subtext could drive a climax to their relationship plot—a point at which things change irrevocably: In the next scene, Benny could end his friendship with Ali, or decide to tell him how he feels about the request rather than going along with it, or lay down an ultimatum that Ali must do his own work.

Authors can best create subtext by creating complicated characters; staying aware of all of their complexities as they write; and then revising individual scenes to bring in more of those complexities/dimensions consciously, if they didn't come out in the scene the first time around. Subtext is often the real guts of the scene—the reason the action matters, even if the characters can't say it out loud—and a lot of the best scenes in fiction involve the subtext of a scene rising to the surface as the characters' conflict strips them down to their essential natures.

In this *Marcelo* scene, what the two men are really discussing is how "normal" Marcelo should be. Marcelo insists on his right to be different; Arturo feels strongly that he should try to be normal; their conflict will play out through the rest of the novel in sometimes surprising ways. If you have a scene that feels like a just-a-cigar scene, look at it again and see how you can pull out those underlying dynamics.

- **Which player in the scene gets what he wants?** That is, who wins? Sometimes nobody does, sometimes both characters do, but in this case, it's pretty clearly Arturo.

5. Where are the beats, and do they build consistently to a clear climax?

"Beats" are nuggets of dialogue or action focused on a particular subject and in a particular emotional register. In our *Marcelo* scene here, I'd identify the beats as follows:

- First beat: Small talk. The two characters discuss the events of the day, allowing us to see their status-quo dynamic.
- Second beat, beginning at "I have a proposition I want to discuss with you": The proposal and its stakes. Arturo proposes that Marcelo work at the law firm, and says that if he's successful there, he can choose what school he'll attend.
- Third beat, beginning at "There's just one thing": The real world. Both characters ruminate on what this idea means to them, the rules of this real world, and the definition of success. Here they set the terms of their deal, and Arturo tries to conclude it.
- Fourth beat, beginning at "There are some things I cannot do even if I wanted to": Marcelo's limitations and processing. This follows directly out of the previous beat because we see him first responding with fear to the idea of being judged on his performance, and then starting to think through what might happen next.

I do this kind of breakdown a lot during line-editing when the rhythm of a scene doesn't feel quite right to me. First I split the scene into beats, or even break it down by paragraph, taking the topic sentence of each paragraph as its subject. Then I summarize each beat in a phrase, as I did above, and check to see if any of those phrases cover the same material, which would indicate that one beat or another could be cut. After that, I look to see if the beats are in the right order for a logical and emotional flow (recognizing that human beings are not always entirely logical in their shifts in topic or emotion, but still hoping the reader can follow the character's, or author's, line of thought).

And as you may have noticed, this logical and emotional flow is pretty much Freytag's pyramid, as the beats above fall neatly into the structure of exposition/inciting incident/escalating and complicating events/climax/resolution. The exposition happens with the first beat, when Arturo calls Marcelo over and engages him in small talk. The inciting incident is the proposal, the escalating and complicating events the rules and definition of success. The climax happens at the end of the third beat, when Arturo asks, "Is it a deal?," pulling all of the preceding dialogue into a sharp, clear point. And then our resolution shows Marcelo putting off a decision and processing the conversation.

Do you see the structure there? Isn't that neat? Certainly not all scenes will fall into the pattern as clearly as this one does, but most will end up following it in the course of the protagonist negotiating the scene's obstacles. If a scene doesn't work or feels flat, it usually has to do with the climax: Either the climax beat is misplaced within the scene, or there's no climax at all. The climax should be the moment everything is working up to, the moment of highest tension, the moment at which something changes. If that happens too early in the scene, or gets buried under other information, rearrange the beats so that this moment falls toward the end and stands out. And if a scene *doesn't* have a climax, create one, to help the reader see that something has changed here. If that's not possible based upon the material, consider cutting the scene.

6. Is the balance among various kinds of narration appropriate to the nature of the scene?

We will go into the theory of this subject in the next chapter, but on a practical level, if a scene feels stuffy or slow to me, I highlight each of the following types of narration in different colors:

- Internal narration: This is the character's self-talk—the narration that's happening inside the viewpoint character's head—as when Marcelo says, "I hoped to enter the house without him seeing me. I am not ready for the discussion that I know will take place and I need more time to anticipate his questions and memorize my replies."
- Dialogue.
- Action: physical movement, which can be as simple as a line like, "I get out of the car and head for the back door."
- Description: Something the character sees, as when Marcelo says, "I'm looking at the red needle of the thermometer attached to the grill. It is moving past three hundred degrees." (There isn't a lot of description in *Marcelo in the Real World* in general, in keeping with Marcelo's more inward-looking nature.)

If you try this highlighting as an exercise on one of your own scenes, don't worry too much about what type of narration each sentence belongs to. Just go with your instincts, and when you're done, look at what color predominates on the page. Is that type of narration appropriate to the experiential point of the scene? For instance, in an exciting chase scene, you should have more action than any other type of narration. If not, it's likely those other elements are weighing down the scene and keeping it from moving at heart-racing speed. If it's a scene meant to introduce us to the wonder of a new planet where our protagonist has landed, then there could be a lot of description and internal narration as she observes her new environment closely and processes what the sights mean for her life there. This *Marcelo* scene is almost entirely dialogue and internal narration, which feels right for a scene where our hero is negotiating with someone he doesn't fully trust and working through the implications of the conversation step by step.

7. Does it have an establishing shot and an appropriate fermata?
These two items are a final check on the information the reader has going into and out of the scene. An *establishing shot*—a term taken from film—

establishes the location of the action and often its time of day. (On a TV show, any long shot of a building from the outside that precedes a scene inside is a textbook establishing shot.) It does not have to be the first line of the scene, but it will usually appear somewhere in the first paragraph or two to orient readers and bring us up to the present time. Here, "I see Arturo in the backyard grilling steaks" lets us know that Marcelo and Aurora have arrived at home and it's dinnertime.

In music, a *fermata* (⌒) indicates a note that should be held for an extended period of time. I'm borrowing the term for a rule of thumb: The last line of a scene should serve as a fermata in the reader's mind, setting and holding the emotional tone the reader should take away from that scene. Suppose the *Marcelo* scene had ended on, "Namu, who has been lying at my feet all the time, walks by my side," or "'You are getting too old to live in a tree house,' I hear Arturo say behind me." The first would have created a sense of Marcelo having more allies and strength in this situation than he actually does. The second would have given Arturo the last word, which might have been appropriate for his manipulation of Marcelo here, but which would have been more of a victory than he deserves, since Marcelo is still holding out against him. The actual last line—"I pretend his words do not reach me"—gives Marcelo the victory of sorts here, if a hollow one, and leaves the reader with a feeling of falsehood, disconnection, and uneasiness. All of this is just right for the nature of the scene, and it makes me want to read on to find some comfort.

The pure jolt of emotion in a good fermata can redeem a flabby scene and push the reader forward, but it's better not to have a flabby scene in the first place! Pay attention to the points of your scene as well as its negotiations, subtext, beats, and balance of narration, and write it tight.

CHAPTER 12

Movement and Momentum

Controlling Your Pace and Prosody

We've created characters here. We've imagined actions for them, and set up a structure in which those actions will unfold. Now we have to make those characters carry out their actions within the prose, in a manner that allows the reader to envision the external action while sharing the protagonist's thoughts and feelings, and maintains the reader's interest via a steady drumbeat of events. This means it is time to talk about pacing and prosody: the speed and flow of the action, information, and language in a book.

Before we go any further, please look back at what we established as your experiential point many chapters ago. Again, this is what you want your reader to *feel* as a result of the book, the overarching emotional experience you want her to have in the course of reading it. If you wrote "exciting" or "suspenseful," then that likely demands a quicker pace for your novel, full of high-stakes action and cliffhangers, to get readers' hearts pumping and keep them turning the pages. If you wrote "sad," "reflective," or "romantic," then a fast pace might end up working against you, because readers wouldn't have time to experience the emotions you'll create as deeply as you want. If you wrote out a mix of experiences—laughing, exhilarated, terrified—you'll need to vary the pacing to allow each of those moments their own emotional space. And in every case, we need to keep the action moving steadily in order to keep readers involved.

With that experiential point in mind, we're going to talk first about four factors that influence pacing, then drill down and look at the novel's flow on a plot level, a scene level—where we'll get into what I call prosody— and a sentence level. The choices you make at each of these levels affect your pacing all the way through.

Defining Your Pace

Four major factors will determine your novel's pace:

The Time Frame of the Action

This is the amount of narrative time that passes between the inciting incident and the climax of the book. Does your novel take place in fewer than twenty-four hours, like *Nick and Norah's Infinite Playlist*? Or might it cover years, if not decades, like *Brown Girl Dreaming* or *Ella Enchanted*? Most middle-grade and YA novels focus on one particular experience of growth in the protagonist's life, which takes place in a time period ranging from a few weeks to up to one year. (The school year is an especially standard measure—think the Harry Potter books, or *The Perks of Being a Wallflower*.) In general, the longer the time period your action needs to cover, the more events you're likely to have, and the more you're going to need to narrate the action, because you will not be able to dramatize all of those events in depth.

Some books cut back and forth among multiple timelines, where the action and information from each separate plotline combine to form a super-plot of their own. In *I'll Give You the Sun* by Jandy Nelson, Jude's story in the present unfolds in alternating chapters with her twin brother Noah's experiences two years earlier. In adult fiction, the first half of *Gone Girl* by Gillian Flynn juxtaposes Nick Dunne's view of his wife Amy's disappearance with excerpts of Amy's diary from years earlier. The action in both novels can only move so fast, because each timeline must stop to cut over to the other every so often; but this cross-cutting also creates suspense, as we must wait to find out what happens in the timeline we aren't in. Novels like these are incredibly difficult to execute well, because each event must work within both its individual timeline and the larger plot and pace of the overall book. That said, editors and agents *love* novels that can pull off these kinds of unconventional time structures, because they're extremely easy to sell to other readers: All we have to do is describe that structure, and the structure itself will generate questions, conflict, and suspense.

=== **EXERCISE** ===

How much time passes between your inciting incident and climax? (A calendar may be useful in figuring this out, and in mapping and pacing your events altogether.)

Narration vs. Dramatization

The difference between narration and dramatization can best be shown through example:

Norah bites her bottom lip.

"Thinking about it?" I ask uneasily.

"No. Just thinking about where to go. Somewhere nobody will find us."

"Like Park Avenue?"

And Norah tilts her head, looks at me a little askew, and says, "Yes, like Park Avenue."

And then she utters a word I never in a zillion years thought I'd ever hear her utter:

"Midtown."

It's ridiculous, but we take the subway. Even more ridiculous, it's the 6 train that we take, the most notoriously slow local in all of Manhattan. At four in the morning, we're on the platform for a good twenty minutes—the time it would've taken us to walk—but I don't mind the delay because we're talking all over the place, hitting *Heathers* and peanut butter preferences and favorite pairs of underwear and Tris's occasional body odor and Tal's body hair fetish and the fate of the Olsen twins and the number of times we've seen rats in the subway and our favorite graffiti ever—all in what seems like a single sentence that lasts the whole twenty minutes. Then we're in the weird fluorescence of the subway car, sliding into each other when the train stops and starts, making comments with our eyes about the misbegotten drunkards, business-suit stockbroker frat boys, and weary night travelers that share our space. I am having a fucking great time, and the amazing thing is that I realize it even as it's happening. I think Norah's getting into it, too. Sometimes when we slide together, we take a few seconds to separate ourselves. We're not to the point of deliberately touching again, but we're not about to turn down a good accident.

—*Nick and Norah's Infinite Playlist* by David Levithan and Rachel Cohn

The long paragraph that ends this excerpt is a textbook example of narration. The authors aren't spelling out every word Nick and Norah say here; rather, they're skimming over the conversation, dipping in and out of specifics, letting us readers watch the action on fast-forward. The paragraph covers about thirty minutes of narrative time, but it requires less than thirty seconds to read, so the authors are able to take us through a lot of conversation in very little readerly time and page space.

In contrast, the first half of that excerpt *does* spell out every word the characters said and every movement they made, from Norah's biting her lip to her utterance of "Midtown," covering about fifteen seconds of both narrative and readerly time. That is dramatization. Dramatization always carries more emotional and narrative weight than narration in part *because* it takes more time. (As a rule of thumb, the significance of a character/item/storyline/anything in a novel is usually proportional to the time and space spent on it.) More importantly still, dramatization allows us to feel like we are witnessing this action in real time, and we get to develop our own opinions on it; we're not dependent on a narrator to tell us what happens and how it feels. Thus we become active players in the drama, and that, in turn, increases our interest in the story and the plot.

If you've heard the writing rule to "show, not tell," dramatization is showing, while narration is telling. Contrary to that rule, telling can be a very good and useful tool to employ, as we can see from the example above: I wouldn't *want* to spend a half hour reading about waiting on a subway platform, much less hear about Tris's body odor in detail. If you dramatized every event in your book for readers, you'd likely waste much of their time, because not all events are equally important and not all action deserves it. At the same time, I do want significant events or scenes to be dramatized for me, so I can experience their power myself. Here are some more rules of thumb for choosing between narration and dramatization for events:

- If your protagonist is directly involved in an event and it counts as action—that is, it makes a significant difference in your central plots or subplots—then dramatize it.
- If your protagonist is directly involved in an event but it doesn't count as action or doesn't make such a difference (like, say, his going to school each day): Narrate it, or just don't mention it. Readers will assume daily life stuff happens without your telling them about it.
- If your protagonist is not directly involved in the event but it makes a difference in the plot: If your novel uses multiple points of view and it's useful for us to see it, dramatize it. If it sticks close to his perspective, dramatize his reaction to hearing the news, so we can share in the emotion of his reaction and the event makes an impression on us. (This happens a lot in the Harry Potter series, when Harry is at Hogwarts and he learns about events in the wider wizarding world.)
- If your protagonist is not involved in the event and it does not make a difference in the plot: You can mention the event in passing if it's part of the world-building. If not, skip it altogether.

As one more very rough, unscientific rule of thumb, I think 80 percent of the action in any middle-grade and YA novel should be dramatized. The novel will then consist of a series of dramatic scenes, joined together by narration that covers the time passing between them.

═══ *EXERCISE* ═══

Find a dramatized scene in your work in progress and narrate it in two paragraphs at most.

The Cashore Principle

The third factor influencing pacing returns to what you wrote down for your experiential point. In a blog post in July 2010,* Kristen Cashore, the author of the excellent YA fantasy novels *Graceling, Fire,* and *Bitterblue,* laid out a writing principle that resonates across plotting, pacing, and voice: "If you're describing a place or an emotion or *anything* that is simple and peaceful, your writing should be simple and peaceful. Match your style of writing to the feeling you wish the reader to feel."

On the plot level, the principle means you need to create story events that match the experiential point you intend: If you want the novel to be exciting, the events should be, too. On the scene and sentence levels, consider these two examples:

> The evil of the actual disparity in their ages (and Mr. Woodhouse had not married early) was much increased by his constitution and habits; for having been a valetudinarian all his life, without activity of mind or body, he was a much older man in ways than in years; and though

---

* http://kristincashore.blogspot.com/2010/07/writing-lesson-about-trees.html

everywhere beloved for the friendliness of his heart and his amiable temper, his talents could not have recommended him at any time.

—*Emma* by Jane Austen

He would not think about that. That was not his business. That was Golz's business. He had only one thing to do and that was what he should think about and he must think it out clearly and take everything as it came along, and not worry. To worry was as bad as to be afraid. It simply made things more difficult.

—*For Whom the Bell Tolls* by Ernest Hemingway

Emma is about a Regency-era upper-class woman who believes she knows how to arrange other people's lives, and tries to do so, and the rhythm and vocabulary of the passage imply leisure, education, ampleness, relaxation. . . . Just the fact that it's *one single sentence* tells us it's from a period when people had time to talk like that! And as Jane Austen's experiential point always includes some humor, it has a nice little kick of a joke at the end. *For Whom the Bell Tolls*, meanwhile, is about a young American man who has joined a guerrilla movement to fight the Fascists in the Spanish Civil War. The short, compact sentences, with short, plain words, create an appropriate sense of carefully controlled tension and focus. In both cases, the pacing of these sentences and their vocabulary matches the experiential points of the works as a whole—as Cashore puts it, "the feeling [these authors] wish the reader to feel."

Information

Everything that readers know about the world and people of a novel comes word by word, phrase by phrase—nuggets of information. That means that information has to come in the right order, and at the right speed, for readers to take it in, and for it to be meaningful to them. (You could just make a numbered list with all the information you're inventing for your book, but nobody would enjoy reading it.) You do not want to supply any more information than the reader needs, and neither do you want to supply any less. You want to supply only what's relevant and necessary.

Editing is the art of putting information in the right order. In nonfiction, you're putting the information in order so that it adds up to a cohesive argument and/or narrative. In fiction, you're putting the information in order so it adds up to a cohesive narrative, thematic argument, and emotional experience. Oftentimes, especially on the sentence level, controlling the pace really means controlling the flow of information—how fast it comes at the protagonist and reader, and how much time both protagonist and reader have to take it in.

Plot-Level Pacing

Beyond those four factors, the pace of the novel will be determined by readers' investment in your characters, the stakes, and the narrative questions. If readers care about your protagonist and she comes under threat, from something as large as a dragon or as small as a best friend moving away, readers will share the character's sense of jeopardy and read faster to try to get beyond it. Along similar lines, the more the character can gain or lose through the stakes, the more readers stand to triumph or fall as well. As a result, as a rule of thumb: the higher the stakes for a character we're invested in, the faster we read. Similarly, the more narrative questions you have in play at any one time (and are managing well), the more tension readers will experience about getting them answered, and the more we want to relieve it. If you can increase the temperature and degree of readers' investment in the protagonist, the stakes, or the questions, the novel will grow tighter and more suspenseful in turn.

As I edit a novel, I try to pay attention to what I think of as the "breathing pattern" of the book—its inhalations, when tensions are rising, and its exhalations, when they recede. (To have a tenser novel, include fewer exhalations.) I track a novel's breathing pattern through its phases—one last refinement and use of the bookmap, which can best be shown through an example:

MARCELO IN THE REAL WORLD PHASES

- Chapters 1–4: Marcelo's Internal Music, Arturo's proposal, the stakes. We meet Marcelo, see and like his innocence, and distrust Arturo.
- 5–7: Marcelo's first day at the law firm—a nest of vipers, pretty much, besides Jasmine.
- 8–14: Getting to know Jasmine and Wendell.
- 15–17: Marcelo finds the picture of Ixtel—a "girl with half a face"—and he and Jasmine react to it.
- 18–21: Marcelo and Jasmine examine the picture and locate Ixtel's lawyer, Jerry Garcia. Jerry asks for Marcelo's help getting a document that would prove the law firm's culpability. Marcelo reaches a point where he needs to make a decision between his father and Ixtel.
- 22–24: The trip to Vermont. Marcelo finds a place of refuge from the suffering of the world, determines to pursue "the right note," and feels connected to Jasmine.
- 25–26: Wendell gives Marcelo a letter from Jasmine that shows she once kissed Arturo, and in unaccustomed jealousy, Marcelo feels in darkness about what to do for Ixtel.
- 27–28: Marcelo gives Jerry Garcia the document he wanted, and the law firm reacts.
- 29–31: The consequences for Marcelo, and conclusion.

As you can see, a phase is a set of events in a certain limited time frame, focused around one certain character, setting, narrative question, or subject, which together accomplish one significant step in the story's development. Some phases might have their own little internal plot structures: The trip to Vermont, for instance, begins with Marcelo and Jasmine traveling quietly, each in their own heads, and ends and climaxes with Marcelo "feeling how it is to no longer be alone." Moreover, all of the phases build on each other in classic plot structure form, leading to the climax of the book as a whole. They need to happen in a specific order for the book to function properly; you could not arrange them in any other way. Given this last fact, phases are a useful way to look at the overall arc of the story and see how each set of events builds toward the climax.

It's also worth looking for a novel's *turning points*. Turning points are the events in a novel where the action and emotional plots cross—an external event that has such an impact on the protagonist that he changes his internal orientation to move in a new direction. In *Marcelo*, both his discovery of the picture and his receipt of Jasmine's letter to Arturo serve as turning points. Turning points signpost the character's growth and signal more action to come, and as a rule of thumb, every novel should have at least one. However, if you have more than three, that will likely end up exhausting your reader (never mind your poor protagonist). To identify your turning points, pick out all of the events in your novel that force your character to move in a new direction, either in terms of the action or their personal growth. (Hint: They will likely be at the end of a phase, or a series of important phases, as they are very much like the act breaks in a screenplay.) If you can't find them, think about what *is* making your character change, and whether it might be worth bringing that change out more strongly through an actual event that can serve as a turning point.

=== EXERCISES ===

Use a fresh copy of your bookmap to write in next to each
scene as many of these labels as are appropriate in
describing its major action:

- Physical action (a chase, a fight sequence)
- Revelation (the character learns something significant)
- Nonreality (a dream or fantasy sequence)
- Dialogue (the focus of the scene is on a conversation)
- Reflection (a significant part of the scene is spent showing us the character thinking through some event or piece of information)
- Flashback (a scene from an earlier point in the novel's timeline that fills in or contrasts to its present events)
- Turning point

This is another way to see the breathing pattern of your novel visually—what kind of scenes you're writing, how they flow together, and whether that mix matches the overall experiential point for your novel. If your experiential point was to write a thrilling fantasy novel filled with drama and betrayal, for instance, but you have many more dialogue and reflection sequences than physical action or revelations, you may need to reverse that balance. Flashbacks, reflection, and nonreality sequences can all slow a novel down because they step outside the normal flow of narrative time. If you want to pick up your novel's pace, be sure that all of those sequences are clearly contributing something to the action plot of the novel. (Indeed, with flashbacks and nonreality sequences, you should confirm how essential they are to your plot or points even if you feel your pacing is just fine. It's very easy for those to feel self-indulgent and bog down a novel's action.)

Draw lines between each phase in your bookmap, or write the phrases out separately, as in the *Marcelo* example. Then, without thinking about it too much, write in:

A. A one-sentence synopsis of each phase.

B. What changes or what the protagonist discovers in the course of the phase.

C. What event makes the character move on from that phase (or put another way, "What is the climax of each phase?").

D. Within that list, identify your turning points. What is the character turning from and to?

Generally, phases should increase in tension as they build toward the climax, as the stakes accumulate, the ticking clock counts down (if applicable), and the action comes to a head. When you read through the answers in (A.), does that hold true here? Conversely, you might want a quieter period in the midst of a lot of action. Katniss's peaceful days with Rue and Peeta during the Hunger Games are precious partly because the rest of the action is so intense. Would a contrasting phase like that be useful to your book?

If you complete the exercises above and discover that you need to tighten your pace, try layering. As most novels have more than one plot going on at the same time, an inciting incident from your romantic main plot may be followed by a scene that introduces a clue for your mystery subplot. If you layer those two things into one scene, so that the inciting incident also establishes that clue, you could then cut that second scene, which would tighten up the novel that much more.

This layering might truly be more work than you need to do. Tightness is not the highest virtue in a novel, rightness is, and the right breathing pattern for the book may necessitate two separate, excellent scenes. But if your novel feels overly long or baggy, look for opportunities to layer more information or plotlines into a scene that isn't doing quite enough work on its own. The more closely you can weave all of the plots and subplots together, the more elegant and efficient your book will become.

Prosody: How a Story Moves

Here we turn from talking about the pace of the novel as a whole to talking about the movement of the prose itself. The dictionary definition of "prosody" is "the study of metrical structure of verse." I'm borrowing the term to refer to the rhythm of fiction: specifically, the rhythm with which information is introduced into and narrated within a story. Unlike poetic prosody, there is no highly regimented system here, nor very strict forms; but there are some general patterns that are useful for writers to know.

In Chapter 11, "Obstacles and Negotiation," I asked you to think about a scene's balance of internal narration, action, dialogue, and description. I classify those categories into three types of narration: descriptive, immediate, and internal narration. Descriptive narration covers things that exist outside the present narrative time: backstory and description. Immediate narration describes things that happen in the present narrative time: action and dialogue. And internal narration shows what our viewpoint character is thinking in reaction to both of the other kinds of narration. To demonstrate, here's a passage from *Bobby vs. Girls (Accidentally)* by Lisa Yee (‡),

where I've left the descriptive narration in plain text and marked the immediate narration in bold and the internal narration with an underscore:

> The whole town of Rancho Rosetta, California, turned out for the
> annual Labor Day Fiesta at Wild Acres. **Bobby could hear a rock band**
> **playing in the distance as the riders exited Monstroso, laughing and**
> **giving each other high fives. Some people got right back in line to go**
> **on again. Bobby shook his head.** <u>The only ride worth going on over</u>
> <u>and over was the bumper cars. He also loved the Circus Train, but that</u>
> <u>was a little kid ride.</u>

The pattern you see here recurs over and over in fiction: A descriptive line
sets the scene or establishes an object for the viewpoint character and the
reader to observe; an immediate line introduces and develops the action
around it; and an internal line lets us know what this scene or action means
to the viewpoint character.

In first-person or close third-person narration, descriptive details are
introduced into the scene through what I call a "senseline." In "Bobby
could hear a rock band playing in the distance as the riders exited Mon-
stroso," the positioning of "Bobby" within the sentence establishes him
as our camera on the action. This means that readers cannot see or hear
something before Bobby sees it, and only once he looks at or hears something can we get a description of it. (This pattern can be less noticeable in
books written in first person, because *everything* we experience there is
filtered through our narrator, but the rule still holds.) Along similar lines,
when an external action introduces a thought of the character's that we
then get to hear, directly or indirectly, I call that a "thoughtline." "Bobby
shakes his head" is a thoughtline to the internal narration that follows.
Senselines or thoughtlines should introduce and anchor most internal
narration. If a paragraph's rhythm feels off, it's often because we're getting
internal narration when we haven't yet "seen" the material covered by the
descriptive or immediate narration.

As a rule of thumb, we should get all the major description of a person or object the first time our viewpoint character sees it. Suppose said character is meeting a new girl named Mina: "She was short, even though her boots had four-inch heels, and her brown eyes sparkled beneath garish green and gold eyeshadow." We shouldn't go through four or five paragraphs of action with Mina and then hear more details in passing, like, "She was wearing a blue fringed dress," unless there's some reason our viewpoint character wouldn't have noticed that dress the first time he saw her (when he did notice a detail like the height of her heels). It's also useful to move the "camera" in a description in a steady linear flow: Rather than jumping from Mina's heels up to her eye shadow and then back down to her dress, try starting with her eyes, then moving down to her dress, then to her heels. That allows readers to easily assemble a coherent picture of Mina in their heads.

If you struggle with organizing the flow of your information, try to structure your paragraphs with topic sentences and conclusions. You likely learned about these in school, when you had to write a five-paragraph argumentative essay, and it's an immensely valuable model for conveying the development of any sort of thought, including description and narration. A topic sentence is the first sentence of a paragraph, which sets forth its main idea or hypothesis. Look at the second-to-last paragraph in the *Marcelo* excerpt on p. 205. It starts with a topic sentence/thoughtline setting forth the paragraph's premise: "As vague and broad as [the term 'the real world'] is, I have a sense of what it means and of the difficulties that it entails." Then Marcelo backs up his assertion of understanding the real world with evidence that shows us what he's just told us: "Following the rules of the real world means, for example, engaging in small talk with other people. It means refraining from talking about my special interest." The conclusion provides an emotional culmination to these thoughts: "Even though I am trying to look calm, a wave of terror comes over me as I imagine walking the streets of Boston by myself." That "wave of terror" re-anchors the reader in Marcelo's immediate physical experience, rather than his internal narration, and readies us to hear his father's next line.

Internal narration shows us directly how the viewpoint character interprets, and how the reader *might* interpret, the action taking place. I divide internal narration into the categories of commentary and reflection (or processing). *Commentary* is the character's immediate internal response to events. *Reflection* is the character thinking out loud in his head, or pulling together various bits of information to arrive at a new conclusion, which will usually set up his next course of action. In the *Marcelo* excerpt, the lines "There is no chance of ever changing the subject with Arturo," or farther down, "This is a total surprise," are both examples of commentary, helping to guide the reader through the minefield of this conversation by showing Marcelo's reactions to it moment by moment.

Later, Marcelo observes, "Now he pauses. He knows I will need time to sort this out. One summer at the law firm versus a whole year at Paterson. I miss out on Fritzy's early months, but I still get to train him next year." That is Marcelo reflecting, figuring out what this proposal means for him. The last long paragraph at the end of the chapter also demonstrates reflection, as he accepts his father's proposal and starts to think about its implications for his summer. Internal narration, and especially reflection, help the reader know what in the descriptive and immediate narration is important to the character and what the character is taking away from it.

With that said, internal narration is a tool that should be used carefully and sparingly, because it can easily become redundant and slow the action down. If it's obvious to the reader from the immediate narration what the viewpoint character is feeling or doing, for goodness' sake, don't add internal narration on top of it! This can be especially dangerous in dialogue scenes, where you might be tempted to add a line of commentary or description after every line of speech—what the other person's face looks like, how each one reacts. Look back at the passage from *Nick and Norah's Infinite Playlist* on p. 218, and compare it to this version:

> I get a crazy idea that just bursts out of my mouth before I completely consider it. "Like Park Avenue?" I say, naming the soulless boulevard that runs from Union Square to Harlem, lined with giant office towers and apartment complexes, and bisected by the wedding cake of Grand Central Station and the gleaming hulk of the MetLife Building.

Norah tilts her head, looks at me a little askew with those eyes as brown as ripe chestnuts, and says, "Yes, like Park Avenue."

And then she utters a word I never in a zillion years thought I'd ever hear her utter, a word I never thought I'd find sexy, a word that turns me on in this moment more than I could ever imagine:

"Midtown."

Dialogue takes place in real time as well as immediate narrative time, so if there's commentary after every line of dialogue, as here, the conversation becomes incredibly stilted, as readers have to pause after every spoken line to digest additional thoughts about it. Even the interesting lines in the commentary, like the "wedding cake of Grand Central Station," distract us from the scene's point: a brief, funny exchange that should get the characters on the way to Midtown. As a rule of thumb, include commentary in your dialogue scenes only if it's necessary for us to understand the protagonist's thoughts or emotional process.

Indeed, it's very much worth remembering that *all* internal and descriptive narration takes place within the time established by the immediate narration, as well as in real time; and you must keep the immediate narration (action) moving and complete any scenes you start. If you have one or two beats of dialogue and action in Scene X, and then your narrator indulges in a four-page Flashback Y or offers six paragraphs of reflection on Subject Z, your reader will wonder what was happening in Scene X during all this internal narration, and then how Flashback Y or Subject Z relates to Scene X, considering so much more page time and reading time are being spent on them compared to the action of Scene X. As a writer, you'll need to both complete Scene X at some point (perhaps your narrator was just staring into space with Scene X going on around him while those four pages of immediate time passed?), and justify all of that page time with some narrative payoffs for the flashback or reflections.

One of my primary rules in editing is *stay with the action of the scene*. Stay with the immediate narration: Don't stop it in the middle for an info-dump of descriptive or internal narration. Stay with the flow of thought: Every reference or bit of commentary or reflection should be linked with a preceding thought or action. And most of all, stay with the emotion: Don't throw in a hilarious two-paragraph digression in the middle of a really tense horror sequence, make references that force the reader to stop and think in the grip of an action scene, or do anything else to distract the reader from the drama of your story and its accompanying feelings.

Here's one final example of an effective flow of narration, starting at the end of Chapter 17 in *The Hunger Games*:

> It's a child's scream, a young girl's scream, there's no one in the arena capable of making that sound except Rue. And now I'm running, knowing this may be a trap, knowing the three Careers may be poised to attack me, but I can't help myself. There's another high-pitched cry, this time my name. "Katniss! Katniss!"
>
> "Rue!" I shout back, so she knows I'm near. So *they* know I'm near, and hopefully the girl who has attacked them with tracker jackers and gotten an eleven they still can't explain will be enough to pull their attention away from her. "Rue! I'm coming!"
>
> When I break into a clearing, she's on the ground, hopelessly entangled in a net. She just has time to reach her hand through the mesh and say my name before the spear enters her body.
>
> **[Chapter 18]**
>
> The boy from District 1 dies before he can pull out the spear. My arrow drives deeply into the center of his neck. He falls to his knees and halves the brief remainder of his life by yanking out the arrow and drowning in his own blood. I'm reloaded, shifting my aim from side to side, while I shout at Rue, "Are there more? Are there more?"
>
> She has to say no several times before I hear it.

Most of that (brutal) excerpt is just straightforward immediate narration, as every line describes action or dialogue that is happening in the present moment. But note the use of internal narration here: "knowing this may be a trap . . ."; "So *they* know I'm near, and hopefully the girl who has attacked them . . ." Katniss's commentary has the effect of slowing down the action, delaying her getting to Rue, at a time when readers are *desperate* for her to get to Rue. That frustration of our desire increases our agony that much more. The cliffhanger at the end of the chapter serves the same purpose, ending on a moment of high drama that makes it impossible to put the book down. (Most of the fermatas in *The Hunger Games* are cliffhangers, which contributes to the book's immense speed.) The point of the scene is to create a readerly frenzy, to have us share in the mad fear and desperation that Katniss feels, and the rhythms of the narration here serve that point perfectly.

You'll note that I used the term "the point of the scene" above. Again, it's always useful to ask yourself, "What is the point of this scene from an informational perspective? From an action perspective? What emotion do I wish the reader to feel? Or *need* the reader to feel, at this point in the action?" Once you have an intention for the scene, write or revise it as necessary. (You may sometimes have to throw out entire scenes and write new ones to get the right information or emotion at a certain moment.) In particular, once you know the experiential point of the scene, you should know what speed it should move at, and you can distribute or cut down its narration appropriately.

=== **EXERCISE** ===

Find a dialogue scene in your WIP and highlight all of the commentary and reflection. How much do you have? How much could you do without?

Sentence-Level Pacing

The pace of a book is set as much by its sentence structures as its plot. Every scene in your book could feature high-stakes action, but if it's written entirely in long, dense sentences that are hard to decipher, the pace could feel glacial nonetheless. Here, then, are four principles for determining your pace sentence on the level:

The structure and syntax of your sentences should match their intended emotional effect. Just to restate this: The Cashore Principle applies on the sentence level, too.

Effective sentences have a clear flow of thought and thereby emotion. Remember how we were talking about beats in a scene in Chapter 11, "Obstacles and Negotiation"? There are beats in a sentence as well, as basically every phrase or new nugget of information within a sentence forms a beat unto itself. In good prose, there should be a recognizable line of connection between those beats. As a positive example, let's go back to that sentence from *Emma* quoted earlier:

> (1) The evil of the actual disparity in their ages (1a) (and Mr. Woodhouse had not married early) (2) was much increased by his constitution and habits; (3) for having been a valetudinarian all his life, (4) without activity of mind or body, (5) he was a much older man in ways than in years; (6) and though everywhere beloved for the friendliness of his heart and his amiable temper, (7) his talents could not have recommended him at any time.

Every phrase in this sentence is directly linked to the next, as we can see if we break out the individual beats:

1. There is a kind of "evil" (meaning "danger, trouble, cause for concern") in Emma and her father serving as each other's primary companions, given how many years these two people are separate in age.
1a. Aside: Mr. Woodhouse had married at a late age.
2. That danger was increased by his nature and behavior.

3. Explanation of that nature and behavior: He's been a valetudinarian—what we modern readers would call a hypochondriac—for a long time.

4. Which is further explained by the next phrase: He hasn't seen or done very much, so he has little to think about besides himself.

5. And thus he acts much older than he is chronologically.

6. And while he is a nice guy,

7. He is not the sharpest tool in the shed. (This again reinforces the idea of the problem Mr. Woodhouse presents, because Emma is a talented young woman, in the vernacular of Austen's age, and she should hang out with people who are her equals.)

When I edit, I spend a lot of time thinking about this kind of phrase and sentence linkage—how one thought flows into another—because that's ultimately how one emotion flows into another, and good novels sweep readers into their sensibility. The smoother you can make the links between phrases, between sentences, and between paragraphs, the more elegantly the thoughts will flow, and the faster the book will read.

To accomplish this, think about the informational point of your sentences first and foremost, and make sure that point is conveyed clearly. (See the "Victorian house" example on p. 4 for an example of rejiggering a sentence's structure to serve its informational point.) Second, keep an eye on your prepositional and appositive phrases (like "without activity of mind or body" above), as they can easily clog up a sentence's flow. Cut the ones that aren't essential or distract from the point. Finally, run consecutive sentences on the same subject or in the same emotional register together into paragraphs where possible. Every paragraph break creates a little pause in the aural flow of the language and signals a potential change in subject or feeling; if the sentences are continuous, the reader's experience has a better chance of flowing likewise.

First and last = most. As a rule of thumb, the first or the last clause in a sentence (or sentence in a paragraph) usually has the most emotional weight, and therefore it should be the clause that drives home the sentence's point. As long as that *Emma* sentence is, its first clause defines its reason for existing, and the rest of the sentence simply provides backup for it. When this principle is applied, readers can discern the sentence's meaning even amid a welter of appositive and dependent phrases.

Or look back at practically every sentence in the *Hunger Games* example: "It's a child's scream, a young girl's scream, there's no one in the arena capable of making that sound except Rue." The weight of that sentence is on the last clause (the longest clause in the sentence), while the rolling clauses before it drive the sentence onward to it, all of which highlights Rue's importance. Collins uses that rolling technique over and over in her prose, and their cumulative technique increases our reading speed as well. We readers tear through *The Hunger Games* quickly because the author literally designed her sentence structures to create that effect.

Choose what information to include based on the speed of the action and the feeling you want to create. Later in that *Hunger Games* example, the action rockets forward so quickly that Katniss doesn't actually narrate all of it. The boy from District 1 dies without our being told she shot him; we see him fall, and then she says, "I'm reloaded," not "I pull out another arrow and nock it." She's moving so fast, and Suzanne Collins wants us to read so fast, that Katniss bounds over steps in the narration. To show the opposite effect, I'm going to cite again this example from Leah Bobet's astonishing *Above*:

> We're late, near the last: Hide is already shuffling back-forth back-forth on his little patch of ground, and Heather's fingers are tapping 'gainst the arm of her wheelchair, the one that used to belong to Reynard before he died and we put him in the ground. Seed's hand's caught her other, fingers tangled together, talking broad-smile low to Jiélì's ma Kimmie, while the little girl squirms and fidgets and makes her singing noises in her mama's arms. I count heads: near the full forty-three people who shelter in Safe. Forty-three Tales in the back of my head; forty-three offerings to make a Tale of tonight.

These four sentences pack in six characters with at least one identifying detail for each; three relationships in both past and present; and two significant nouns that aren't usually capitalized, Safe and Tale. Having to process that much information in that compact a form makes us read much more slowly. But the density of the prose matches the lives of these characters, which are rich with secrets and subtext, and deciphering the language forms part of the pleasure of reading the novel, so it's entirely appropriate for the novel's points. Don't worry about making your prose read quickly in every circumstance; worry about making it suit the emotional tone of the scene and novel.

Even more than all the other mental activity involved in writing, controlling the pace of a novel can sometimes feel like playing a three-dimensional game of chess, where you must keep track of your book's overall story and character dynamics on one axis, satisfy the needs of the particular scene you're writing on a second, and craft good prose on the third. It is never easy to do well, but the more you can get these basic rhythms into your brain—narration and dramatization, sight lines and thoughtlines, staying with the scene, and so forth—the more attention you can pay to the other levels, because you can trust the prose to hold up its end. Pacing also relates intimately to the aspect of writing we'll discuss next—if you turn the page.*

---

* Hey, look! A cliffhanger! Hee.

CHAPTER 13

Person and Personality

Fundamentals of Voice

Earlier I quoted the wonderful line, "All art is where you put the camera." The metaphor comes from film: When you shoot a picture or movie, the world narrows to what you can see through a particular lens or frame, and thus what you say is determined by where and how that lens is positioned—what the camera is able to focus on and take in. Here's a wide-lens description of my former living room on a Sunday morning:

> The gray light pushed at the red-striped curtains and finally muscled through, exhausted. It fell weakly upon the table in the center of the living room, strewn with books, magazines, two cups of now un-sparkling water, and an iPhone; it reached out to the stiff green chairs huddled together in one corner, and the paisley couch that ruled the room with its sure, solid squareness.

I could stop and zoom in:

> The couch was not young, and its misshapen back cushions, scarred upholstery, and occasional staining testified to a long biography of owners spilling objects, drinks, food, and themselves onto it with great

force. But it was well-loved for its length, its comfort (no couch ever made a better visitor's bed), and that peach-and-scarlet, seafoam-and-black paisley that somehow absorbed all the colors of this disparate room and united them in harmony.

And then zoom out again:

But the light moved on toward the kitchen, and even—did it dare?—the archway into the hall, lined with bookshelves on the way to the bedroom in back.

The story would change with my angle on the room. If I were writing a story from the point of view of a cat sitting on the floor, the cat would be looking at the same scene, but what it could see would be the legs of the table and chairs, the shoes scattered about, the cracks in the wooden floor. Or suppose the camera was focused tightly on the cat itself:

The cat's ear twitched. He looked away disdainfully. Twitch. Twitch. Tail flick. Twitch. He sneezed, untucked his front paws, and sat upright, glancing quickly from side to side. Nothing needed his further inspection, so he yawned and sprawled luxuriously across the floor, stretching front legs, back, tail, returning to his contemplation of dust motes in the light. Tail flicks: One. Two. Three. Nose twitch now. Blink.

Of course, if the cat were narrating this scene, or narrating the actions of his own face in the mirror, he would most likely pick up on other details and describe himself completely differently, based on his own feline interests and vocabulary and sentence rhythms. Or suppose I took the perspective of a fly buzzing around the space:

I buzzzzzzzzzzzzzzzz. Green! Yum! Cloth. No! Green! Better! Fuzz! Food? No food. Wood buzz wood buzz wood buzz WATER! Shine flat shine flat red fuzz feel, feel, feel, feel. Crumb. Yum! Crumby crumb crumb.

This draws on a lot of the same details as the first example above, with the light, but it narrates them in a more compact form, and with very different ideas of what's important within the scene—in this case, the texture of the chairs and the availability of crumbs upon them. It also moves at a much higher speed than the leisurely narration of the first example, with shorter sentences; fewer verbs, descriptors, and details; and less punctuation (and much punchier punctuation when it's there). All of this combines to create an emotional atmosphere of fluttering frenzy.

In every case here, I've been describing the same room—but it's completely different depending on, first, where I put the camera, and then how it moves through the action, at what speed and depth of detail. Ultimately, those choices determine the kind of story I end up telling: a calm, domestic, Sunday sort of story about a paisley couch and a watchful cat, or a frenetic rushing story about a fly's fight for survival.

The camera in film equals the narrative voice in written fiction—the way we move through your novel. When I talk about "voice," I am thinking of not just a novel's point of view, but its emotional atmosphere, its narrator's thought patterns and vocabulary, how it tells a joke or opens and rounds off a scene. This amplitude is made more complicated still by the uniquely and directly emotional nature of the narrative voice. Readers are affected by the characters when they come to care about them, and affected by the plot after they get involved with the action; but the sounds and rhythms of a voice can create an emotional effect in and of themselves (a point we've discussed before with the Cashore Principle). So if you know your points, and you know you need your novel to move at a specific speed or take a specific attitude to achieve those points, then you can construct a voice to help you reach those ends. We're going to look at three fundamental components of voice here:

- The degree to which the narrator is involved with the story—that is, the *point of view* and *person* in which the story is told.
- The temporal distance between the storytelling and the events of the action—also known as the *tense*.

- And the ways in which this voice reveals the consciousness behind it—what we'll call the *personality*, and then we'll talk about six aspects of that.

I believe the most important responsibility of a narrative voice is to give a connective flow to the facts the story reveals. It must lead the reader steadily through the story, except for the times when the author intends some sort of break in that flow in order to achieve a specific effect, and it will convey an emotional tone to the story through merely existing, as we said above. Your enemy as a writer here is anything that violates the transparency principle to remind readers that these images flooding their brain aren't real, or anything that interrupts the narrative flow or emotional tone against your intent.

Point of View and Person

The most important choices you make in your storytelling are the point of view (POV) and person. In her excellent book *The Power of Point of View* (which I was introduced to by the equally excellent middle-grade novelist Linda Urban), Alicia Rasley defines POV as "the perspective from which the reader experiences the action of the story"—in other words, the camera. She adds that it allows readers an "amazing cognitive doubling trick: They can descend entirely into the experience of a compelling character, while maintaining the distance of the outside observer."

The person, meanwhile, involves distance as well, as it's the mental space between that narrating POV-camera and a character within the book, usually the protagonist. In first person, where the character is an "I," there is no space whatsoever; the camera peers out from the character's eyes. In third person ("he" or "she"), at least some space exists, as the camera is able to observe the characters from the outside, but may also have access to their most intimate thoughts. Second person ("you") elides the distance between the character and *reader*, with the camera supposedly in the reader-character's perspective. It increases the distance between the character and narrator, however, as the narrator becomes a figure dictating actions that the "you" character completes. We'll walk briefly through each of these three options below.

First Person

In first person, the camera is set up so that readers experience the story exclusively through one character's eyes, mind, and heart. That means that all of your novel's informational and plotting requirements will have to work within the bounds of this character and her experiences. In exchange for accepting that limitation, readers receive access to all of the character's thoughts and feelings as she reveals them to us. Ideally these thoughts and feelings have enough personality, specificity, and sensibility that the character attains credibility:

> I laced up my new sneakers, then unlaced and laced them better. Pulled the tongue of the shoe up. Scrubbed the toe with a spitty finger. Gotta be perfect. You never know who might be at this party. Might be the finest woman I ever seen, and she might be looking for a smooth brother like me, with clean shoes.
>
> —*When I Was the Greatest* by Jason Reynolds

As a reader, I instantly believe in and like this narrator because of the easy conversational tone of his narration, which sounds like real speech, and his sweet and equally realistic preparations for this party—driven by a desire for connection, which I recognize and appreciate. In first person, once a reader-character bond like this is established, the reader's remaining in this fictional world is dependent upon the character's continued existence, so any time that character is in jeopardy, emotionally or physically, we experience his distress as our own. This makes first person terrifically intense, which is why it is often appropriate to YA: It takes those frequently stormy adolescent feelings of isolation and importance, and embodies them in a narrator who *is* isolated and important to readers.

Of course, people who feel isolated and important are not always the most reliable narrators, and no first-person perspective is ever an entirely trustworthy point of view. Every human being has blind spots, irrationalities, secrets, false postulates, and things they simply don't know. When first engaging with a text, readers (and child readers especially) tend to forget these limitations and trust the narrator, unless an author immediately gives them reasons not to do so. Smart authors use this readerly tendency to their advantage—first drawing readers in, so we like or feel for the character, then using the character's blinkers to hide information crucial to the book's story. Authors might then build the plot of the book around the character's coming to understand the things her internal postulates have kept her from seeing. (This is the narrative strategy of *Pride and Prejudice* and *Emma*, for example, even though they're written in third person.)

Other books call attention to the ways in which the narrator's perspective isn't wholly reliable. Consider the delightful opening line from Lisa Yee's *Millicent Min, Girl Genius* (‡, co-edited with Arthur Levine): "I have been accused of being anal retentive, an overachiever, and a compulsive perfectionist, like those are bad things." The reader knows or can intuit that anal retentiveness, overachieving, and compulsive perfectionism *are* questionable values, and "accused of" indicates that Millicent is aware of their questionable status as well. But with the "bad things" phrase, she blithely dismisses their questionability, and the confidence with which she does that—the faith in anal retentiveness as a positive virtue, no matter what—creates the humor that suffuses the book.

Rasley points out that this doubled reader reaction is created through the difference between what the reader knows and the POV character says, and what the reader can hear and the character can't. If we can see those informational gaps—in this case because Millicent is thrusting them in our face—that might weaken our level of trust in her (though not her credibility as a real human being, as real human beings leave gaps all the time). But those gaps also increase our engagement with the book as a whole, as we know we must then read carefully to discern the objective truth beyond the character's highly subjective lens. *Okay for Now* by Gary L. Schmidt,

244 | The Magic Words

Justine Larbalestier's *Liar*, and E. Lockhart's *We Were Liars* are all excellent examples of this strategy.

As *Millicent Min* shows, first person can actually operate on three levels of feeling. On the first level, we participate in the POV character's emotions, which saturate her perspective and thus our view of this world. Katniss narrates *The Hunger Games*, so when Rue dies, we experience Katniss's grief simply by reading her narration. At the same time, we mourn Rue, independent of Katniss, because *we* liked Rue, who was clever, and generous, and innocent. On this second level, because we readers have "maintained the distance of an outside observer," as Ms. Rasley says, we have thoughts and feelings about the action separate from—even if they're ultimately the same as—the thoughts and feelings the POV character offers us.

On the third level, we have thoughts and feelings about our POV character's thoughts and feelings, which can intensify or weaken the overall emotion depending upon how much we both trust and like the character at this moment in the text. The more we trust and like Katniss, for instance, the more strongly we identify with her grief for Rue, and thus we have both of the first two levels reinforced. If we like but don't trust her, we might pity her grief, but we won't participate in it as much, because we can't believe it's genuine. If we trust but don't like her, then we might pity her grief *because* we know it's genuine; but we won't participate in it so much, as we feel separate from her rather than sympathizing with her. Authors can use this level to create gradations in the first two levels of emotion, and again increase the reader's overall engagement with the book.

Not all first-person books use all of these possible levels of emotion. *The Hunger Games* sticks pretty much with levels one and two, allowing us to sympathize with Katniss and develop independent feelings within the action (albeit ones that mostly mirror and reinforce Katniss's), but not leaving much space or time for us to question her choices. That means we share all of the horror and trauma that she goes through within the trilogy, serving Suzanne Collins's long-term thematic and experiential points of illuminating the terribleness of war. In *Millicent Min*, on the other hand,

Lisa Yee uses all three levels to show us Millicent's perspective and feelings; allow us to establish our own independent liking for her, rooted partly in the (unconscious) humor of her perspective and feelings; and engage us deeply in the book and with Millicent, because we constantly weigh her reactions against our own. This expertly serves Lisa's experiential point to be hilarious, while treating Millicent's underlying emotional concerns with the seriousness they deserve.

While the most basic requirement of every narrator is to tell the story clearly, a first-person narrator labors under two additional obligations. First, he has to have a personality beyond the mere recitation of the facts of the story, as no human worthy of being a protagonist ever reported merely the facts. Second, we readers have to be compelled by that personality, in all the ways we discussed compellingness in Chapter 8: We have to like our narrator, or appreciate the expertise or enthusiasm with which she's telling the story, or be intrigued by the secrets she's keeping or the jeopardy she's in, and so forth. If a reader isn't emotionally engaged with the first-person narrator of a book, then the reading experience feels like being stuck on a cross-country flight with someone who irritates you and yet won't shut up. (When I stop reading a first-person manuscript, eight times out of ten it's because something puts me off the narrative voice.)

As an aside, one particular thing that can disconnect me from a first-person voice is its similarity to a second first-person voice in the text. That is to say: If you're writing a book with more than one first-person narrator, every narrator in the book has to be distinct from each other one, as well as any third-person voices, in all the aspects of vocal personality we'll discuss below. After all, every narrator within the book will come from a different groundwork, where they will have learned different styles of telling stories and absorbed different vocabularies. If two narrators from different groundworks put a punch line on a joke in the exact same manner, that undercuts both characters' credibility, because the similarity draws attention to the fact that they are created characters rather than living human beings. Juggling several first-person voices credibly within a text is one of the most difficult and admirable feats a writer can accomplish, in my opinion, since the writer must sustain multiple distinct patterns of thought and speech across the entire book. See Jaclyn Moriarty's Ashbury/Brookfield series for brilliant examples of this feat in action.

In children's and YA fiction, this question of engagement is also tied to believability, as first-person narrators said to be a specific age need to be credible to readers as being people of that age. Lisa Yee's first four books were all written in first person, and so was her fifth, a chapter book called *Bobby vs. Girls (Accidentally)*—in the first draft, anyway. Here's an excerpt from that draft:

"What's this?" Annie eyes the lumps on her plate.

"Pancakes," Dad says, proudly. "I made them from scratch."

I glance warily around the kitchen. It looks like something exploded. There's even a pancake slowly sliding down the refrigerator door.

Recently, my father's become a stay-at-home dad. He doesn't want Mom to know, but things like cooking and cleaning confuse him. I've caught him staring at the vacuum cleaner like it was something that fell out of the sky.

"I love pancakes!" Casey squeals. To prove her point, she flings one at me. I try to catch it but miss.

"Stop it, Casey," Annie grumps as she peels the pancake off her helmet.

"Sock," I point out.

"What?" Annie scowls, then sighs. "Oh, thanks." She pulls a sock off of her jersey. Dad's biggest battle used to be the opposing football team. Now it's static cling.

"Take off your helmet, Annie," Mom orders. She closes her eyes and savors her first sip of coffee.

"But it's for protection," Annie protests.

Mom's eyes flutter open and for a flash she looks surprised to see us. She sets her mug down. "Don't be silly, Annie. There's nothing dangerous about breakfast."

My sister and I look at the lumps on our plates, then exchange glances.

My boss Arthur Levine and I co-edited this book, and we instantly loved all the characters in Bobby's family: the spunky older sister and princess-obsessed younger sister, the dad who's a professional football player turned househusband. But we actually had a hard time connecting to Bobby, our narrator, who's a nine-year-old boy. Why? Because he was apparently the kind of kid who would say, "I glance warily around the kitchen," and, "Dad's biggest battle used to be the opposing football team. Now it's static cling." That voice uses adverbs like "warily" that I wouldn't expect the average nine-year-old boy to use in his everyday mental processes, and it makes observations, like the one about the battle with static cling, that I wouldn't expect a nine-year-old boy to think. (There's only one thought I expect the average nine-year-old boy to have about static cling, and that's, "Cool!")

Now, it was entirely possible that Bobby could be an *extraordinary* nine-year-old boy, one who does speak with this much precision and sense of detachment for reasons Lisa would make clear to us. (For example, Millicent Min is a child prodigy, which is why it's believable that she could be an anal-retentive, overachieving, compulsive-perfectionist eleven-year-old.) But the action in the rest of the novel showed that Bobby's greatest strength was actually his everydayness, his wonderfully standard nine-year-old boy combination of curiosity, earnestness, mischievousness, and sweetness, so an extraordinary perspective seemed unlikely. Rather, it felt like the novelist's voice was coming through here instead of Bobby's voice, and that was distancing us from the action, because it was hard to believe in and connect with the main character.

Arthur and I talked to Lisa, who had two choices to solve this problem: (1) She could rethink everything Bobby says, and recalibrate all his observations to be more authentically those of a nine-year-old boy; or (2) she could rewrite the book in third person. Lisa is really, really good at first-person voices—Millicent is truly one of my favorite narrators of all time—but in this case, she decided to go with option two. What did that look like?

Well, to find out, let's talk third person.

Third Person

In third person, the camera is positioned outside of the characters, recording their action from a distance . . . but that is the only thing consistent to all third-person narration! Third person requires writers to make three decisions from the outset:

How much does the narrator know? In *omniscient third person*, a narrator knows everything about everyone, including their thoughts, feelings, future actions, and ultimate destinies. This allows the narrator to comment on the action, foreshadow events, move from character to character, or zoom from extreme close-up to a high crane shot. Take this glorious example from Terry Pratchett's *The Wee Free Men:*

> Then there is Tiffany's face. Light pink, with brown eyes, and brown hair. Nothing special. Her head might strike anyone watching—in a saucer of black water, for example—as being slightly too big for the rest of her, but perhaps she'll grow into it.
>
> And then go farther up, and farther, until the track becomes a ribbon and Tiffany and her brother two little dots, and there is her country.
>
> They call it the Chalk. Green downlands roll under the hot midsummer sun. From up here the flocks of sheep, moving slowly, drift over the short turf like clouds on a green sky. Here and there sheepdogs speed over the grass like shooting stars.

This omniscient narrator can shift back and forth between Tiffany and the witch who is watching her via that saucer of water, then pull the camera up into the clouds to give us a god's-eye view of the Chalk. Contrast that to *personal third person* (also known as "limited omniscient" or "close third person"), where the narrator can see only the thoughts, feelings, and actions of one or more characters on the ground, and has access only to the information they possess. This is where *Bobby vs. Girls (Accidentally)* ended up:

The Ellis-Chans were already eating when Bobby slid into his seat.

"What are those?" Annie asked, pointing to the flat brown blobs on her plate.

"Pancakes," Mr. Ellis-Chan said proudly. He was wearing a new blue apron. It still had its price tag on. "I made them from scratch."

Bobby glanced warily around the kitchen. It looked like something had exploded. Dirty pots and pans were everywhere. A pancake slowly slid down the refrigerator door. "I loooove pancakes!" Casey squealed as she flung one across the table. Bobby tried to catch it, but missed.

"Stop it!" Annie grumbled. She peeled the pancake off her football helmet.

"Sock," said Bobby as he poked at a pancake with his fork. It was hard.

"What?"

Bobby pointed to her shoulder. "Sock."

Annie sighed. "Oh, thanks." The sock made crackling noises as she removed it from her jersey. Their dad's biggest battle used to be the opposing football team. Now it was static cling.

"Take off your helmet, Annie," her mother said. Mrs. Ellis-Chan was wearing her peach-colored business suit. Bobby thought she looked like the pretty dentist in that commercial where people sang about clean teeth. Mrs. Ellis-Chan closed her eyes as she took her first sip of coffee.

"I need to wear my helmet!" Annie protested. "It's for protection,"

Mrs. Ellis-Chan's eyes fluttered open, and for a moment she seemed startled to see everyone. "Don't be silly, Annie. There's nothing danger-ous about breakfast."

Bobby and his sister exchanged glances.

The narration not only stays with Bobby's perspective, it sometimes echoes the way he would think and speak: ". . . she looked like the pretty dentist in that commercial where people sang about clean teeth." Thanks to that mental mirroring, close third offers writers the same intimacy and depth of character development we see in first person alongside the free-dom of an external observer.

The final form of narrator knowledge is *objective third person*, which functions almost like a recording of a play; the narrator cannot go inside characters' heads, but simply describes all their action and dialogue from the outside. Given the emphasis on emotion and connection in children's and YA literature, few novels in the genre use it.

Within close third, how many points of view can the narrator access? Do we see the action primarily from one character's perspective, like Bobby above? Or does the camera move among multiple members of a cast? In *The Great Greene Heist*, the point of view shifts smoothly among Jackson Greene and his friends (and occasionally enemies), staying with each one long enough to let us see that character's unique gifts, knowledge, or understanding of the situation. That allows us to form an emotional connection with all the characters and become a silent member of the heist team, while also giving us more information than any one character has.

What tone does the narrator take toward the action? In the Pratchett example, the narrator calls Tiffany's face "nothing special," but adds, "perhaps she'll grow into it"—an almost familial combination of honesty and affection that directs us to feel the same kindliness toward Tiffany. Or look again at the Austen and Hemingway examples on pages 221–22: They're both written in third person, but Austen's tone is amused, ironic, gently but firmly opinionated, while Hemingway's is controlled, stoic, sorrowful but accepting in the face of war. Those differing attitudes profoundly influence readers' feelings about these situations.

~

If you decide to write in third person, play with different answers to these three questions to find the level of knowledge, number of perspectives, and tone that feel most right for your story. For a Victorian potboiler, you may want an omniscient narrator with a clear relish for drama. For a novel about a contemporary small town uniting after a school shooting, a close third with multiple perspectives and a compassionate tone might embody the unity and acceptance the community needs to find.

I'd like to go back to the *Bobby* example for a moment here and contrast it to the earlier draft, as it changed (and improved!) a great deal in the shift from first to third. In the first-person version, the "static cling" lines showed a lot of personality, as a first-person voice is required to have. But that personality conflicted with the second requirement—Bobby's credibility as a nine-year-old boy. In third person, that second requirement is removed, so the observation about static cling comes off as amusing rather than fussy. Likewise, the "warily" works in third because it's so unexpected—this is an average American suburban kitchen; what could be dangerous enough to cause wariness? We soon learn it's Mr. Ellis-Chan's cooking, and thus Bobby's wariness becomes not only justified but funny. Third person frees writers up to create more evocative language, richer insights or observations, and more nuanced tone than many first-person narrators can offer.

These two *Bobby* examples also demonstrate some of the limits of both first and close-third POVs. In both, the camera must stay firmly inside the head of our point-of-view character for that scene; it cannot slip into other characters' minds. Look again at that line toward the end of the first-person example: "She closes her eyes and savors her first sip of coffee." How does Bobby know that his mom's savoring her sip of coffee? Maybe she's actually strategizing on a work project later that day, or wishing she were still in bed and her kids were far, far away. Bobby can guess at his mom's thoughts, but he can't know them, and that little slip out of his perspective jars the camera for a moment, just as it would in a movie if we suddenly switched camera positions. That slip is known as head-hopping, and it is an enemy. To fix it, you have to recast the head-hopped feeling as something that the main character can witness from the outside. Here, once *Bobby* went into third person, Lisa simply took out the part about savoring, and the "surprised to see everyone" showed the reader that Mom had mentally exited the room for a minute there, without the narrator jumping into her head.

Another notable enemy is info-dumping, where the writer needs to supply a piece of information to the reader for plot purposes, and includes it without regard for whether the character would believably know it and say it. (Info-dumping is also a danger in situations where an author has done a lot of research and wants to work it all in.) In the first-person Bobby excerpt, the paragraph about his dad is a fairly minor bit of info-dumping—"fairly minor" because it does flow naturally out of the action that Bobby's witnessing, and readers will accept a little info-dump at the beginning of a novel if it helps them get oriented within its fictional world. But it is something to watch out for, especially if there isn't any immediate narration to prompt that piece of information, or if you have a lot of facts you need to convey to the reader. (Look at the *One Crazy Summer* excerpt on page 149 for an example of excellent information integration.)

A related enemy is "elbow-jogging"—info-dumping in miniature, where tiny, unnecessary details clog the smooth flow of the narration. (The term comes from critic Anthony Lane, who defined "elbow-joggers" as "nervy, worrisome authors who can't stop shoving us along with jabs of information and opinion that we don't yet require." Consider the line, "Six-year-old Bridget McShea skipped along the path to her grandmother's house": "Six-year-old" is a bit of elbow-jogging, slipped in because the author wants the reader to know Bridget's age, not because the reader needs to know that yet (or possibly at all, if her exact age isn't relevant to the plot). If you find yourself doing a lot of info-dumping or elbow-jogging, try to pull back and focus on what your narrative camera would naturally take in, and trust that your readers are smart enough to pick up the information they truly need.

In close third narration, the character's thoughts can be reported on the page directly—"*I really hate cream cheese*, Juniper thought with a shudder"—or indirectly, in a style known as free indirect discourse: "Juniper put the bagel down and pushed it away. Why did people ruin a perfectly lovely baked good with cheesy paste?" (Note the thoughtline the push creates with the internal narration.) Rasley points out a fascinating difference between first and third person: "In first person . . . we expect some lying or deliberate misinformation; but in third person, we are in someone's head, so what we 'hear' is what the narrator actually thinks, not what he's 'telling' us." In other words, as a rule of thumb, third-person internal narration does not lie. That doesn't mean you can't use third person to deceive, however, especially if you have access to multiple narrators. A key plot twist in *The Great Greene Heist* happens in plain sight of one viewpoint character, but the action seems so insignificant that neither the character nor readers notice it at the time. When we discover the twist later in the book, the fact we were fooled is part of the pleasure.

Indeed, the switch in perspective allowed by third-person voice is often used for plot or thematic purposes. The vast majority of the Harry Potter books are written in an intimate close third on Harry, but J. K. Rowling used other characters' perspectives for the opening chapters of books one, four, six, and seven, which allowed her to establish the wider circumstances of Voldemort's evil and create mysteries that permeate the rest of the volumes. *George* by Alex Gino is the story of a transgender third-grader who knows herself to be a girl named Melissa, even as the rest of the world perceives her as a boy named George. As Linda Urban points out, the third-person narration in the book refers to the main character as "she," establishing Melissa's primacy firmly within the text. The disjunction between the feminine pronoun and other characters' references to "George" makes us feel Melissa's discomfort personally—one of the thematic intentions of the novel, I think, in connecting us so intimately with her experience. Again, if you decide to use third person for your novel, spend some time playing with all the possibilities it affords.

Second Person

One more perspective is available to writers: second person, where the protagonist is "you." That creates a peculiar intimacy, and also a divide, between reader and novel, as the "you" of the narrative goes about the action described in the text, while actual "you," the reader, are simply reading a book. Second person is thus most appropriate for stories that benefit from either a reader's active participation, which the "you" invites, or the slight sense of alienation the disjunction creates.

Linda Urban points out that most instances of "you" in novels fall into two categories. In true second person, it's a kind of self-talk, where the protagonist seems to be narrating her actions to herself:

> Your feet are ice. The flip-flops were a stupid idea—what were you thinking? The playground swings are freezing and your hands ache, but you hold on, walk yourself back a few steps, and let your body fly.
>
> —*Goodbye Stranger* by Rebecca Stead

Eavesdropping on the character's thoughts and actions like this can feel wonderfully intimate—or claustrophobic. In the second category Linda identifies, a first-person narrator addresses another character or the reader as "you" within the text, as in *When You Reach Me*, also by Rebecca Stead and *Cut* by Patricia McCormick. Despite the use of "you," those remain first-person books.

Which Person Should You Use?

So which person is right for your book? Well, you should only write in first person if you can make your style credible as the voice of a character of your protagonist's age, personality, and circumstances. If that's not an issue, consider your points, and what kind of narrator might best serve them and your story. Some questions to ask:

- **What are your informational needs?** If you choose to write in first person, how will you negotiate the informational limits that imposes? If you use multiple perspectives, how will you split the story's information among them?
- **Whose story is this?** Is it one person's story of growth and action, or a community's story of irruption or transformation? (If the latter, more perspectives might be useful.)

- **What emotional effect do you want to create?** Will that effect best be experienced from inside the head of a person going through that emotion directly, or by someone on the outside? (In a horror novel, will we be more terrified in the first-person perspective of the babysitter heading into the basement, or if we watch her go down the stairs in third person?)
- **How comfortable do you want the reader to be?** Keep in mind that you are writing for an audience of a particular age, and you may need to calibrate your sense of effect and comfort to theirs. A gory scene in that basement may not shock *you*; the same sight could traumatize a younger reader.
- **What member of your cast has the most intriguing or entertaining voice?** Who do you *want* to write?

Linda Urban adds two excellent questions about first-person narrators:

- **To what degree is this character able or willing to tell the literal (objective) truth?** Katniss and Marcelo have no reason to lie to us or present a partisan view of their experiences to us (they're both the virtuous heroes of their stories, after all), and thus they seem to offer fairly accurate accounts. In contrast, Millicent *thinks* she's presenting an accurate view of reality, but it's filtered through her (justified) ego and fears, so the reader must read "through" her narration to the truth—an extra layer of pleasure and work.
- **To what degree is the character unable or unwilling to tell an emotional truth?** Millicent cannot directly admit that she is wrong or frightened for a great deal of the novel, because she hides so much of her feelings behind her emotional façade. Similarly, Melinda in *Speak* is both unable to and unwilling to talk about what happened to her prior to the book's beginning—but that silence forms the action and emotional plot of the entire novel, which chronicles her journey to being able to tell that truth.

=== *EXERCISE* ===

Even if you are 100 percent committed to the narrator you've chosen, pick a scene from your manuscript and rewrite it in another person. (If you don't have a work in progress at present, use the *Marcelo* chapter on p. 202, or try writing a fairy tale in first person.) What do you find yourself changing beyond the pronouns? What does that teach you about person?

Tense

The tense of a novel specifies the time the action takes place in relation to the present moment. From a grammatical perspective, all fiction is written in the declarative mood in past or present tense. (You *could* write a novel in future tense—I say doubtfully—but you would need to find a way to turn the words "will" or "would," which would have to appear in nearly every sentence, into a strength of the text rather than a deadening defect.)

In present tense, the action is unfolding at the very moment the reader's eyes run over the page, which creates a great deal of tension and anticipation, as anything could happen at any moment. Many YA novels in the past few years—most notably *The Hunger Games* and its dystopian descendants—use first-person present tense, which, in its combination of an intimate perspective and that constant anticipation, offers the greatest emotional intensity that a reader can experience, especially when combined with high-stakes action. But it can also be a powerful tool in more interior stories: For Francisco X. Stork's *The Memory of Light* (‡), the story of a young woman recovering from both a suicide attempt and clinical depression, Francisco chose to write in first-person present tense to convey the moment-by-moment unsteadiness of his heroine's mind, and allow readers to see her growth as she learns to master the mental lies her depression feeds her.

Third person, present tense, is likewise very good for setting us on edge. That anticipatory tension remains present, but we feel less certain how our protagonist might react, since we don't have full access to her thoughts:

> She throws down her cigarette and mashes it on the sidewalk, kicking it over with a pile of a dozen others. She breathes out one last, smoke-filled breath and almost smiles. There is still a little pretense left. She slips a peppermint into her mouth and lifts the latch of the gate. It groans, low and heavy, whispering
> *Don't go in, don't go in.*
> But she does.
>
> —*A Room on Lorelei Street* by Mary Pearson

In this novel, teenage Zoe lives a difficult, hand-to-mouth existence, as she strives to put together a better life for herself. Our distance from her, our concern for her, and our unease from the present tense combine to create a constant guardedness that feels very similar to Zoe's own emotional stance. The person, tense, and plot thus support each other just the way they should.

With past tense, the action has already been completed, so events are fixed, settled, certain. It's thus a better choice for stories where you want readers to feel relaxed or at home in the action. (It's also very common and useful in speculative fiction, in part because there's already so much world-building material for readers to digest that setting them on edge with the tense can feel almost unkind.) Look at the two examples above from *Bobby vs. Girls (Accidentally)*, where the tense changed alongside the person. I think past tense would have been the right choice for Lisa to make even if the book had stayed in first person, because this is essentially a reassuring story about a domestic world that would be familiar to many young readers—not a world where we need the reader to be held in a state of uncomfortable suspense.

So, again, which one is right for your book? Think about your experiential point—the state you want readers to be in as they experience your book. If it's a state of (relative) comfort or relaxation, use past tense. If it's a state of suspense or unease, try present tense.

Once more, even if you are 100 percent committed to the tense you've chosen, take a scene from your work in progress or another novel and rewrite it in the opposite tense. (Or try future for kicks!) What are you changing beyond the verb forms? What does that teach you about tense?

Personality

The great English writer Evelyn Waugh defined the three elements necessary to a writer's style as "lucidity, elegance, individuality." Individuality is personality, and a writer's personality should be as distinctive as a fingerprint, utterly unique to that writer or narrator and generally unduplicable by anyone else. It includes a writer or narrator's linguistic choices, such as their grammar, syntax, and diction; emotional patterns, like their attitude, volume, and overall temperament; and mental patterns, such as the well of cultural references they draw from, or the dominant sense through which they experience the world. It should be present by definition in a first-person voice, but I also love seeing it in third person. Personality is usually the least conscious aspect of creating a voice, and may be the least controllable, as it is much more difficult to change the rhythms of one's sentence structures than it is to undertake the largely mechanical work of switching tenses or fixing thoughtlines. While no rubric could cover all of its nuances, I'm going to discuss six key elements here (four of which were drawn from Nancy Dean's *Voice Lessons*, with admiration).

Diction

Diction is word choice—a devilishly interesting and difficult set of choices indeed, as the vocabulary of the narration and dialogue provide not just the overt content of the information, but the subliminal content of the characters' natures and groundworks, based on their language. Consider these twelve words that all imply "blue":

Navy	Periwinkle	Indigo
Lapis lazuli	Cerulean	Sky
Sapphire	Azure	Ultramarine
Slate	Cobalt	Turquoise

Clearly these are not all the same color, and some would be more appropriate than others for describing whatever blue a narrator might see. But if a first-person narrator remarked in the opening pages of a novel, "The sky was a lovely lapis lazuli," that would tell me this character is fairly well educated or well read—or perhaps he's a bit of a show-off, or he likes being accurate even if he's accused of pedantry, or all of the above. His knowledge of "lapis lazuli" would then need to be integrated with his backstory and internal qualities. If this narrator was a ten-year-old boy who had just emigrated to the United States from Vietnam, for instance, and he was still learning to speak English, his use of "lapis lazuli" without some narrative explanation of how he picked up such an obscure term would ring false to me. Diction always needs to be consistent with all the other elements of character.

In children's and YA fiction, this question of diction is further complicated by the fact that the target audience might not be familiar with all the words you may want to use. In this case, the rule of thumb is to choose the word that your protagonist would be most likely to employ, because your protagonist's age will likely reflect the age of your intended reader. If you're concerned about vocabulary levels, the *Children's Writer's Word Book*, available from Writer's Digest Books, offers lists of words keyed to reading levels.

The concept of diction brings me to another enemy of a good narrative voice: overactivity or overspecificity. I know that most writing books tell you to use strong, vivid verbs, adjectives, and nouns over weak or vague parts of speech, and not only is this a good rule of thumb, specificity is one of my own fourteen principles. But strength is not the be-all and end-all of writing, and ironically, overly strong language can often get in the way of the action. For example:

> The linebacker torpedoed the running back. Then he pummeled the tundralike ground with his meaty paws, rocketed up, and caterwauled, "WHO'S THE HEAD HONCHO? WHO'S THE HEAD HONCHO?" Chortling with jubilation, he tarantellaed around the pouting prone player.

This is vivid, all right. But there is so much readerly effort involved in deciphering and picturing those specific actions, which in turn are highly charged with emotion, that I feel exhausted reading just that paragraph—I can't imagine reading three hundred pages of similar prose! Contrast that with:

> The linebacker tackled the running back. Then he pounded the ground with his fists, leaped up, and shouted, "WHO'S THE BOSS? WHO'S THE BOSS?" He danced around the running back, laughing in triumph.

We could certainly debate the choices made in writing and editing these examples; "HEAD HONCHO" provides more texture and interest than "BOSS," for instance. But overall, because the second example uses more natural speech and word choices, it is much easier and more pleasant to read, and thus I would much rather spend time with this second narrator than the first. In all your writing, whether in first person or third, don't worry too much about using active, strong words. Worry about using the most natural and accurate diction for the voice you're writing in, and the activity should take care of itself.

═══ *EXERCISES* ═══

Are your characters' diction choices each distinctive to who they are? Think about the sources of that diction, for your protagonist especially. What books might she have grown up reading? Where else would she have been exposed to rich language—church, theater, rap, the oral tradition? Steep yourself in those sources and draw some of your word choices from them.

What is your protagonist's favorite word, and why?

Syntax

Syntax is the sentence structure of your narrator's speech—its rhythms, repetitions, patterns, and variances in length. We've established via the Cashore Principle that the mere sounds of your sentences and words can have a direct emotional effect on the reader. Thinking about syntax means thinking about how those sounds (especially the sentence rhythms) can be manipulated to serve your informational and emotional ends. Consider the first paragraph of the *Marcelo* excerpt quoted earlier:

> I get out of the car and head for the back door. I see Arturo in the back-yard grilling steaks. I hoped to enter the house without him seeing me. I am not ready for the discussion that I know will take place and I need more time to anticipate his questions and memorize my replies. But Aurora yells at him from the back door.

What can we learn about Marcelo from his sentence structure?

- **Many sentences start with I.** Think of all the different ways Francisco Stork could have chosen to phrase the information in that second sentence. The "I see" isn't essential to the information about Arturo grilling steaks, so including it, and then repeating "I" as the subject of most of the other sentences in that paragraph, puts a special emphasis on Marcelo and his action of seeing. Neurodivergent people often focus strongly on their individual sensory perceptions, so this authorial choice subtly reemphasizes Marcelo's unique perspective.

- **Very plain, straightforward sentence structures, with few commas, pauses, or interior clauses**. Again, the style emphasizes Marcelo's straightforwardness, his reliance on and appreciation of solidity and truth.

- **Very plain, straightforward thoughts, with more or less one thought per sentence**. These are the facts, and again, Marcelo loves facts, which are things he can trust in a world where people are often confusing.

Just the syntax of that one paragraph allows us to construct a profile of Marcelo's personality. If you have a first-person narrator, could you do the same for him or her based on one paragraph of prose?

In either person, you can use syntax to achieve specific emotional effects, as demonstrated by the rolling clauses of *The Hunger Games* we discussed earlier, or the work of Kristin Cashore herself here:

> She saw him, suddenly, in the reflection of the window. He was leaning back against the table, as she had pictured him before. His face, his shoulders, his arms sagged. Everything about him sagged. He was unhappy. He was looking down at his feet, but as she watched him he raised his eyes, and met hers in the glass. She felt the tears again, suddenly, and she grasped at something to say.
>
> —*Graceling*

The passage starts out with Katsa looking at this young man, Po, establishing her senseline; zooms closer into a description of his physical location and posture; deduces his emotional state from them via a thoughtline; and then, when he raises his eyes to look at her, the camera pulls back to identify her own emotion and resume the present action. As the zoom-in on Po takes place, the sentences get shorter, culminating in, "He was unhappy." Where a long sentence might bury that point in verbiage, this short sentence plus the zoom effect makes the thought hit both the reader and Katsa hard. As this shows, when you want to draw attention to something within the text, try changing the syntax to highlight it.

Finally, syntax, like diction, can be a powerful tool in dialogue and for the characterization of nonviewpoint characters. Suppose that Marcelo, Katniss, Millicent, and Bobby all gathered in a room together, and their conversation was transcribed by a third-person narrator. No one would ever mistake a line of Bobby's dialogue for a Marcelo one, and a reader of the transcript could likely diagnose the personalities of these disparate people from their language alone. That is your goal in all dialogue scenes: Because no two people ever have the exact same syntax and diction, your characters should each speak with their own unique rhythms and words, identifiable as that character even if a line is removed from context. Perhaps your character has key phrases he repeats or returns to, like Arturo's fondness for talking about "the real world," or particular habits of speech, like Bobby's best friend Chess, who loves using big words like "indubitably." Details like these can help supporting characters become three-dimensional people and round out your entire cast.

EXERCISES

Read your dialogue aloud, or better still, have someone read it aloud to you. When you hear it spoken, does it sound like something a real person would say in general? Something this character would say in particular? If not, in either case, rewrite it.

What is your native syntax—the form, length, and rhythm into which your sentences naturally fall when you write? Do you struggle with changing that for your characters? If you find it difficult, you could work backward from it to develop an appropriate first-person narrator who might naturally use that syntax.

At a gathering with a group of friends or family who will forgive you if they find out, tape ten minutes of conversation without telling them. Transcribe it later. What patterns do you see in their speech patterns and the conversational flow? How might those reflect what you know of their personalities?

Check your sources. Syntax can be influenced by the same sources as a character's diction. (You can blame all the long, semicolon-laden sentences you're reading in this book entirely on Jane Austen.) How might your character's linguistic sources have changed his everyday speech?

Tone

Tone, in Nancy Dean's words, is "the expression of the author/speaker/ narrator's attitude toward his or her listeners, audience, or subject matter." Emotionally, it establishes the energy level and atmosphere of the story. Consider this excerpt from *The Porcupine of Truth* by Bill Konigsberg (‡), where seventeen-year-old Carson Smith has come to Billings, Montana, from New York City, and is now stuck at the zoo:

> I'm here because after we landed and got our rental car for the summer, my mother suggested she take me for "a treat." We cruised past multiple Arby's and shops that sell discount mattresses and a Wonder Bread thrift store, whatever that is. She dropped me here, at the zoo, and told me she'd pick me up in a couple hours, after she got us settled in at my dad's house. She suggested that the zoo might be a place to "locate and center myself" before seeing him for the first time in fourteen years.

> My mom, a therapist-slash-school-counselor, "hears" that I feel like she's ripped me out of my normal summer, but "what she wants to say to me" is that I need to stop moping. And what better place to drop off a mopey seventeen-year-old boy in a strange new city than at the zoo? Had she just asked me where I wanted to go, I would have been like, I don't know, a coffee shop. A movie theater. Any place a guy in his summer before senior year might want to hang. But whatever. My mom is down with the kids and how they all just want to stare at monkeys all day.

The tone here is strongly conversational, thanks to phrases like "whatever that is" and "I would have been like, I don't know," and even more sarcastic, especially toward his mother, who receives both the skeptical-quotation-marks and the old-person-trying-to-talk-like-a-hip-young-one ("down with the kids") treatments. This makes Carson's narration entirely believable as a teenage voice, but also hints at his deep anger toward his mother, which will become a conflict subplot within the book. Moreover, the tone creates a tense, nervous energy that powers much of the rest of the novel, as Carson searches for a sense of connection and inner peace that his very tone denies.

Contrast Carson's tone to the family scene in the *Bobby vs. Girls (Accidentally)* excerpt on page 228. Its third-person POV is naturally more detached, but small touches throughout—like the "static cling" line, with its wry commentary upon Mr. Ellis-Chan's domestic travails—create an affectionate and humorous tone in keeping with the action of the book as a whole. Your narrator's attitude toward the action and characters will shape the reader's attitude toward them in turn (pending the reader's relationship with the narrator as well), so be sure that tone serves your overall points.

EXERCISES

Find an excerpt in this book, identify its tone, and rewrite the same content with the opposite tone. (*Anne of Green Gables* on p. 109 might be interesting to try.)

How would you characterize the tone of the narrator in your WIP? How does this serve the book?

If you're writing in first person, does your narrator have a defined purpose in telling this story to us? If so, what is it, and who does she conceive as her audience? How might having an audience change what she would say?

Observations

As Carson's mom drove him through Billings, he noticed "multiple Arby's and shops that sell discount mattresses and a Wonder Bread thrift store, whatever that is." The third-person voice of the *Bobby* excerpt comments on Mr. Ellis-Chan's battle with static cling, and when Bobby observes his mother's suit, he "thought she looked like the pretty dentist in that commercial where people sang about clean teeth." In the chapter from *Marcelo in the Real World,* Marcelo distinguishes between the faces of "Arturo the father" and "Arturo the lawyer." These patterns of thought help characterize our narrators and POV characters by revealing what is important to them—what they judge worth calling out for informational or emotional effect. The nature of the observations also shows us their individual frames of reference, as Carson sounds like a cranky New Yorker, Bobby draws from TV, and Marcelo works hard to understand others' facial expressions and accompanying emotions. Finally, the observations themselves can have an effect independent of their narrators, as we experience the apparent cultural barrenness of Billings or smile at the line about static cling.

In choosing your observations, consider: which of the five physical senses is most important to your protagonist? A musician traveling the same road as Carson might miss the multiple Arby's because she's fussing with the radio, while an aspiring chef might observe them with even more disapproval. If you can build that sense into a majority of the character's observations, it provides another powerful means of integrating character and voice.

═══ *EXERCISES* ═══

Freewrite for five minutes about your present location and situation. (Do not read the rest of these instructions until you're done.)

- ✎ Read through what you wrote. Did you focus more on large objects or small details? What kind of sensual details do you call out most often— colors, textures, sounds, smells? What sort of comparisons or connections do you draw in your descriptions? Is this in keeping with your own domi- nant sense or other interests?

- ✎ Freewrite for another five minutes, and whichever sense dynamics you called on the first time, try to reverse them (e.g., if you focused on colors last time, describe textures here).

What is your protagonist's dominant sense? Why? How is that shown in the text?

Latitude

"Latitude" is my term for the range of references, subjects, images, dic- tion, and types of and examples of figurative language that a particular narrative voice can include. If you're writing a first-person voice with a six-year-old narrator, latitude traces the limits of what that six-year-old could know: he likely couldn't refer to "Titian hair" in describing a redheaded friend, for instance, or liken his first-grade teacher to Norman Bates in *Psycho* (unless, of course, you had a very particular six-year-old with very lax and/or highly cultured parents, which you'd have to show in the story to explain how he could make such references). But this six-year-old might also make some fresh new metaphor about something he's just discovering—the veins in leaves, or the swoop of a roller coaster—because those items would be wholly new to him. A football-obsessed first-person narrator might think of life in terms of a game, with quarters and downs and a goal line, and that might be reflected in the way she tells her story. The latitude of a Christian novel will include God and Jesus as real and present actors, while a secular novel might think of them as ciphers; the latitude of a fantasy or adventure novel will be wider than that of a realistic domestic novel, because it can include magic, or dragons, or quests for Mysteriously Capitalized Objects. To pretentiously quote Shakespeare for a moment, latitude is what is dreamt of in a voice's philosophy, and the limits on that dreaming.

Latitude can also be seen in anti-examples, which violate those limits to achieve specific, often comedic effects. *Pride and Prejudice and Zombies* was a huge hit off its concept alone because it opened the action and latitude of Jane Austen's elegant narrative world to brains-starved zombies. *The Onion* takes the anodyne journalistic voice and visual style of *USA Today* and widens its latitude to include subjects mundane and surreal. If we widened the latitude of common children's and YA experiences, what might a school look like? A best friend? A sports team? Those could be interesting narrative directions to explore.

Image systems also grow out of the latitude of a voice. "Image systems" is another term I learned from Laurie Halse Anderson. They are the physical embodiment of the objective correlative—actual physical objects or ideas in the text that symbolize the character or aspects of their journey. (I hate using the word "symbols," though, because that makes them sound pretentious and separate from the action, and your goal is to make them real and integrated within it.) For instance, if you've read Anderson's *Speak*, you know that trees are an important image system in it: The story starts in winter, when everything is dead, and so is our narrator, inside. She's taking an art class, where she's assigned the word "tree," and as a result, she draws and carves trees through the months that follow. As the story moves from winter to spring, she begins to feel hope again and talk to people—budding out and regaining leaf, metaphorically speaking. In *Glory O'Brien's History of the Future* by A. S. King, Glory is a photographer who analogizes her depression to the "max black" of developing film. Marcelo of *Marcelo in the Real World* sleeps in a tree house at the beginning of the novel; by the end, when he's accepted his place as part of the real world, he decides to move back into his family's home. Image systems like this aren't essential to a novel—you can write a perfectly good book without them. But they reveal character and embody theme in one neat image that ties to the action, subtly providing unity and coherence and lifting your writing to the next level.

The latitude of your voice will likely emerge naturally as you discover what kind of story you're telling and the narrator who's telling it. Don't worry too much about it in the first draft, but as you're revising, keep an eye out for references that may be inappropriate for the latitude of your narrator, possible image systems emerging from the text, and any other ways to further integrate the voice of your book with its content.

═══ *EXERCISES* ═══

Can you list three mental preoccupations of the narrator of your book? What are three things, in contrast, that s/he would never think about (or, to be more accurate, would never talk about, like graphic sex or dinosaurs in a Jane Austen novel)? What sets those limits for your narrator?

Think about your novel not as a conglomeration of words, but an accumulation of images. What picture comes immediately to mind when you think of the book? What objects are important to your main character? What does she love or work on? Write down all of these things and see if you can find resonances between these objects or images and the action or emotional or thematic ideas of your book. Perhaps there are ways you can integrate those images and ideas throughout the text as Anderson does. Or perhaps you'll find you want to change one of those object elements to better reflect the themes.

Details

Details are the physical representation of the specificity principle—the small things that make a story believable and therefore real. Details include the gestures the characters make or typical phrases they say; the specific objects or brand names a character calls out in his observations (like Arby's); and the small sensual touches that make a setting come to life in the reader's mind. In the *Bobby* excerpt, for example, the detail of the pancake sliding slowly down the refrigerator door instantly sets up the cheerful domestic chaos of the Ellis-Chan household. Likewise, the different views of Arturo's face in the *Marcelo* excerpt provided a wonderfully telling detail about him as a person as well as showing us more of Marcelo's sensitivity to his father. The best details encapsulate the emotional heart of a character, relationship, or scene.

With that said, as with any element here, it's important not to go overboard. Every writer I edit has at some point received a note in their manuscript saying, "Extraneous detail," which I write when I feel some topic is getting more time or information than its role in the narrative warrants. Details become extraneous when they describe some object for the object's sake, or exist solely for the sake of the author's own interests or pretty writing—when they no longer feel relevant to the story. Keep in mind the principles discussed in Chapter 12, "Movement and Momentum," about balancing immediate, descriptive, and internal narration, then choose just a few important details, and make them count.

=== *EXERCISE* ===

Can you find at least two revealing details or moments in each scene of
your book?

~

If the enemies I listed earlier are avoided and the aspects of voice I've just
discussed are used well, so the book has a narrator I believe in, employing
words, images, and sentence rhythms that serve the emotion and action, and
revealing details and observations that make it all real, then the voice moves
from having just personality into authority for me. *Authority* is the feeling
that I am in good hands, that I can trust the person who's telling me the story.
That happens when I know the writer and/or narrator are giving me the honest truth, reality as they see it, and that truth they're telling resonates with
the reality I know about the possibilities of human behavior and the facts of
physical laws. It comes from the surety that these are the right words, in a
distinctive order, saying something interesting, and that the narration will
likely remain interesting for the rest of the book. That surety lets me know I
can relax into the novel and trust the narrator to take me somewhere good.

Authority is probably the most important quality I seek in a narrative
voice because it's the summation of so much else—reality, competence,
interestingness; I'll finish an entire manuscript with a good authoritative
narrator even if I find the story flagging, just because I enjoy hearing what
the narrator has to say. If you ever hear editors say that they're looking for a
really distinctive voice, what we mean is that we want a voice with authority to grab us and carry us along.

So now we can create a formula where:

Voice = Person + Tense +
    (Diction + Syntax + Tone + Observation + Latitude + Details)

And for the last time: Each one of those aspects should be chosen and shaped to serve your points. Of course, the fact that you'll probably discover said points as you write the book, using whatever voice might come to you at the beginning, means that some revision may be required after you finish the draft . . . and revising a voice is a gigantic pain, I admit, because in some cases, like changes of person or tense, it can require rewriting nearly every line in the novel. But once you find the right voice for the book—the right place to put the camera, to document your characters and plot in their best lights—everything else should lock into place. If the idea for your next book starts with a character or a plot concept, and not a voice that speaks to you from the Muse (as some writers are fortunate enough to experience), experiment with different combinations of elements in the formula above, to find the voice that's most comfortable for you and right for the project in total before you move forward with it.

CHAPTER 14

Teases and Trust

What Makes a Good First Chapter

Y ou could replace the word "Chapter" in the title above with "Line," "Page," or "Scene"; the good ones all have at least four of the following elements, and the more the better. After we take a look at them all, with representative examples, I'll talk about how to integrate them successfully into a first _____.

Credibility. To return to a key principle of this book, when readers open a novel, they should be able to see immediately that its world has been imagined and thought through in full, and it's waiting there on the page to engulf us: We believe in it. Often this credibility is established via another principle, specificity:

> My name is India Opal Buloni, and last summer my daddy, the preacher, sent me to the store for a box of macaroni-and-cheese, some white rice, and two tomatoes and I came back with a dog.
>
> —*Because of Winn-Dixie* by Kate DiCamillo

Every phrase here attests to the plain but wholesome reality of this character and her life. "My name is India Opal Buloni": What an intriguing name, and where did she get a name like that? I want to know. "My daddy, the preacher": Huh. I don't read a lot of novels with preachers as characters. That's different and interesting. "A box of macaroni-and-cheese, white rice, and two tomatoes": As I picture all of these simple, colorful items in my head, this world starts to take on solidity. Then the lack of a comma after "tomatoes" tumbles me forward into "I came back with a dog"—and instantly I want to know how that happened, how that straightforward grocery list transformed into a canine. I'll read on to find out.

This is what I think of as a *situation beginning*, where the author lays the opening situation out in the first paragraph or scene to draw us in, then backtracks to dramatize how the character got into the situation and what happened next. Situation beginnings are good for books whose strengths lie in either their domestic realism or their action, because they anchor us in the physical world from the start.

Credibility might also be gained through a statement of a truth we recognize, which surprises us with the fresh way it's stated:

> It is a truth universally acknowledged, that a single man in possession of a good fortune must be in want of a wife.
>
> —*Pride and Prejudice*, by Jane Austen, of course

This line has been delighting readers for two hundred years, through vast changes in gender roles and the overall social fabric, because gossipy interest in other people's love lives never goes away, nor does the sense that single men must be interested in *someone* romantically—for the good of society, if not themselves. I call first-line statements like these *insight beginnings*, which offer a truth that makes readers laugh or nod in recognition. Once that happens, boom, they're hooked. (You should only use an insight beginning if your novel is going to make a pattern of such insights throughout; otherwise, it's a bit of a false promise.)

A Distinctive Tone. The very sentence structure of *Winn-Dixie* evinces the forthright goodness of the book, as India announces her name in the most straightforward syntax and diction possible. Austen's first line contrasts the universal acknowledgment of a truth with the lone single man who has to live it out, setting up the book's examination of societal vs. individual lives and choices, and establishing the narrative tone of ironic amusement. These tones are both distinctive to the books and writers and appropriate to their story's intents and content, and their specificity and personality pulls us along: We want to hear how this voice will continue to bend reality to its own vision.

A Tease. This might be an obvious mystery; it might be a reference to something we don't know about yet, with the promise that we'll find out. Either way, a tease sets up a narrative question with as little as a single word.

> Lyra and her daemon moved through the darkening hall, taking care to keep to one side, out of sight of the kitchen.
>
> —*The Golden Compass* by Philip Pullman

What is a daemon? Heck if I know. But my curiosity will make me read on, and the fact that Lyra and this creature are trying to stay out of sight of the kitchen signals that something forbidden is happening, which is intriguing as well. I also want to call out *The Lightning Thief* by Rick Riordan in this category, as it uses a situation beginning, a direct address to the reader (another factor that sucks us into the book immediately), and two major, major teases for a brilliant opening:

> Look, I didn't want to be a half-blood.
>
>   If you're reading this because you think you might be one, my advice is: close this book right now. Believe whatever lie your mom or dad told you about your birth, and try to lead a normal life.

A "half-blood"? Half of *what*? Why wouldn't our narrator want to be one? And then he insinuates that the reader might be one too, but the readers' parents might have lied to them, which is outrageous and infuriating and an absolutely terrific tease. When combined with a warning not to read the book, devouring it becomes nigh-on irresistible.

A Compelling Character

> They say I was born with a caul, a skin netting covering my face like a glove. My mother died birthing me. I would've died too, if Mama Ya-Ya hadn't sliced the bloody membrane from my face. I let out a wail when she parted the caul, letting in first air, first light.
>
> —*Ninth Ward* by Jewell Parker Rhodes

I think of this as a *description beginning*—an in-depth still shot of a person, place, or object that will be integral to the novel, limning its details and foreshadowing the story to follow. This description of Lanesha's birth signals her specialness and her will to survive, which she will need when Hurricane Katrina strikes New Orleans. Description beginnings can feel a little old-fashioned, as modern readers usually expect to be pulled straight into an action or situation. But if you're writing a novel that's deliberately somewhat retro, or you want to fix one significant image firmly in the reader's mind for the rest of the novel, a description can be a fine way to start.

When a manuscript introduces us to the protagonist in the first chapter, as here, I'll watch her carefully to see what action she takes and what kind of things she says. Is she kind to others? Snarky? Resourceful? As noted earlier, whatever she does first in the novel, that is who she will be to me, and it will take a lot of additional experience with her to change that first impression. In order to be sure you're making the *right* first impression in this reader-character relationship, look back at the list of compelling qualities in Chapter 7, "Identity and Choice," and build in action demonstrating the traits you want that character to show the reader.

Action, Promising More. To state outright a principle inherent in all of these examples: The first lines portend action, movement, trouble. The chapters that follow fulfill that promise, as India's future dog knocks down a store display, Lyra witnesses a potential poisoning, and Lanesha demonstrates her ability to see ghosts. Of course, many first lines simply thrust us right into the actual action:

> Dreadlock Man, with his fierce fists and suspect jump shot, sets his stuff ($1.45 sandals, key to bike lock, extra T-shirt) on the bleachers and holds his hands out for the ball. It's ten in the morning and Lincoln Rec has just opened. Sticky's at the free-throw line working out his routine while all the regulars come swaggering in. *Come on, Little Man*, Dreadlock Man says. *Give up the rock.*
>
> —*Ball Don't Lie* by Matt de la Peña

This is an *action beginning*, where we move through the novel's world in real time alongside the characters, instantly equally embroiled in whatever action is going on. An action beginning is perhaps the most immediately grabby of all the choices here because it activates readers' wild-beast instincts to follow the movement and see what will happen next. It can also be trickier than it looks, as the author must introduce and connect us to the characters and delineate the world around them while simultaneously keeping the action of the scene rolling forward. If you're starting your book with an action beginning, try to stay with your narrative camera in the first draft and record the scene with as little commentary as possible, trusting readers to pick up the information they need. Here, for instance, we get a sense of Deadlock Man's strapped-for-cash striving from just the list of his stuff, and the players' mix of affection and condescension toward Sticky (who will be the book's protagonist) in the nickname "Little Man." Our curiosity about where the action will lead combined with the reality we're glimpsing here will compel us to read on.

Zooming Out. Start with one particular image, character, situation, or incident. Establish it within the text, giving readers a clear picture of it alongside a strong sense of the dynamics at play (lack, conflict, desire) and how we should feel about them. Then pull the camera back to introduce character, situation, or incident #2; and then back further still to develop #1 and #2 or introduce #3. Trying to do more than one of these character/situations/incidents at a time will muddy the readers' understanding of what's going on, and weaken their engagement and interest thereby.

As an example here, it's easy for longtime readers of the Harry Potter series to forget that it doesn't start with Harry himself or in the wizarding world. Rather, J. K. Rowling spends the first few pages of *Harry Potter and the Sorcerer's Stone* on the proudly unimaginative Dursleys, dwelling on their small-mindedness and self-satisfaction (characters, #1). The Dursleys are so awful that we enjoy our superiority to them. Then, as the camera pulls back and strange events start to happen around them—people in capes, an abundance of owls (situation, #2; developing characters, #1)—as noted earlier, we automatically like anything that the Dursleys disapprove of, so we are intrigued by these hints of magic. Then the camera changes direction entirely to introduce Professors Dumbledore and McGonagall (characters, #3), both interesting, empathetic people. They discuss Voldemort's attempt to kill baby Harry (situation, #4), and the grand narrative begins. This chain of characters and events gives us just enough information about each one to awaken our interest and pleasure in that new topic, then expertly manipulates our emotional responses to make us feel sympathy for baby Harry and a fascination with the wizarding world.

Because this chapter takes place ten years before the action of *Sorcerer's Stone* proper, it could have been presented as a prologue . . . but I'm glad it wasn't, as prologues are controversial in children's and YA publishing. A prologue is one to five pages of text included before Chapter 1, which frames the real-time action of Chapter 1 within a character's reflection, a flashback to events prior to the book, or a flash-forward to high-stakes events later in the book. (Prologues thus usually function as situation or action beginnings, really—just different situations and actions than what we'll see in Chapter 1.) The flash-forward in particular lets the reader know that while the actual story may begin somewhat quietly in Chapter 1, the book will get exciting later, so readers should hang in there.

Many editors and agents hate prologues or will tell you to cut them, as they feel prologues simply get in the way of the actual inciting incident and start of the story. I am not automatically opposed to them, but I do think the flash-forward trick is terribly overused; any sort of "If I knew then what I know now" reflection can easily feel pretentious and should be regarded with a great deal of side-eye; and it's altogether better if you can incorporate whatever you're trying to get across in the prologue in Chapter 1 instead. On the flip side, prologues can work if they have a distinct, effective tone to them, and they show one single episode that provides essential (*truly* essential) context for the rest of the book. They should also be kept as short as possible. If you want to use one, know that many people dislike them, and proceed with caution. For examples of effective prologues, see *The King of Attolia* by Megan Whalen Turner; *Irises* by Francisco X. Stork; *The Peculiar* by Stefan Bachmann; *The Killer's Cousin* by Nancy Werlin; *Shadow and Bone* by Leigh Bardugo; and *The City of Ember* by Jeanne DuPrau.

Easing In. We readers don't want too much information or figurative language thrown at us right off, as this can feel overwhelming without a strong story or character to anchor us. Nor should the emotional volume of the book be set at 9 on a scale of 1 to 10, because we are likely coming into the book at more of a 3 or 4, and we want time to adjust to the novel's sound and speed. Starting at 9 does the author no favors, either, as it doesn't leave you much room to develop the emotional dynamics, and sustaining the action at that volume is exhausting! Thus we want to ease in, allowing facts and details to accumulate over time as we settle into this new world. It helps when the characters themselves are at the beginning of something—a new home, the first day of school or vacation—because then, as they explore this new place or meet the new people there, we can build those connections alongside them and share their feelings at what they discover.

The opposite of easing-in is what I call "conceptitis," where writers feel so eager to convey their super-awesome and original plot concept for the novel, or are so anxious that readers will put the book down if they aren't highly stimulated at every moment, that they give the whole shebang away on the first page. Here's an anti-example of such faults:

> "Elyria!" I heard my mother call as I fled into the woods.
>
> I threw back my head and screamed, "LEAVE ME ALONE!"
>
> "I hate her," I whined to myself. She was such a harpy! Ever since my stepfather, Cleve Lorain, became High Toledron of Columbra, she had been begging me to stumble into his archenemy, the beautiful Toledra Cindayton, and step on her foot with my deadly poisonous left pinky toe. I knew my real father would never ask me to do anything so degrading—if only my mother would tell me who he was.

This opening doesn't just give away the key concept of Elyria's magical left pinky toe and the powers it endows her with, it presents us with a whole mess of concepts: conflict with her mother, high and deadly politics in the fantasy world of Columbra, a missing father, and a secret about his identity. It's hard to have a sense of where the larger story is going because there are so many stories on the page already. Moreover, the fact that Elyria is fleeing, screaming, whining, and making extreme declarative statements like "My real father would never" sets the emotional volume at 11, not just 9; and because I haven't seen any of the circumstances that led to these hysterics, I feel more alienated from her than connected to her.

I also feel disconnected because she's an angry, whiny teenager, and again, I believe firmly that protagonists who are meant to be likable should not whine. A few years ago, I told a writer how bored I felt with YA manuscripts with whiny first-person teen or preteen protagonists, and she said, "But that's how my kids talk to me, so that's an authentic teen voice, isn't it?" Whininess *is* authentic to one of the voices and emotional registers that teenagers often use, God love 'em. But it's hardly their only or their most attractive voice, and it's one that's difficult to connect with, I think, especially on the first page of a novel. If you're a parent writing YA, I don't want to read a voice that mimics how your kids talk to you; I want to read how your kids talk to their friends, with a warmth and enthusiasm and wider range of emotion than you might get to see.

Two other sins of this Elyria piece before I move on: Both the stepfather's name and the beauty of the Toledra are elbow-jogging us with as-yet-unnecessary details that hamper the narrative flow. And the "real parent" gambit is so common in children's or YA fiction that it makes me roll my eyes a little. That does not mean it's not true or believable or a necessary element in many stories—the desire to know oneself by knowing one's family; only that it's such a familiar plotline, I wouldn't lead with it on Page 1. Hook the reader with some other, more original elements first.

A Complete Scene or Reflection. Once you've established a number of the elements above and zoomed out and eased in to the overall narrative, I expect to see a dramatically or emotionally complete scene or reflection, in the terms discussed in Chapter 11, "Obstacles and Negotiation," including a full Freytag's pyramid and possibly the inciting incident. (If the first chapter doesn't include the inciting incident, there should be plenty of clues laid toward it by the chapter's end, so it can follow fairly quickly in Chapter 2.) As a rule of thumb, I recommend avoiding any space or time breaks in the scene until you feel confident readers will be thoroughly hooked into the narrative. A break is an opportunity for readers to put the book down, and you don't want to give them that chance until you're sure they'll stick around.

Questions. While I want the scene to feel complete, this is still a novel opening, not a short story, so I also want some clear narrative questions leading out of this first chapter—or even the first scene, or first page, or first line. What drives the protagonist? What is he hiding? What else is he capable of? Will he get out of his present danger? Or the simplest and best question of all: What will happen next?

Authority. I understand that writers are told over and over again to capture a reader on Page 1; I've probably given that advice myself at some point. But as I said in the previous chapter, I believe that the number one thing that hooks readers is authority—a sense that the writer is in complete control of the story and how it's being told. An author with authority isn't in a rush to give away the central plotline of the book on the first page, because she knows she has a good plot, and she takes the time to set it up right. Nor is she sucking up to or desperate to attract the reader, which is often how a case of conceptitis comes off, and which loses my respect in turn. Rather, she can offer little details, hints, shafts of light that illuminate the characters and world that's about to open up to us, and help us get anchored within that world, so when the inciting incident happens, we readers already have an emotional relationship with the setting and characters. The action then leads us to become even more deeply involved with them.

So how do you gain authority and write a great first chapter? Choose your type of beginning and write your first line, possibly with a tease in it, definitely with a tone. Execute a zoom-out according to the formula above, building in more teases and introducing your compelling characters, all without overwhelming the reader with information. Point everything toward the inciting incident (here or in Chapter 2 or 3)—an interesting event that sets up clear lines of activity and/or mystery. Then wrap up the scene, leaving some action or questions for the reader to follow into Chapter 2.

In sum: Write your first chapter like you're performing a striptease, not going to a nude beach.

EXERCISES

Choose three novels of your genre from your bookshelf and look at their beginnings. Do they fall into one of the categories named above (insight, situation, action, description)? Why was that the right approach for that novel (or was it)? If one novel takes a different approach, how would you describe it? What is the first situation presented in these books? At what point is the protagonist introduced? What is his or her first action in the book? How is other information (especially teases and credible details) integrated into the text?

If you have a situation or action beginning, choose one character or object within it, and write a description beginning instead. Or, if you were to distill the entire situation down to one pithy line, what would it be? There's your insight beginning, if you want to try it.

Complete the first page/chapter checklist on pp. 284-85 for your book.

FIRST PAGE / CHAPTER CHECKLIST

What kind of beginning do you have?

(A mix is perfectly acceptable—indeed admirable.)

Insight	Situation	Action
Description	Other (What would you call it?)	

Which of the following elements does your beginning include?
You don't need to have all of them, but the more, the better.

Credibility: What details or other factors make the action and characters you're presenting here believable?

A Tone: Note two examples.

A Tease: Note at least one.

A Compelling Character: What details make her compelling?

Action, Promising More: What actually happens in this chapter?

Zooming Out: At what rate are your characters and plotlines introduced?

Easing In: On a scale of 1 to 10, what is the emotional volume of this first scene? How many proper nouns and adjectives inhabit your first page? (More than six in either category is questionable.)

A Complete Scene or Reflection: If this is a dramatized scene, does it fulfill Freytag's pyramid?

What narrative questions does the reader have at the end of the first sentence?

The first page?

The first scene?

The first chapter?

CHAPTER 15

Worlds and Wonders

Writing Speculative Fiction

I f you're an adult who first fell in love with children's or YA fiction in the early 2000s, the odds are good that you came to it through one of three series: Harry Potter, Twilight, or the Hunger Games. These three series transformed children's and YA publishing from a reliable but not especially notable moneymaker into one of the few segments of the industry with consistent sales growth. I believe (as you'll know by now) these series became popular through strong story concepts that unfold via emotionally rich writing about compelling characters. But they are also speculative fiction, aka science fiction and fantasy (SFF)—narratives that incorporate supernatural or presently nonrealistic elements into the DNA of their stories. Good SFF offers readers the security of the familiar in its characters and relationships, combined with the thrill of the new in the magic or technology it presents. These three series' plot concepts (wizards, vampires, battles royale) were both just familiar enough to be accessible to and just foreign enough to thrill the many, many people who did not usually read speculative fiction, and hook them on children's and YA books for good.

But of course fantasy and science fiction have been a part of children's literature since its inception, from the Grimms' fairy tales and Andrew Lang's fairy books, to the Victorian fantasies of *Alice in Wonderland* and

George MacDonald, to *The Wonderful Wizard of Oz,* to *The Chronicles of Narnia* and *The Hobbit,* to *A Wrinkle in Time* and Diana Wynne Jones and Ursula K. Le Guin. In the modern era, many of the best fantasies for children and young adults use magic to externalize an emotional or societal situation and examine or solve it thoughtfully. Edward Cullen's vampirism in *Twilight* is a metaphor for what many young people experience in falling in love for the first time: an attraction so powerful it can kill you, entwined with an insatiable fascination with its source. In *Shadowshaper* by Daniel José Older (‡), a white anthropologist tries to take over a group of spirit-workers of color, who practice a form of magic rooted in their connections to their ancestors. The book's exploration of the real-world problems of appropriation and gentrification results in a fantasy that has political and social depth to it as well as magical thrills. If you're interested in writing fantasy, it is of course delightful to think about magical powers and rich and strange new worlds—what I will call "the fantastic fact" below; but spend an equal amount of time thinking about the thematic questions that interest you and how those could be externalized, or what the deeper implications of your fantastic fact will be.

Before we go any further, I'll offer some definitions of terms. These are not definitive definitions, as the lines between genres are hotly debated in the speculative fiction world, and not only are the categories broad, they frequently overlap. Everything after "fantasy" and "science fiction" are subgenres of those major divisions.

Fantasy. A novel that incorporates a supernatural power of some kind, creatures not presently known in nature, or both. Fantasies rooted in our real world (like *The Chronicles of Narnia,* the Harry Potter books, and *Twilight*) are often more accessible to beginning and nonfantasy readers than novels set entirely in a magical world. Notable children's and YA fantasies include *The Hobbit* and *The Lord of the Rings* by J. R. R. Tolkien; the Earthsea books by Ursula K. Le Guin; the Dark Is Rising Sequence by Susan Cooper; the Song of the Lioness Quartet by Tamora Pierce; *The Hero and the Crown* by Robin McKinley; the His Dark Materials trilogy by

Philip Pullman; *Skeleton Man* by Joseph Bruchac; the Percy Jackson and the Olympians series by Rick Riordan; *Hero* by Perry Moore; the Graceling Realm trilogy by Kristin Cashore; *Zahrah the Windseeker* by Nnedi Okorafor-Mbachu; *Silver Phoenix* by Cindy Pon; *The Graveyard Book* by Neil Gaiman; and *The Jumbies* by Tracey Baptiste.

Science Fiction. A novel that includes technology or other elements extrapolated from present scientific theories or developments. These elements can be prodigious expansions on our real world, like time travel or aliens, or the novel might be set in a distant future or another world that takes such items for granted. (*Frankenstein* by Mary Wollstonecraft Shelley is often called the first science fiction novel, and as such, it is always worth calling out that the genre was invented by a seventeen-year-old girl.) Notable titles include *A Wrinkle in Time* by Madeline L'Engle; *Have Space Suit—Will Travel* by Robert Heinlein; *Ender's Game* by Orson Scott Card; *The Ear, the Eye, and the Arm* and *The House of the Scorpion* by Nancy Farmer; *Feed* by M. T. Anderson; *Zita the Spacegirl* by Ben Hatke; the Uglies books by Scott Westerfeld; *Tankborn* by Karen Sandler; *Archer's Quest* by Linda Sue Park; *City of Ember* by Jeanne DuPrau; *Killer of Enemies* by Joseph Bruchac; and *The Monstrumologist* and *The 5th Wave* by Rick Yancey.

Alternate History. A science fiction novel where some event in the history of our real world unfolded in a different fashion, leading to new and often dire conclusions. (If that event included magic, then I'd probably classify the novel as a "historical fantasy" below.) Notable titles include *The Year of the Hangman* by Gary Blackwood; *The Only Thing to Fear* by Caroline Tung Richmond; and *Leviathan* by Scott Westerfeld.

Steampunk. A science fiction or alternate history novel where the technology is built out from or has the appearance of technology from the Victorian or Edwardian eras, e.g., steam engines and dirigibles, and lots of wood, metal, and pipes. Note that this excludes anything involving computers. Notable titles include *Larklight* by Philip Reeve; the Finishing School series by Gail Carriger; *The Unnaturalists* by Tiffany Trent; *The Clockwork Three* by Matthew Kirby; and (again) *Leviathan* by Scott Westerfeld.

Dystopia. A science fiction novel featuring a futuristic alternate society that was set up after some traumic event in its past, which created lasting damage our protagonist will likely try to rectify. This trauma could be a war, an environmental event (including the loss of water, gas, and/or electricity), a political coup, or some other cataclysm. Led by *The Hunger Games*, dystopias took over YA publishing for a period that has largely passed as of this writing; interestingly, the trend never filtered down into middle-grade books very much. Notable titles include *The Giver* by Lois Lowry; *Divergent* by Veronica Roth; the Chaos Walking series by Patrick Ness; *Matched* by Ally Condie; *Shatter Me* by Tahereh Mafi; *The Summer Prince* by Alaya Dawn Johnson; *Legend* by Marie Lu; and *Little Brother* by Cory Doctorow.

Paranormal. Our real (and usually contemporary) world with one or more supernatural elements added, such as ghosts, vampires, werewolves, or angels, or a protagonist with a unique supernatural ability, like ESP. YA paranormal novels frequently feature a strong romantic plotline, which has pretty much come to define the subgenre. Notable titles include the *Twilight* saga by Stephenie Meyer; the Shiver trilogy by Maggie Stiefvater; the Mortal Instruments books by Cassandra Clare; *The Coldest Girl in Coldtown* by Holly Black; and *Shadowshaper* by Daniel José Older.

Horror. A paranormal novel that is explicitly designed to evoke terror, dread, or disgust in readers by setting our protagonist in extreme jeopardy, often from some kind of supernatural creature. In middle-grade, notable titles include the Goosebumps series by R. L. Stine; *Wait Till Helen Comes* by Mary Downing Hahn; *Coraline* by Neil Gaiman; or the classic collection *Scary Stories to Tell in the Dark* by Alvin Schwartz. In YA, examples include *Anna Dressed in Blood* by Kendare Blake; *This Is Not a Test* by Courtney Summers; *Charm & Strange* by Stephanie Kuehn; *This Dark Endeavor* by Kenneth Oppel; *I Hunt Killers* by Barry Lyga; and *Miss Peregrine's Home for Peculiar Children* by Ransom Riggs.

Urban Fantasy. A fantasy or paranormal novel that uses the unique energy and landscape of a city as a backdrop. Notable titles include *The Blue Girl* by Charles de Lint (who arguably invented the genre); *Neverwhere* by Neil Gaiman; *Tithe* and the Curse Workers trilogy by Holly Black; the Mortal Instruments books by Cassandra Clare; *Gone* by Michael Grant; and *Shadowshaper* by Daniel José Older.

Magical Realism. A novel focused on our real world with occasional non-realistic elements presented matter-of-factly. These elements may play a role in the plot, but they or the powers they evoke do not necessarily shape said plot in the way that most other fantasies wrestle with them; they are simply present in a story that explores other thematic or emotional concerns. The subgenre has particular resonance within the Latin American literary tradition, where it began. Notable titles include *Ninth Ward* by Jewell Parker Rhodes; *Bigger than a Bread Box* by Laurel Snyder; *Breadcrumbs* by Anne Ursu; most of the novels of A. S. King; *Above* by Leah Bobet (‡); *Summer of the Mariposas* by Guadalupe Garcia McCall; *The Strange and Beautiful Sorrows of Ava Lavender* by Leslye Walton; *Bone Gap* by Laura Ruby; and *A Snicker of Magic* by Natalie Lloyd.

Epic or High Fantasy. A novel set entirely within its own invented world, usually involving a young hero coming of age, quests, and/or grand conflicts between good and evil forces or among several morally ambiguous kingdoms. Notable titles include the complete works of J. R. R. Tolkien and Tamora Pierce; the Chronicles of Prydain by Lloyd Alexander; *The Hero and the Crown* by Robin McKinley; *Sabriel* by Garth Nix; the Graceling Realm trilogy by Kristin Cashore; *Throne of Glass* by Sarah J. Maas; and *Shadow and Bone* by Leigh Bardugo.

Historical Fantasy. A novel that introduces magical elements into a historic setting, which could be either a real historical period or an alternate world that strongly resembles one. It may also be used to describe realistic novels set in imagined historical worlds. Examples include the Queen's Thief series by Megan Whalen Turner; *Plain Kate* by Erin Bow; *Grave Mercy* by Robin LaFevers; *A Curse Dark as Gold* by Elizabeth C. Bunce (‡); the Moribito books by Nahoko Uehashi (‡); *Huntress* by Malinda Lo; *Chime* by Franny Billingsley; *The Inquisitor's Apprentice* by Chris Moriarty; and *Razorhurst* by Justine Larbalestier.

Fairy Tale Retelling. A novel that expands the plot of a classic fairy tale to book length, where it explains or justifies the tale's strange, magical, or less obviously psychologically realistic elements within the story. Notable titles include *Ella Enchanted* by Gail Carson Levine; the Whatever After series by Sarah Mlynowski; *Book of a Thousand Days* by Shannon Hale; and *Grounded: The Adventures of Rapunzel* by Megan Morrison (‡) on the middle-grade side; and in YA, *Beauty, Rose Daughter* and *Deerskin* by Robin McKinley; the Lunar Chronicles by Marissa Meyer; *Ash* by Malinda Lo; *A Curse Dark as Gold* by Elizabeth C. Bunce (‡); *Fire and Hemlock* by Diana Wynne Jones; and *Tender Morsels* by Margo Lanagan.

Animal Fantasy. A novel in which the majority of the characters (including the protagonist) are animals, real or supernatural. These are nearly always published for middle-graders or younger. Sometimes these creatures have been anthropomorphized, which allows the writer to comment on human situations with some distance or humor; in other books, they act as the animals they are. The characters might share a world with humans, or they might live in a self-contained fantasy world. Notable examples include, on the classic end, *The Wind in the Willows* by Kenneth Grahame; *Winnie the Pooh* by A. A. Milne; *The Mouse and His Child* by Russell Hoban; the Redwall books by Brian Jacques; and *Watership Down* by Richard Adams (one of the rare animal fantasies for adults); and more recently, *The Tale of Despereaux* by Kate DiCamillo;

the Warriors series by Erin Hunter; and the Wings of Fire series by Tui T. Sutherland.

Science fiction and fantasy not only allows multiple crossovers among categories, it also blurs the lines between age groups, as YA fantasy readers might read down for a retelling of a fairy tale they love, while many kids make their first forays into an adult section of the bookstore via the genre. If you've written a speculative fiction book and you aren't quite sure how to classify it for a query letter or other purposes, identify three comparison titles and follow their lead.

∾

If you're interested in writing a fantasy or science fiction novel, it will usually start with what I call "the fantastic fact": one or more presently nonrealistic elements that so profoundly alter a world and the people who inhabit it that the story becomes speculative fiction. This thing might be a dragon or a daemon; warp drive, sentient robots, or time travel; witchcraft or wizardry (not the same things); werewolves, aliens, or ghosts. (Note that a fantastic fact could also be a scientific fact, like climate change carried to a future extreme.) Whatever it is, the entire logic of this world will catch on and warp around this point. Accordingly, once you've found your fact(s), you must world-build around it—that is, you must create a world that integrates this imaginative element seamlessly into its characters, society, landscape, and natural and social laws.

As an example, let's say the fantastic fact in your novel is telekinesis, and every human on earth can move objects with their minds. Here are ten categories you could explore to develop this new power, the resulting world, and some possible story lines within it:

- **Definition of terms.** What is this power? How do you define "objects" and "minds"? Can you move living beings? Could a person in a coma practice it unconsciously?
- **Procedure.** How would a character wield this power? Do they have to envision the object in their mind and say certain words or complete a gesture? Or is a look and an intention enough?

- **Abilities.** How far does this power extend? Can someone move an object a mile away, or does it have to be within their line of sight? Is there a weight limit on how much the power can lift? Can it create force (e.g., push a button, pull a drawer open), or is it simply capable of lift? Can you apply it to yourself—that is, can you make yourself fly? How fast can an object move?

- **Equity and society.** Do all humans have the power in equal strength, or do different people have it in different degrees? What differences (age, gender, physical strength, etc.) would determine those degrees? How have people reacted to differences in this power: by revering those with more of it, or by repressing or ostracizing such people? What new connections or communities have come out of these practices?

- **Origin.** Where did this power come from? Who or what created it? Who was the first person to discover it, and how? How has that origin story (a creation myth, really) been integrated into the culture?

These preceding five elements create what is known in fantasy as a magic system. It doesn't have to be as logical or rule-bound as my questions here might indicate; many classic fantasies use a more airy, free-floating concept of "magic," while modern ones often tend toward this more scientific approach. If you were writing a science fiction rather than a fantasy novel, with a scientific fact of some kind in place of a fantastic one, then the "Abilities" and "Equity and society" questions might be most applicable, along with the categories that follow:

- **Government, economics, technology, and culture.** What sort of laws has the government passed in order to regulate this power? If I could just walk by a jewelry store, pick up a diamond bracelet with my mind, and fly it out to my wrist, what's going to stop me? Did the store put new guards at every door, or tie down every object, or invent a new tracking device? What new terms, jobs, or industries have been created to accommodate these changes? What sort of artwork would artists or choreographers create with telekinesis? How has language changed?

- **One day, one month, one year, ten years.** What did this world look like one day after the onset of this power, as people reacted to it? One month, as they settled into it? One year, as it became a fact in their lives? And ten years, as it turned invisible to them?
- **Landscape.** These questions may apply more to novels set in alternate worlds than to in this one, but: What does the landscape of this fantasy world look like? What are its natural resources? Where does this society get its water and food or energy? What is its economy based on? How might magical powers or these new scientific realities affect the way people treat their resources, particularly the land?
- **Historical analogues.** While you should investigate this with great caution, are there historical parallels to this situation that might inform your understanding of human behavior in these new circumstances? For instance, as telekinesis could move both objects and people: How did human thinking and behavior change after there was a reliable postal service to ship objects securely? Or once there was regular plane travel? Reading up on the evolution of such models might help you discern patterns that can be brought into your present work.

As you can see, answering one of these questions leads to a whole host of other questions and story directions. The more you can build out and weave together both the foundations of your fantasy world and its details here, the richer that world will feel. That does not mean you should put all of the details you imagine into the book—quite the contrary, since, as with any backstory, all those details can easily overwhelm the frontstory. Many speculative fiction writers compare world-building to an iceberg: Only 10 percent of it should appear above the narrative surface, but the mass and integrity of the whole will give it tremendous power.

While the fantastic fact may change the society you're portraying, the action of the book should still abide by the laws of the real world in terms of human characterization and relationships. I would venture that in speculative fiction, more than any other genre besides romance, readers want to feel connected to our protagonist, as he or she will provide a human anchor and orientation in this unfamiliar world. Thus you might want to use a number of the connective strategies from Chapter 8, "Interest and Change," in introducing him to us. If something about the fantastic fact or the culture it created renders the characters or their relationships different from what readers know in the real world, then you should make that clear early on, to allow readers to adjust their expectations accordingly. For example, if this fictional society now reproduces entirely by cloning, so every baby is raised in a group home and parent-child relationships no longer exist, that would be a crucial fact in the backstory of all of the characters, as it could profoundly affect their sense of authority and their emotional connections.

The action of a speculative fiction novel will usually involve our protagonist discovering this fantastic or scientific fact, or, if it's a long-settled part of her universe, wielding it, exploring its implications, or dealing with its malfunctions. This can be especially pressing if that fact involves power: How should this power be wielded? What limits exist on its use? How do others employ it, and how does our protagonist feel about those methods? (These questions all point toward a conflict plot, you may note, if our hero and another character have different values.) Where did the power originate, and how has it been used or abused in this world in the past? (There you have a mystery plot, as characters discover the power and trace its history.) In middle-grade, and sometimes YA, fantastic power often also points to a lack—a missing family member, who may have been a great practitioner of this power, or some kind of perceived deficit in our protagonist because the magical power has not yet manifested within him. Gaining the power then becomes a story of the protagonist's finding an identity, both as a member of his family and as a person who chooses how to wield power. Consider also changing up these dynamics, as there have been hundreds of Chosen One narratives already. What would a Chosen Eight story be like? An un-Chosen Community? Or the servant of the Chosen One: What stories might she have to tell?

Once you've settled on a plot direction, you can make the action as simple or complex as you like, depending on how deeply into your fantastic fact and world-building you want to go. Continuing with the idea of tele-kinesis, suppose our heroine wakes up tomorrow as the only person in our present-day world with this power at this time. You could show her using this new ability to pull off a heist: That's one layer of world-building, com-bined with a conflict plot. Or suppose the novel is set two hundred years in the future, after scientists have discovered that telekinesis doesn't work through aluminum. So all the rich people live in high-walled, aluminum-lined compounds, while the poor scrimp and steal, and our starving hero-ine needs to pull off a heist if her community is going to survive. Now you have three layers of world-building, in the original fact and the scientific and societal response to it, and a conflict plot with much larger implica-tions. The questions you choose to broach under this fantastic fact should be appropriate to the characters' and readers' age and emotional develop-ment; if you're writing a unicorn fantasy for seven- to ten-year-olds, for instance, you should probably skip the part of unicorn mythology that involves virginity. The climax of the book will be the culmination of the character's new knowledge within the bounds of other plots (conflict, mys-tery, or lack) as described earlier.

Narratives of power have tremendous resonance for young readers, as they get to vicariously experience authority through a book in a way they often don't have it in real life. Fantasy and science fiction can call out those dynamics even more strongly by making a power a physical force in the text. Develop your fantastic and scientific facts; by all means, have a mar-velous time building your incredible world. But never forget the uniquely emotional dimension of this genre for these age groups, and honor that in your storytelling as well.

CHAPTER 16

Perspective and Polishing

Considering Charlotte Keene

Here's the first scene of a YA novel by a writer whom we'll call Charlotte Keene. (I've annotated it for our use.)

> (1) Madison bent over and placed her hands carefully on the rough surface. (2) She bent her knees and thrust her gluteus into the air, feeling the pull of the muscles in her back and along the backs of her thighs. (3) On both sides of her, three other young women felt the same pull. (4) They all shot forward when the gun sounded. (5) Madison quickly took a commanding lead, rounding the first curve of the track nearly ten feet ahead of the seven other girls. (6) Her feet pummeled the turf, her arms pumping like oil jacks, her head cocked back like the safety on a gun. (7) She pictured her father in her mind's eye, shouting at her, "You want to qualify for State, Maddy-girl! Can't you run any faster?" (8) She thought about how satisfying it would be to run past him, run out of the stadium, run down Schuyler Street to Highway 47 and out of Duluth forever. (9) She wished she could forget the scouts in the stands, the track scholarship from the U, the drama with Jeff, and run all the way south to her mother in New Orleans.

(10) The end was in sight. (11) Madison glued her eyes to the strip of plastic stretched across the finish line. (12) The 400 always went so fast! She could hardly believe it was almost over already. But out of the corner of her eye, a yellow Asics running shoe with blue laces and purple racing stripes poked into her vision on her right side. Madison knew those shoes. (13) It was Betsey Alejandro. Madison hated her, ever since Betsey defeated her in the 800 at last year's Northfield Relays. (14) The sight caused her to pick up her pace, (15) but the Lafayette High runner's kelly-green jersey and shorts still came more and more into view. (16) She heard the crowd. It was screaming louder than the wind in Madison's ears.

(17) Betsey smiled as she pulled even with that bitch, Madison George. (18) She had taken her down in Northfield and she would do it again here. See if *she* got to run at the U next year.

(19) There were only ten feet left to the finish line. Nine, eight, seven, six, five, four, three, two . . . (20) Madison put her head down and thrust her chest forward. She threw her arms in front of her, then swept them back like the wings of an angel. (21) Her right arm smacked into something soft. Then suddenly that arm was grabbed by something that then yanked it up. (22) Madison tripped and fell, hitting something else soft on the way down. Madison realized there was a kelly-green uniform on the ground next to her. (23) Her face hurt. Had she won the race? Or had she lost to Betsey yet again? What made her trip and fall? Those were the latest Asics sprint shoes—how had Betsey scored them? Had they even crossed the finish line?

(24) "Madison!" Her coach, Peggy Reynolds, a tall white woman with white-blonde hair she wore in a fashionable pixie cut, stood over her. She held her gray plastic Motorola 4500X stopwatch in her hand. "Are you all right? Do you need a medic?"

(25) "My face hurts . . ." Madison moaned.

(26) "Don't move," Coach Reynolds commanded peremptorily. "You're bleeding. What happened here?"

(27) "I was running and my arm hit something, I guess?" Madison narrated as she ran her fingers over her face until she felt something warm and sticky. She looked at her red fingers, then put them back on her face to apply pressure to the wound. "Then we both went down." She pressed harder to stanch the bleeding, then noticed her elbow was bleeding as well. "What was my time?" Her left hand came up to press that elbow.

The coach told her, "Your time? Fifty-three point eight seven five. It's a new personal best for you, if they let it stand."

"Let it stand? You mean, I could be disqualified?" Madison whined.

(28) Betsey's body rolled back and forth over the rough track surface as she clutched her knee. (29) A track official, Gilbert Seabury, knelt over her. (30) "She tripped me! She tripped me! She tripped me!" the girl was screaming.

(31) Madison felt indignant. (32) The two girls had been neck-and-neck the whole race. Then, at the very end, Betsey had started to pull ahead. (33) She hadn't tripped the other girl! If anything, Betsey had tripped *her*. She must have been the one to pull on Madison's arm as they approached the finish line. That was completely typical of Betsey, who had cheated in Northfield as well, which was why Madison hated her.

(34) It had been free of humidity, eighty degrees, and cloud-free—a perfect day for a track meet. Madison had worn her favorite pair of Nikes, which glowed hot pink against her pale skin. Jeff had smiled at her from the stands. Her dad hadn't been there. (35) She had won the 400 and made every other competitor eat her dust. Then it came time for the 800, which wasn't her best event, as she was more of a sprinter than a pacer. Still, she felt great as she approached the starting line for the 800, which she had won at the previous year's championships.

(36) A Latina girl in a kelly-green uniform and garish clown shoes was standing in her starting space. "You're in my blocks, *chica*," Madison joked.

The girl rolled her eyes. "*Chica?* Really? Hope your running is as lame as your Spanish."

(37) Madison in fact spoke Spanish fluently, thanks to her nanny Odelia. It was *on*.

(38) "Of course you could be disqualified. (39) You deliberately tried to block a competitor from crossing the finish line ahead of you! We all saw it. (40) You hit Betsey in the *face*. She was so surprised that she tripped, so she tried to grab on to your arm for support, then her foot went in front of yours and you went down too. She may need surgery. What were you thinking, Madison?"

So, this situation has a lot of interesting raw material for a novel beginning/ inciting incident: the 400-meter race at a Minnesota high school sectional track championships; two competitors who hate each other because of an episode in their past; a protagonist with a father who pressures her to succeed, a distant mother, a love interest, and a potential college scholarship on the line; all concluding in an accident said protagonist may or may not have intentionally instigated, which may have just ruined the knee (and running career) of her rival, and which may disqualify her from competition as well.

But the passage is not even close to reaching its full potential, because Ms. Keene has made a series of unfortunate artistic decisions that render the scene's drama flatter than the track itself. We'll analyze it now to identify its problems and discuss possible solutions. I'm warning you up front that reading the annotations here may make you extremely self-conscious about your writing: "Oh, dear, is that a protagonist + mental verb construction?" "Everything I write has SO MUCH REPETITION!" Please ignore most of these sentence-level ideas and concerns in writing your first draft, and even through any structural revisions, and consider them only in doing your final polish on your prose. After the annotations, you can read a much-improved version of this scene written by Kass Morgan, the *New York Times* bestselling author of the 100 series.

═══ EXERCISES ═══

What do you like about this passage? What problems do you see in it? If it were you writing about these characters, how would you handle the inciting incident? If you were developing this beginning further, in what direction would you take the story?

Before you read the annotations below or Kass Morgan's take on the scene, line-edit it yourself or write your own version, using the same characters and action but adding or changing details as you choose. (The passage is available for download on my website.

An Editor's Annotations

1. The first fault of this sentence is that it's extremely boring as the first line of a novel, with no interesting action or details to draw a reader in. The second is that it doesn't name the object that has this "rough surface," and early in a scene, as here, Keene should be doing everything she can to establish the reality and solidity of her setting and the objects in it.

2. Here we see the first of the many repetitions that will appear throughout this passage, in the two "bents" and the two "backs" of the first couple sentences. Repetitions are a problem in prose because the aural chime of the two words violates the transparency principle; that is, the repetition catches readers' attention and reminds them they're reading words in a book, thus distracting them from the imaginative world. (The best way to find repetitions is to have someone else read your work out loud to you, so you can hear them yourself.) The diction choice "gluteus" here also feels unnecessarily specific and distracting, and the protagonist's derriere is an awkward first image for a novel in general. All of that said,

the description of the tension in Madison's muscles is useful, as it anchors us in the body of this character who is about to become all physical action.

3. This is a POV violation: We were just inside Madison's physicality, having the pull of her muscles dramatized for us, and now we're very suddenly on the outside of this lineup of girls, having *their* physicality told to us. Does this mean *they* will be our POV characters as well? How many other girls are running this race, anyway— four? Seven (three on each side)? It's not clear from the text.

4. This sentence represents a huge wasted opportunity. The dramatic action of this scene literally begins with a gunshot, which would instantly grab the reader's attention. Yet this shot is buried deep within the paragraph and even the sentence, as it's mentioned only in passing as the competitors start to run. If I were editing Keene, I might suggest pulling out this detail and making it the first sentence of the scene/book, since even a line as simple as, "The gun went off," would inspire readers to want to know *what* gun, *who* shot it, *why* it was shot, and what the consequences are. All of that would be a huge improvement over Keene's first sentence, because it would make readers curious about what happens next; and if you can get someone to read your second sentence, you've won the first battle of your novel.

That said, as cool as the gunshot is, a multitude of approaches could make this opening more compelling. Start with Madison and Betsey lining up next to each other, each girl fully aware of the other, but outwardly ignoring her to prepare for the race in her own mental fashion. That would highlight the differences between the two girls beyond their ethnicities (which is actually one of the most reductive facts about them) and provide readers with a fascinating choice: Whom do we want to root for? Or start with a description of Madison's warm-up routine: Which muscles does she stretch, in which order, and why? Does she have a pre-run mantra or ritual? What's her lucky charm? If those details can be rendered in a rich and cred-

ible manner, then we'll be drawn into Madison's reality and want to
see what will happen to her. Or start with a simple, ominous insight:
"Only one runner can win a race." Any of those openings (and any
others you might brainstorm here) would establish Keene's authority,
and the reader's interest in the text, better than the current beginning.

5. This book has not yet set a consistent pace for its prosody: We experienced real-time dramatic action with the description of Madison's
careful movements and that pull in her muscles in sentences (1) and
(2), but the text moved into narration with (3) and stayed there for
(4). This sentence takes us even further out of real time by narrating
the first few seconds of the race, then cuts back to the dramatized
action as Madison approaches the first curve of the track. That tog-
gling back and forth between real time and narrated time makes
readers feel disoriented, like frames have been cut out of our film
reel. Keene's tone here is also a bit more sports-reportorial than
novel-personal, yet at the same time she reports the facts wrongly,
as she states there are eight girls on the track, but (we know from
the "three girls" line earlier) there are actually either four or seven
runners. Good writing keeps its fictional facts straight.

6. Suddenly we're back in close focus on Madison, possibly in real
time, observing how she runs. With three strong verbs and two
similes in one sentence, the language here feels overblown.

7. Now we're inside Madison's mind. The redundancy of "picturing"
someone "in her mind's eye" here is outweighed by a problem I
call the "protagonist + mental verb distancing effect," which also
appears in (8) and (9). In all three sentences, the key idea of the
line—the pressure from Madison's father, her desire to run away,
her longing to forget her present dilemmas and find her mother—is
filtered through a verb that takes place in her head: "She pictured,"
"She thought," "She wished." These repeated reminders that Madison is thinking slow down, and weigh down, the action as a whole,
and keep us from experiencing the full power of what she's looking
at or thinking about. (Other verbs commonly involved in creating

this effect: *watch, look at, see, hear, listen to, feel, think, remember, wonder, imagine, realize, understand, know*.) The easy fix is to cut the protagonist + mental verb phrases as follows:

> (7) She pictured her father, shouting at her, "You want ot qualify for state, Maddy-girl! Can't you run any faster?" (8) How satisfying it would be to run past him, out of the stadium, down Schuyler Street to Highway 47, and out of Duluth forever. (9) Forget the scouts in the stands, the track scholarship from the U, the drama with Jeff, and run all the way south to her mother in New Orleans. . . .

In this revised (8) and (9), we experience and share her thoughts directly, so these sentences now draw us closer to Madison and make her problems feel more immediate. The revision also eliminates the repetitions of "run" and "She _____," which were especially notable as they all fell in the same position within the individual sentences of (7) through (9); the changes vary the subjects and structure of the sentences and make the prose more interesting. I did leave "She pictured" in (7), as it serves as a transition from the exterior action to Madison's interior thought; if the fact of a mental process is the key idea of a line, it's fine to show that mental process happening. As with any writing technique, this is a sentence-by-sentence judgment call. But most often, removing these phrases is a quick and effective way to show, not tell—to dramatize more and better. Go forth and cut.

8. My remaining beef with this sentence is a straightforward one: Highway 47 doesn't run through Duluth, and good writing keeps its real-world facts straight as well.

9. This sentence introduces a third kind of repetition, after the words in (1), (2), and (8) and the phrases in (7) through (9): The sentence structure here exactly replicates the structure in the preceding line, with an interior thought of Madison's followed by four phrases describing her longings. It isn't terrible, especially as the key ideas of the two sentences are more or less continuous, but the fact that the

structure is used twice in two sentences makes me feel like Keene isn't paying attention to the details of her language, which gives me less reason to pay attention, too.

Finally, throwing all of these plot elements into the last sentence of the opening paragraph gives it a case of "conceptitis," as described in Chapter 14, "Teases and Trust." This scene would feel stronger and more confident if Keene indeed trusted the inherent drama of her present characters and situation and stayed focused on them.

10. "The end was in sight"? Last we heard, Madison was rounding the first turn on the track! Granted that a lot of real time might have gone by while she was thinking in (7) through (9), and the 400 is an extremely fast race, but it again feels like a few frames were cut out of the film reel. I would have liked to get at least one or two more updates on the race before I hear that it's ending.

11. Gluing her eyes to something is the kind of "creative" writing that ends up causing more trouble than it's worth, as the literal meaning here is so painful that it distracts me from the sentence's actual intent.

12. Madison is running at extremely high speed in the homestretch of a 400-meter dash. She does not have time to catalog all the details about the shoe that are given here; indeed, she should barely notice this shoe at all, if her eyes are truly glued to the finish line. Keene should simplify this description to what Madison's mental camera could truly take in at this moment—probably the shoe and its color at most—if that detail is really the best way to signal Betsey's approach.

13. As with (4) above, the fault here lies less in the sentences themselves than in the wasted dramatic opportunity they represent. We're meeting our protagonist's greatest nemesis, the Veronica to her Betty, the Tonya Harding to her Nancy Kerrigan (assuming Madison is the innocent one here) . . . and Betsey is introduced through flat statements of her identity, her backstory, and Madison's feelings toward her, without any juicy drama or detail to show why she

warrants all this attention. Moreover, we're in the last fifty meters of what should be an extremely exciting race; ideally, we would have gotten all the information we needed about the competitors earlier in the scene, so we could concentrate here on which one of them will take home the trophy. Info-dumping backstory at this point further diminishes the drama.

14. The "caused her to" construction always sounds awkward. Either use "made her" or cut the phrase: "She picked up her pace."

15. Keene renames Betsey as "the Lafayette High runner," employing a technique writers use a lot when they don't want to feature a character's name too often in the text. I always find this technique a little jarring because it requires me, as a reader, to stop and connect this new identifier with the character I already know. Here that connection is made more difficult still because this is the first time "Lafayette High" has been mentioned in the text. If you're going to rename characters like this, be sure the terms are comfortably established well before you do so.

16. If I were line-editing this passage, I would probably switch the "she" and "Madison," so the lines would read "Madison heard the crowd. It was screaming louder than the wind in her ears." That improves both sentences by putting a strong proper noun in the active subject position, while relegating the weaker pronoun to the possessive. (Yes, editors do pay attention to such details!) A better fix would be, "The crowd was screaming louder than the wind in Madison's ears," or superior still, something like, "The crowd screamed as the girls pounded down the track"; the first correction would address the protagonist + mental verb problem and combine two uninteresting sentences into one, while the second would put the sentence in the active voice and add a last dose of drama.

17. Here we head-hop from Madison to Betsey, as signaled by the text abruptly naming Madison "that bitch." Both the hop and the term feel harshly out of tune with the preceding action. As a reader, I have barely started getting to know Madison as a character and investing

in her as the protagonist; should I now make a similar investment in Betsey? Only time will tell: If we return to Betsey's POV, then yes, I should pay close attention to her. (Since it turns out this is a onetime jump, the whole paragraph should be deleted.)

As for the word "bitch," I find that children's and YA writers sometimes use expletives to indicate that a character is "tough" or "gritty"; but if that language doesn't feel of a piece with the overall tone and atmosphere, then those attributes remain in quotation marks. Treat expletives as you would any other matter of diction, and choose the most natural words for both your voice and the character.

18. If you *do* head-hop consistently, make it worth the reader's time: Give us some new information or insights from this point of view. Here Betsey's thoughts just repeat Madison's anxieties without adding any dimension to either character.

19. We're now back in Madison's POV, as we learn in (20), moving in real time and even real distance. However, this is another case where I don't believe Madison's internal voice would actually count down the last ten feet in so many words, if she's truly focused on putting on speed to win, and I would cut the countdown altogether.

20. After you finish reading this sentence, please set this book down and move through the actions that the text describes: put your head down, thrust your chest forward, throw your arms in front of you, then sweep them out to the sides. It takes a few seconds, doesn't it? Both the action and the sentence feel awkward because the four movements don't flow together, and the narration calls attention to each one individually. (They also represent a waste of energy and motion for a runner trying to win a race, which is worth noting when it comes to Madison's intentions below.) Having Madison's actions described in such detail certainly creates a mini-movie in the reader's mind, but this mini-movie halts the larger and more exciting and consequential film of the race, which is irritating when our protagonist is two feet from the finish line. When you're describing a character's movements, especially in an action scene,

I suggest including only those motions that have consequences for that larger action—in this case, her arms sweeping out—and cutting everything else. (I frequently act out the gestures described in a book I'm editing to see how natural they feel and how long they take. If the actions require more time to read than they do to perform, that's usually a sign something needs to go.)

21. The first "something" here feels justifiably vague, as Madison should be looking toward the finish line and wouldn't know what her arm hit. The second "something" starts to violate the clarity principle, and the reader's right to know what is going on.

    Additionally, "that arm was grabbed by something" is an example of passive voice—that is, a grammatical mode in which the thing that performs the action in the sentence is diminished or obscured by the sentence's construction. (Lawyers use passive voice a lot to separate their clients from their actions and thereby minimize the clients' responsibility. My favorite example: When a recruiter asked a lawyer friend of mine about his past drug use, my friend said, "Some pot was smoked by me.") Passive voice can be useful when the thing doing the acting is not that important to the sentence, or when the writer wishes to highlight the object being acted upon; you'll note that the first sentence in this paragraph is partly in passive voice, because I wanted to emphasize "the thing that performs the action." But in Keene's case, passive voice slows down the action, and Madison could surely feel and identify what's grabbing her arm already: A hand? Teeth? Claws? I would suggest rewriting this sentence as, "A hand grabbed her arm and yanked it upward," or even better, combine it with the previous sentence for speed: "Her right arm smacked into something, then a hand yanked it upward."

22. In keeping with the idea from (20) of focusing on the most important physical movement, Keene could rewrite this passage to focus on Madison falling and hitting her head, with Betsey tumbling down next to her. As it is, the action feels very stop-start and slow for what should be a split-second sequence, and it jumps back and

forth between physical action and internal thought in a manner that doesn't develop either one effectively. (As a side note, any "There was" statement is also passive voice, and the sentence can also usually be improved by eliminating that phrase and rejiggering it with an active verb: A girl in a kelly green uniorm lay on the ground next to her.")

23. This sequence of questions feels a little stagy, but more importantly, it's a place where the "first or last = most" principle could be used to much better effect. The most important question right now is, "Had she won?," so that should be at the end of the series, with all the other questions arranged to build up to it. The shoes thought is irrelevant right now and should be cut.

24. This line creates a good visual full of specific detail, but it's entirely too *much* detail about the coach at this moment, when we readers want to focus on the drama of the crash and the end of the race. Also, the use of elbow-jogging brand names in a text, like "Motorola 4500X," often distract the reader through too much specificity and can date the book in the long term. I'd rewrite this as, "Coach Reynolds stood over her, stopwatch in hand."

25. "My face hurts" repeats what the narration already told us above in (23), which makes it a waste of words. Give us something new. I'll also point out the pattern of speech verbs in this dialogue beat: "moaned," "commanded," "narrated," "informed," "whined." Writers often employ such speech verbs to lessen their use of "said" and to show emotion in general. However, these verbs press their emotions on the reader with almost physical force, as every line carries a huge emotional charge, and as a result, the conversation becomes exhausting. Moreover, what both characters are feeling is perfectly evident from what they say; Keene doesn't need the strong dialogue words to reinforce that. Use dialogue tags like these only when justified by the extremity of the emotion or volume. Otherwise, use "said" or other emotionally neutral tags, and let the content and punctuation of the dialogue carry the emotion.

26. Along similar lines, the adverb here is redundant with both the verb "commanded" and the nature of the statement itself, and thus should be cut. (Editors do not hate all adverbs—witness how many I'm using in this text—but we do look at the ones attached to dialogue tags with great suspicion.)

27. One very important question underlies what Madison says here, as well as this entire scene and all the action that might follow: Did Madison hit Betsey deliberately? That is, did she sweep her arms out in an intentional act of unsportsmanlike conduct, or was it just an unfortunate accident? If it was deliberate, how long had she been planning that act, and what prompted it? (If Betsey is going to be seriously injured, the motivation might need to run deeper than a silly conversation in Northfield.) If it was an accident, how will Madison feel about it? If I were working editorially with Keene, I'd talk with her about Madison's intentions, how much we want to show those intentions in the scene, and how much readers should like or be invested in Madison in general before either of us edited this text. Depending on the answers, we might want to add some internal narration here or earlier to delineate those intentions more clearly, or rebuild the action so those intentions are clearly a mystery (as that mystery might be, in fact, the point of the scene, or even the book).

    On a strictly prose level, we get much more information here than we need about Madison's movements, with a detailed action following every line of dialogue, which slows down the conversation considerably. Yet we don't hear the most important detail for the reader's mental image of her: What part of her face is bleeding?

28. The camera cuts abruptly to Betsey. As an editor, I would suggest adding a senseline featuring some sound here to attract Madison's attention away from Coach and thus prompt the visual cut. I might also recommend moving the fact that Betsey is clutching her knee to the start of the sentence, as that image (and the event that caused it) is significantly more consequential than her rolling around on the track.

29. The official's name is utterly irrelevant at this moment, and even if it does become relevant later—if, say, the next scene consists of a hearing with the two girls, their coaches, and this official—readers can learn it when Madison learns it. To get it earlier is elbow-jogging.

30. Two repetitions of "She tripped me!" might be enough here.

31. I'm always suspicious of the words "feel" or "felt" in a text, because if a writer has to tell me how his protagonist feels, then that probably means he hasn't succeeded in anchoring me emotionally in the protagonist and action. When I have that anchor, then I come to share the protagonist's emotions organically, via my connection with the character and my reactions to the action. The rule of thumb I would like to lay down here is, "Do not use any variations of the word 'feel' as telling statements," but the word *can* be okay if the statement provides a confirmation or summation for readers of what both they and the protagonist were already feeling. "Madison felt great" in (35), for example, is earned by the many preceding details that set up why Madison would feel great at that particular moment (her shoes, Jeff, her dad's absence, the 800). Both showing and telling have their place in fiction, even with the word "felt." Here, however, Madison's feelings are just announced with no context, and it feels (eek!) flat.

32. This kind of character-POV recapitulation of action we've already seen is almost always an automatic deletion for me, unless it's showing us something new, which isn't the case here.

33. I don't mind these next few sentences as much because we are seeing Madison thinking, putting together the events at the end of the race (and possibly her cover story). Thus it feels more active than (32).

34. These next two lines serve as an establishing shot for the flashback to Northfield. A rule of thumb: Try to minimize or eliminate flashbacks in first scenes. A writer has quite enough work to do in establishing the characters, setting, and forward action in the present timeline. Cutting away to a past event requires reestablishing all of those elements in the flashback and detracts from the present drama. All of which is to say: As an editor, I would cut the next four

paragraphs and find a way to build in what created the girls' enmity at another moment.

35. A cliché like "eat her dust" signals not very interesting writing and thinking.

36. In contrast to the specificity of (12), this does describe more or less what Madison might see when she casually looks up: "A Latina girl in a kelly-green uniform and garish clown shoes." However, we have not gone deep enough in Madison's perspective to know whether "garish clown shoes" is a literal description or her opinion, and as a result, readers might wonder whether this girl *is* actually wearing oversized clown shoes to a track meet, which would distract us from the action. The "Latina" also feels like ham-fisted elbow-jogging here, though it's probably necessary to set up Madison's equally ham-fisted remark.

37. In (33), this flashback was introduced with a promise: It would tell us how Betsey cheated and why Madison came to hate her so much. It now ends with the promise unfulfilled, unless Madison *really* can't take a mild insult. As a result, the flashback feels pointless.

38. One other reason flashbacks are problematic within opening scenes: They put the current action on hold while the flashback unfolds in the mind of the main character. Our return to the present can then feel abrupt and awkward, as it is here, where we can't tell whether this line is part of the flashback or the present action. This awkwardness could be ameliorated by the addition of an opening sentence that would bring Madison's thoughtline back to Coach—something as simple as, "Coach was talking to her." But I still hold that cutting the flashback altogether, or saving it for later (creating a sort of mystery around what happened in Northfield), would be a better way to go.

39. I might add a "Coach Reynolds said" at the beginning or end of the first sentence here. As a rule of thumb, dialogue tags or actions in mini-monologues like this should be inserted at a point where the character speaking would take a breath or pause. Try not to have more than two such insertions per paragraph.

40. Now it's Coach Reynolds's turn to tell the story of what happened at the finish line. This isn't *great*, but because she provides an outside point of view and can give us new information (why Betsey clutched Madison's arm), it's more acceptable than Madison's recap.

Kass Morgan's Take

I hope that seeing these patterns called out might help you identify and possibly avoid them within your own writing. As an example of what to do instead, here's Kass Morgan's version of the same material, with some brief annotations afterward on points of improvement:

(1) The hardest part of the race was waiting for the shot. Once Madison took off, the rest of the world would fade away, leaving only the thud of her sneakers, the rush of the wind, and the word echoing with every heartbeat: *Go go go.*

(2) Until then, she needed to focus—to stretch, to breathe; to become the girl who would win the 400 here at Sectionals and go on to the state meet in St. Paul. Everything around her seemed heightened already. The other girls strained through their own warm-up routines, though Madison chose to ignore them. As she bent to touch her toes one last time, she could hear the anxious murmur of the crowd, mostly parents and friends, and the giddy cheers of her teammates. She was glad she didn't know where her dad was sitting. Even a hundred yards away, she could hear what he was thinking: *You better give it your all. There's a full ride on the line, Maddy girl.* But that was the problem. Madison *always* gave it her all. And even that was never good enough for her father.

(3) She took a deep breath, shook that thought off, and got into position on the track. The roughness of the turf beneath her palms felt almost comforting. But then a flash of green in the next lane made the breath catch in her chest. *Betsey was supposed to be in a different heat. They*

weren't going to meet until the final. . . . Everything about her rival made Madison's stomach clench. Even the kelly green of her jersey and the swish of her dark ponytail seemed like taunts.

(4) *Don't let her get to you*, Madison told herself. It was easier said than done. A few weeks ago, someone had slashed the tires of Madison's car before a meet, and she'd almost missed her race. That evening, Betsey Alejandro of Lafayette High—who'd easily won that event—had posted a selfie with a tire store in the background on Instagram. Madison had told Coach Reynolds, but Coach said she had an overactive imagination, and she wouldn't do anything about it.

The countdown started, and Madison took another breath, gathering tension in her muscles as she pushed against the ground. For a moment, the air was perfectly still.

(5) Then the shot rang out, and all eight runners surged forward. Madison settled into third place, the position that gave her the best advantage in the home stretch. The frontrunners would tire themselves out, and then she'd go in for the kill. But she still had to run like hell. *Go go go*, her heart pounded. They rounded the first turn, and a girl in a blue jersey pulled up beside Madison. Almost without thinking, she dug in harder. *Go go go*, her sneakers clapped over the turf. A few seconds later, Madison had pulled ahead again.

She was in second place, gaining ground on the small redhead in front. Two hundred meters to go. In the distance, she heard people calling her name. But their exuberant cheers seemed faint compared to the ragged wheeze of her own breath. *Go go go.*

Madison pulled up next to the redhead, matching her surprisingly long stride. Then she gritted her teeth and pushed harder, struggling against the air, the strain in her legs, and the gravity that wanted to hold her back, pull her down. *Go go go.* The redhead fell away from Madison's peripheral vision. Now, there was no one else in front of her. The finish was in sight. She was going to make it. She was going to *win*.

Where was Betsey?

Forget her.

Madison's eyes locked on the strip of plastic stretched across the finish line fifty meters ahead. She could already feel its pull as she strode through it. And then her father's eyes and smile would say the same thing for once. *I'm proud of you.*

(6) Then a flash of movement made Madison jerk her head to the side. Something kelly green.

No. The word echoed through her head. *Not this time.* She dug in harder. Ten meters. She summoned every last ounce of energy to thrust her body forward, throwing her arms back to propel herself toward the finish line. Her right arm smacked into something. Then something else—a hand?—wrenched that arm over Madison's head. Madison gasped, tripped, saw the sky. Then she hit the track with a thud that knocked her breath from her chest.

She could barely process the pain. As she lifted her head with a groan, all Madison cared about was the finish line. The plastic ribbon lay on the ground behind her—and so did Betsey, curled up and clutching her ankle. What had happened? Who won?

"Madison!" Coach Reynolds stood over them, a stopwatch in her hand. "Are you all right? Do you need a medic?"

"I think I'm okay," Madison said, pushing herself up to sit.

"Don't move," the coach ordered. "You're bleeding. What happened?"

(7) "I don't know." Her voice was thick, and it almost felt like something was speaking for her. She looked over at Betsey, who was still on the ground, her coach and teammates gathered around her. "We were at the end, and my arm hit—someone? Then we both went down." She brought her hand to her forehead and felt something warm and sticky. She really was bleeding. Everything started to swim, and Madison put her head between her knees. "What was my time?"

When she spoke, Coach Reynolds's voice was strangely flat. "Fifty-three point eight seven five. It's a new personal best for you, if they let it stand."

"Let it stand? You mean, I could be *disqualified*? I didn't—"

"Don't say anything, Madison." Her tone was still quiet. "Let's see what happens."

(8) The beginning of tears stung Madison's eyes. She couldn't cry. Not now. If Coach didn't believe her about this either . . .

Betsey was rocking back and forth, still holding her ankle, as a track official knelt over her. "She tripped me! She tripped me!" Betsey shrieked.

(9) Madison's face hardened. If anything, Betsey had tripped *her*. She must have been the one to grab Madison's arm as they approached the finish line. "I didn't trip her!" Madison said, her voice rising above the din.

Betsey stopped wailing instantly. "You're such a liar!" she snapped. "I was about to win this, so you smacked me in the face."

(10) She'd just changed her story. Madison looked up at her coach, expecting a look of equal fury at Betsey. But Coach Reynolds was looking down at her instead, with an expression of almost—disgust?

(11) "Maddy," a voice called. She turned to see her father walking toward her, the stony look on his face all too familiar.

An Editor's Annotations, Part II

1. Starting with the gunshot—and already we have a more interesting first line, with a more exciting focus.

2. Remember the zoom-out technique from Chapter 15? Kass demonstrates that beautifully here by first holding her focus on Madison warming up and the people immediately around her, then widening it for just one more character—Madison's dad, who introduces both personal stakes (Madison wants to please him, presumably) and

practical ones (the scholarship) for this race. She cuts all the other narrative threads that gave the original passage conceptitis.

3. Our narrative lens zooms out one more notch to take in the rivalry with Betsey. Note the many great sense-focused details Kass has introduced into the passage: We've heard the crowd; Madison feels the turf under her hands; her stomach clenches at the sight of Betsey's kelly green jersey. . . . All of these things anchor us in Madison's physicality and, brief as they are, make this world feel more real.

4. This paragraph does two positive things compared to the original Keene: It introduces a more immediate and less stupid reason for Madison's concern about Betsey that employs contemporary details relevant to real teenagers' lives (namely, an Instagram account). And yet the reasons for this enmity are still just vague enough that it's plausible this conspiracy *is* in Madison's head, which better sets up the uncertainty at the end. (It also gives us another zoom-out and point of narrative tension as we "meet" her coach and learn there's conflict there too.)

5. The *go go go* provides a nice aural and action motif throughout this beginning, showing us Madison's concentration, and the narration overall moves us smoothly through the race: first the surge forward, then the first turn, and in the next paragraph, they're halfway done.

6. The details—the flash of kelly green, the way Madison throws herself forward, the repetition of "something," even the ultimate fall—are much better calibrated to the speed at which the runners are moving and what Madison might actually see and think in this situation.

7. Hooray for better-paced, more realistic dialogue!

8. A callback to the conflict with Coach in (4), which reminds the reader that there's history here, and Coach hasn't always had Madison's back.

9. Both here and in (8), note the physical action that anchors the internal narration: "The beginning of tears," Madison's face hardening.

10. "She'd just changed her story" is a thoughtline into Madison's expectations, which are then dashed by Coach's expression.

11. Finally, her dad shows up to complete the awfulness of this moment.

By the end of Kass's passage, we've identified who our protagonist is; we've gotten a glimpse of her psychological dimensions; we know her desires; and we've seen multiple conflicts in her life—all of which creates narrative questions that will make us read on. When you write, be a Kass, not a Keene.

CHAPTER 17

Vision and Revision

Twenty Techniques

W hen I talk to writers about how to revise, I sometimes think the key syllable they hear is "vise"—as in a large set of pincers that will slowly crush their spirits, their souls, and the life out of their work. But the word "revise" actually comes from the Latin *revisare* or *revidare*: literally, "to visit again" or "to see again." After you finish a full first draft, I believe your revision process should indeed start with *seeing again*: stepping back to recharge your creative batteries on the project, moving your brain away from solving the practical problems of getting your hero to the climax or perfecting that last phrase, and then thinking through the larger questions of what you've created so far and what you want this book to be. Here I suggest or call back to some practical techniques that should help you consider your work with fresh eyes, and then revise, if not in comfort, at least with less of a sense of impending death by pincer.

You'll see that many of these exercises are redundant, and deliberately so: Different writers are energized by different foci or approaches, and I wanted to provide enough methods that all writers could find ones to their liking. However, if you actually performed all of these techniques on the same novel, I would suspect you of putting off the hard work of actual revising in favor of the (comparatively) more fun work of making collages, highlighting favorite scenes, and constructing charts. Remember these techniques are a means to an end—a fully revised manuscript ready to share with a reader—and not the end itself.

1. Take time off from the project. Again: put the manuscript in a drawer for a minimum of two days and a maximum of two months. You want to be able to read the manuscript and consider its strengths and weaknesses as objectively as another reader might, and that's hard to do when it's fresh in your mind.

2. Before you look at the manuscript again, write a letter to a sympathetic friend. See the second exercise in Chapter 6, "Intention and Invention," on p. 72.

3. State the premise of the story in one sentence. Look back at the exercises in Chapter 4, "Promise and Premise," on p. 46. The mere act of having to define your protagonist's primary action in the book or main problem to solve can help clarify what your book is about, and serve as a useful reminder or boundary line when you're revising. It's also great for elevator pitches, or at family reunions when people ask, "So, whatcha writing?"

4. Write the flap copy. See the instructions on p. 97. Once you've written the flap copy, congratulations! You've pretty much completed your first query letter. But more importantly, you will have just had to set up all of the major narrative elements for a reader who is utterly unfamiliar with them. Looking at them from that perspective: What makes your character compelling? How does your inciting incident change the status quo? What action does your protagonist take? What are the stakes and those key narrative questions? What is the promise of your book? Why would someone want to read it? (You might give the copy to an honest friend or writing partner and have them tell you what sounds great and what feels less exciting.) If you feel dissatisfied with any of your answers, that could indicate an issue to address in revision.

5. Write a synopsis of the book in 750 words or less. This is different from the flap copy in that it is longer; it doesn't have to be written to sell the book to the reader, but just to describe its action—like a kid's book report in school; and it answers the narrative questions by giving away the climax and ending. Like the flap copy, it should include the opening situation, thumbnail sketches of the protagonist and any other major characters, the inciting incident, and the stakes, but it should expand from there to include all of the major events of the book, the climax, and the resolution, with a sense of how the protagonist's life has changed. Try writing it from memory first, without looking back at the manuscript, and then check it against the text to and fill in any missing information.

Once you're done, read the synopsis through. Does the action make sense and flow steadily to the climax? What events or elements did you forget to include when writing from memory? Why did you forget them? What is the overall action, idea, or theme that holds the book together? Can you see it coming through in both the book's events and the protagonist's growth? Again, you may want to share this with a friend and ask him or her to talk it through with you, or consider revisions if you find any of your answers unsatisfactory.

6. Make a book Pinterest board, collage, or playlist. See the instructions at the end of Chapter 6, "Intention and Invention," on p. 72.

7. Look at your word frequency using a word cloud. At WriteWords or Wordle, you can paste your manuscript into a text box, hit the button, and see what words appear most frequently in the text. Are there any surprises in your top one hundred or so words? Those might show a hidden theme, image, or idea lurking in your text that you can expand on in the revision. You can see a Wordle of the text of this book on p. 322:

8. Change the font, then print out and reread the entire manuscript on the page before making any revisions. I really want to emphasize "the page" here. Books read differently on computer screens than they do on paper, and as a majority of your young readers will read your book on

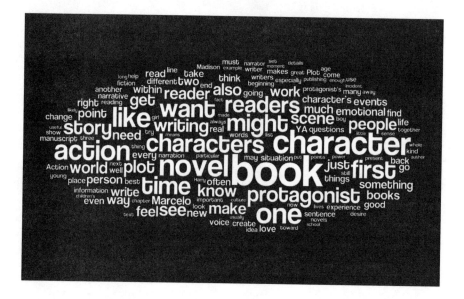

paper, it's important that you have that same experience at least once in editing the book.

9. As you read, take notes on what works and what doesn't. Resist any urge to start revising the actual text; your goal at this stage is to see how the big stuff you envisioned in #2 above—the ideas, the story, what it's all about—accords with what is actually on the page. Note new ideas and large plot or character points you want to revisit. Do not fail to write down things you love in the book (I put star stickers on the page) and pat yourself on the back for what you did well.

10. Bookmap (outline) the action of the novel chapter by chapter/scene by scene. See p. 157 for instructions, and the rest of that chapter for other analysis questions and activities.

11. Diagramming your plot: Three methods

- **Character chart:** Make a table with the name of each significant character in the first column and the following categories across the top: his or her primary identity at the outset; his or her desire or goal at the outset (conscious or unconscious); the perceived reward for the goal; the obstacles in the way; the action he or she takes to achieve the goal; and the final results and how the reader feels about them. Like the Plot Checklist, this is an easy way to map out what happens in your book and identify where you might be lacking stakes (the reward), motivations (the desire/goal), complications (obstacles and action), or conclusions (results).

- **Plot and subplot spreadsheet:** Make a table listing each plot or subplot in the columns on top and the chapter numbers in the rows down the side. Fill in what happens in each plot in every chapter. (To see what this looked like for a portion of *Harry Potter and the Order of the Phoenix*, search online for "J. K. Rowling Plot Spreadsheet.") The character chart above is probably more useful for character-driven novels; this one is more useful for heavily plotted novels, as it helps you get a visual read of the action.

- **Informational spreadsheet.** Put the categories from the bookmap assignment on p. 157 into a spreadsheet alongside any other factors you may want to track: the mood of the scene, the presence of specific characters, the date it takes place, the word count. What patterns do you see?

12. Try Darcy Pattinson's Shrunken Manuscript technique.* In your document file, delete all space breaks, single-space the text of your book, and put it in the smallest point size that is still readable. Then highlight the strongest chapters (or anything else you want to track), print the whole manuscript out, and spread the pages on the floor for a visual map of your book's strengths and weaknesses.

13. Run the Plot Checklist. See p. 200.

14. Take a second look at what you created for steps #2–7 above and compare the results to what you discovered in exercises #8–13. Based on

---

* http://www.darcypattison.com/revision/shrunken-manuscript/

this analysis, compile a to-do list of things to accomplish in a revision. This to-do list will prove extremely useful in keeping track of your larger goals as you work through the minutiae of revising.

15. Remember: You don't have to do everything at once, and all spot changes should resonate in the whole. If you're a person who works best by starting with the first word of Chapter 1 and revising holistically from there, more power to you. Other writers may want to take it "bird by bird," to use Anne Lamott's lovely phrase, and address one item on the to-do list at a time. Again, go with what works best for you.

Remember that the ultimate goal of revising is to have a stronger manuscript that organically integrates all the novel's elements into a satisfying whole. To that end, keep an eye on how each spot revision from the to-do list affects the entire novel, and be sure to give yourself time away from the manuscript occasionally so you can reread the revisions with fresh eyes and see how the changes are integrating into the original framework.

16. Set a deadline for completing each stage of revision, and a reward for each one. It is very easy to get bogged down in the weeds of a revision, so give yourself an end date for completing a new draft or a certain number of pages or items on the to-do list (just before a vacation is always good). Better still, tell a friend or writing partner about this deadline and ask them to keep you responsible to it—either that they'll check in with you occasionally about your progress, or they'll take the manuscript away from you on that date so you can't fiddle with it any further, forcing you on to the next stage in the revision or submission process. Do be kind to yourself in the course of the revision, and treat yourself or take some time off after you reach your goal.

17. Work large to small. Prioritize your to-do list from #14 so you take care of the most far-reaching revisions first, from plot down to sentence polishing. It is unproductive to get the dialogue pitch-perfect in one passage and then discover later that you need to delete the whole scene.

18. Once you're reasonably satisfied you have all the plot- and scene-level changes completed:

- **Cut as many redundant adverbs, telling uses of the word "feel" or "felt," non-"said" dialogue tags, and unhelpful "babies" as you possibly can.** By "unhelpful 'babies,'" I'm referring to the famous writing dictum, "Kill your babies"—that is, "eliminate anything you love solely for an ego/writerly reason." This aphorism often needs to be taken with a grain of salt, as I've had writers ask me, "I really love this. That means I should cut it, right?" No: Babies should die only if they're getting in the way of your larger points or ends. If they serve those ends, please let them live, as the odds are good that your readers will love them, too.
- **Check the balance among descriptive, immediate, and internal narration,** especially in dialogue scenes. See p. 228.
- **Highlight each character's dialogue in a different color, then read through each color in turn.** Does each character speak in a distinctive voice, register, or language? Do any characters sound too much like each other, or like the narrative voice? Are their speech patterns consistent throughout the whole book?
- **Look at establishing shots, topic sentences, conclusions, and fermatas.** Establishing shots are discussed on p. 214; topic sentences and conclusions on p. 229; and fermatas on p. 215.

19. Read the book aloud. There's no better way to discover repetitions or feel the actual pacing of a scene. It's even more useful to have someone read your work to you. Writing partners might perform this service for each other; you can record your own voice and then play it back; or you can find applications online that will convert your text to speech (sans emotion), which leaves you free to read along and take notes.

20. Don't let the perfect be the enemy of the good. The truth is, once you complete this revision and reread it, you may need to do further rewrites;

and once you submit the manuscript to your writing group, agent, or editor, they will likely ask you to make more revisions still. Thus trying to get it "perfect" is ultimately a waste of time. Take the manuscript as far as you can; celebrate your accomplishment in finishing the draft; and send it on its way.

CHAPTER 18

Love and/or Money

Publishing Your Book

S o you've written a manuscript. You've revised it to your utmost capability. You've had at least one other person read it and provide a thoughtful response. You've polished it again based on that response. You have done the very best you can to craft a smart, pleasurable novel, and now it's time to share it with the world.

Welcome to the dating game.

"What's that?" you say. "Dating? I'm married! I don't do that anymore!" Actually, you are fortunate: If you're married, you've been through all of these emotions already. Because the truth is, the book submissions process is exactly like dating—an intensely personal endeavor in which everyone is looking for the right match. Agents and editors are seeking manuscripts they love. Writers are seeking the best home for their work. We're all overwhelmed with information and choices. And if you lose a great potential connection, the disappointment can feel as harsh as divorce.

So how do you avoid that step, and find a happily-ever-after for your book? A modern-day quest begins with a choice: You can enter the dating pool for professional publication, or you can choose to be happily single and self-publish. Which option is right for you depends on your capabilities as a publisher and businessperson, and what you want to get out of having a book in the world.

Self-Publishing: My Way

It's been only a decade since Amazon and Apple came forth with the Kindle (2007) and iPad (2010), respectively, but the changes those two platforms have wrought on the publishing industry can hardly be overstated. They made e-books a viable format in the marketplace, which in turn made it feasible for writers to self-publish their manuscripts digitally, which in turn led to some authors abandoning traditional publishing altogether. Some writers have had great financial success with this model. Many more have put their books out on one of these platforms without making much money, because the competition for readers is intense, and the pricing wars that have ensued from that competition exert considerable downward pressure on prices. Most agents will tell you *not* to self-publish if you want to pursue traditional publication later, as low sales could establish an unfortunate track that the agent would then have to overcome in selling your later work. But if the idea of directing your book's life from manuscript through marketing holds appeal for you, self-publishing is now a fully practicable option.

Many good guides to self-publishing are available online, so I won't rehash the process here. Rather, I'll offer some questions that are hepful in considering publication in general and self-publishing in particular:

What do you want to get out of having the book published? Do you want to become famous? Be rich? Share a story with your family? Would it be enough just to hold a book with your name on it in your hands? While big dreams are great, realistic expectations can be even more useful, especially if you discover you can fulfill them yourself.

How much time are you willing to devote to your publishing vs. your writing? It's extremely satisfying to make a book that looks exactly how you want it to look—but it can also be a lot of work and take a lot of time you might otherwise spend writing.

How much would you enjoy the organizational and business aspects of publishing? These can include everything from proofreading the text, designing the cover, and figuring out a marketing strategy, to coordinating print runs and checking over shipments. If you don't have the skills or interests to carry out these tasks, you can hire freelancers to help, but that could be a significant outlay of cash.

Is your book a serious literary novel, or more of a quick, entertaining read? That could help you determine the appropriate publishing format for it—hardcover, paperback, or ebook. While e-publication has minimal up-front costs, print publication will likely require another outlay of cash to typeset the text, print the books, and store and ship them as necessary.

Who is the likeliest audience for your book? What age group is the manuscript for? What genre is it? If you are thinking of e-publishing first, it's important to know that certain age ranges and genres work better in that format than others do. Romance readers buy a lot of e-books, so YA romance is probably the most successful e-category in children's and YA fiction. Conversely, not many kids under twelve have e-readers, so a middle-grade novel would likely struggle more in e-only publication.

If you did self-publish the book, how would you price it? Are you willing to accept the possibility of fewer copies sold in exchange for a higher percentage of the price on each one? In traditional publishing, you'll receive anywhere from 5 to 15 percent of the cover price on each sale, depending on the publisher and format, while self-publishing allows you to take home as much as 70 percent on certain e-books (as of this writing)—but on a lower cover price. Self-publishing companies usually pay authors on a monthly or quarterly basis, rather than twice a year like traditional publishers.

What means do you have of reaching the likely audience for the book? What is the state of your current platform? How much time are you willing to invest to build up that platform? Publishing expert Jane Friedman defines "platform" as an author's visibility, authority, and proven ability to reach the target audience for the book. Put another way: Your platform is the combination of connections, fame (in whatever circles), expertise in a given topic, or past success that proves you can get the word out about your book to the people most likely to buy it. Since you'll be arranging most of your own marketing if you self-publish, having a strong platform to start from is enormously useful. Traditional publishers also think about an author's platform in making an acquisition decision, and an established one can be an argument in the book's favor; but the lack of one isn't a huge detriment, in my experience.

Writers build their platforms through a long-term effort of establishing credibility and building connections with an audience. When you're still in the writing stage, I'd suggest you concentrate 90 percent of your time on drafting a terrific novel, and the remaining 10 percent on preparing for your novel's submission: becoming familiar with the market, getting to know the children's and YA literary communities, and connecting online and in real life with fellow writers and other literary folk. Be genuine and generous in doing all of this, though; nobody likes someone who networks solely to try to sell you something. People will support you most when you're a great person with an even better book.

Your "likely audience" for a children's or YA novel might encompass everyone between the ages of eight and eighteen in the entire United States. There are ways to narrow this down; if your novel portrays a subculture where you have a platform—horse jumping, say—then you might be able to reach out to horse publications for publicity, or make appearances at competitions, or advertise on related websites. If you're just trying to reach kids in general, however, or their book-buying parents, then you'll want to get wide distribution and media exposure for your work, if at all possible, and that can be very difficult for self-publishers. A platform has also become much more of a moving target in the age of social media, as the likely audience's energy and attention can shift in a blink from one site to the next. Self-publishing offers writers an incredible degree of autonomy and control over their work, but if you're looking for big sales, be prepared for the challenges ahead.

I speak from experience here: In 2011, I self-published the first version of this book you're holding now, under the title *Second Sight: An Editor's Talks* on *Writing, Revising, and Publishing Books for Children and Young Adults*. I enjoyed putting together and publishing the book, and I sold a respectable number of copies, which I credit to having unique content, a strong platform, and a clearly defined, easily reachable audience of children's and YA writers. However, you will note the spine on *this* book says "Norton," because in revising the text, I wanted the editorial support, production resources, and wider distribution that an excellent publisher can provide. There is no one absolutely correct publishing choice for every book. The right direction will depend on the project, the author, her platform, and her abilities to write, publish, and promote the book at a particular moment in time.

Traditional Publication: Love for Sale

Let's say you decide to pursue traditional publication. That means it's time to think about your book not as an artistic work, but as a mind and heart—*your* mind and heart, really—out there in the dating pool, where you want to find the best relationship(s) for it that you can. To know what you're offering, think about how you'd answer the questions in the section above, as well as:

- What is your book about? What makes it appealing to your likely audience?
- We asked this way back in Chapter 4, "Promise and Premise," but it's newly relevant now: What are three comparable titles (aka "comps" or "comp titles") for your book? What makes those books similar to yours? How is your book preferable? (You can be immodest here, we don't mind.)
- On the 1–10 literary/commercial spectrum, with 1 being *Finnegans Wake* by James Joyce and 10 a Teenage Mutant Ninja Turtles activity book, where would your manuscript land?

From your answers, you should be able to create a sort of dating profile for your book, describing what it is and what kind of connections you're looking for. Then you need to get that profile in front of people who might be a good match—that is, agents or publishers who handle your type of book.

At this point, you have a choice: You can submit to editors/publishers directly, or you can approach agents. (You can also do both at the same time, but that often annoys the agents, because if your manuscript has already been rejected by Editor X, that could close off the opportunity for the agent to submit a revised and improved version of the project to Editor X.) In the children's and YA world, quite a few publishers are still open to unsolicited submissions—the method familiarly known as the "slush pile." Three of the most extraordinary novels I've published came in via the slush (*8th Grade Superzero* by Olugbemisola Rhuday-Perkovich, *Shadowshaper* by Daniel José Older, and *Young Man with Camera* by Emil Sher). Writers also have the opportunity to submit to editors directly if they meet at writers' conferences, particularly those sponsored by the Society of Children's Book Writers and Illustrators (SCBWI), which holds conferences in eighty-five regions throughout the world. That said, publishers receive literally thousands of unsolicited manuscripts each year, and submissions in the slush pile are often low on an editor's priority list, because our authors under contract and agented manuscripts come first. And to that end . . .

Agents: Matchmaker, Matchmaker, Make Me a Match

Agents serve as matchmakers in the dating scenario: people who know a wide range of authors and a wide range of editors and do their best to bring the two together. Once they take on an author, some agents will guide the manuscript through a revision—a makeover, so to speak—addressing any obvious aesthetic issues that might block a sale; others prefer to stick with the business side. The manuscript will then go out on submission to a select list of editors. If an editor makes an offer, the agent negotiates the formal and financial details of the contract—the marriage—and later oversees the royalty statements and payments. In return for these services, they take 15 percent of all monies earned by an author on that book.

Given this last fact, many authors balk at getting agents; they'd prefer to take their chances with the slush pile and other contacts, and negotiate contracts themselves or via a lawyer. While I have sympathy for this point of view, especially for picture-book writers, I do generally recommend that novelists try to have agents. Agents will have a sense of which editors would be most receptive to your manuscript, based on those editors' prior publishing and stated wish lists. A submission from an agent will usually be prioritized over slush, as the editor will want to maintain a good relationship with the agent and read and respond quickly. During the contract process, an agent should be able to negotiate more favorable terms and rights splits than a writer could likely achieve on her own, not least because the agent knows what to ask for and which of those terms are most important for the project long-term. In the editorial process, an agent can serve as a sounding board and advocate for both editor and author, should difficulties arise in the relationship, and later help an author navigate the labyrinthine departments and politics of a larger publishing house. And, finally, they can provide essential emotional support and a voice of experience for authors throughout the publishing process. When my authors have good agents, I'm always grateful to have another partner in creating a great book.

Research: I've Got My Eyes on You

Whether you decide to pursue an editor at a publishing house or an agent, the overall process is going to be the same. First, you need to determine what agents and editors might be right for your book? To figure this out:

- Check the acknowledgments of your comp titles or any other books you particularly admire. Does the author thank an agent or editor? Editors and agents want to take on projects they're passionate about, so if one of those professionals loved a book that has qualities similar to yours, they might be interested in yours as well.
- Go to a bookstore or library and pull out a number of books you like, and/or ones that fall in the same place on the literary/commercial spectrum as yours does. Do you see a pattern among the publishers of those titles? In 1997, a writer named Neil Connelly had just completed his

first YA novel. He went to a bookstore, sat down in the YA section, and read the flap copy and first chapters of about twenty books. One of his favorites was *When She Was Good* by Norma Fox Mazer—the very first novel that Arthur A. Levine Books/Scholastic published. Neil sent the imprint a query letter that mentioned his enthusiasm for the book; an editor asked to see the manuscript; and in 2001, we published his *St. Michael's Scales.*

- The SCBWI provides an "Edited by" database on their website that allows aspiring authors to look up the editors of particular books (e.g., your comp titles).

- Literary agents who are members of Publishers Marketplace will frequently have pages on the site listing their current authors, most recent books published, submissions guidelines, and tastes. QueryTracker likewise features excellent agent profiles and offers direct contact information.

- The annual *Children's Writer's & Illustrator's Market* and *Guide to Literary Agents* provide the contact information and publishing interests/formats/genres for many publishers, editors, and agents.

Once you've identified a list of ten to twelve agents or editors/publishers who interest you, dig into Google and see what more you can learn about them. How do their tastes and interests in writing—their styles and personalities as literary people—coincide with yours? You can check out Twitter feeds, websites, Facebook pages, and blogs, but try to read at least one of the books they've handled, too. Once you've done your research, you should be able to narrow your list down to four to six agents or publishers, with perhaps one or two favorites, to whom you'd like to send a query letter.

Queries: I'm Gonna Sit Right Down and Write Myself a Letter

The query letter is the pick-up line of the publishing world: a few words designed to break through the noise and catch the reader's attention with its personality and verve. What sets a yes apart from a no, in dating and in publishing? Your query needs to show:

- Quality: I want to see a solid, saleable premise that makes an emotional promise.
- Originality: The manuscript has something interesting to say that I haven't heard five hundred times before, or offers a fresh take on a familiar story.
- Expression: The description of your plot should sound like jacket or catalog copy for your book, with that same level of compelling story-telling and professional polish. (If you wrote the flap copy as an exercise earlier, you'll have a good start here.)
- Interest in the other person: In your introduction or conclusion, it's very useful if you can point to reasons why the agent or editor might like your book. (This is why you should read one of the books they agented or edited.)
- And—it has to be said—I always appreciate a nice, clean outward appearance, presented like business correspondence, with no copyediting errors.

(There are many excellent guides to writing queries online; see www .cherylklein.com/themagicwords/booklinks.html for a starter list.) Queries don't have to be exclusive; you can send out more than one at a time. But you should try to tailor each one to the agent or editor to whom you're sending it, in terms of the comparison titles cited or the reasons you give for approaching that person. If you are querying several people at the same time, you should note in your letter that it's a simultaneous submission, because just like in relationships, you need to be honest with everyone involved.

When I talk to writers, they often seem nervous about the apparent *rules* of queries. How many pages? Should it include a synopsis? Can they send it to more than one editor in a house? The truth is, there are no rules, in love or in publishing. You should always try to follow an agent or publisher's query guidelines, because you'll only annoy them if you don't. But when I was single, I never turned down a date with a smart and funny guy just because he had a little mustard on his shirt; and today, I wouldn't throw out a fantastic query letter just because it spills onto two pages. Don't worry too much about the rules. Worry about writing the best description of your book that you can, and making that human connection with another person.

So you write a query, you send it, and the agent or editor responds with a yes or a no. If it's a no, it hurts a bit, but you've only invested a little time, so you can get right back out there and try again with another agent or editor. If it's a yes, congratulations! You are now dating. You send your full manuscript to the editor or agent and wait for a response.

On the Publishing Side: Did You Ever Have to Make Up Your Mind?
At this point, it's easy for writers to quietly go mad, because publishing can move at what feels like the speed of tectonic plates. The best thing you can do while you're waiting is write another book. The quality of the work you produce is really the only thing you can control in this process, and if an editor or agent likes one manuscript, they may want to know what else you have lined up.

But still: What makes everything take so long? Well:

Publishing people get *a lot* of manuscripts. Writing is an individual pursuit, that anyone who is literate can participate in, with extremely low technological requirements (as technological requirements go in the modern age). As a result, all you need to write and submit a manuscript is the ability to write in English, access to a computer with word-processing software, and an Internet account so you can send out the result. Thus tens of thousands of people can participate in the submission process, and do.

Writers vastly outnumber editors and agents—an issue made worse when writers multiply submit. We are living in an unprecedented age of access to information about publishers and editors and agents. This makes it extremely easy for writers to research possible homes for their work, and to send manuscripts to all the names they find. I am not complaining about multiple submissions, please note; I understand why writers and agents do them, and those reasons are 100 percent valid. But if we think of the amount of time spent reading a query as quantity X, then one writer submitting to one agent equals a reading time of X across the whole industry. One writer submitting to six agents equals $6X$. Six writers submitting to six agents each equals $36X$ (though note we still have just those same six agents doing six times the work) ... and we haven't even gotten to the agents submitting to editors! Thus it simply takes a while for publishing professionals to get through all of their submissions.

Reading is inherently slow. The writer and publisher Jason Pinter once observed, "The average person reads 250 words per minute—sixty pages an hour. If you give someone your 350-page manuscript, you're asking them to spend the length of a flight from New York to California with you talking to them." His point was that your manuscript should do its best to be good company, which is true. But no matter how good the company is, reading a novel manuscript takes a lot of time. I have days when I wish I *could* fly back and forth between New York and California to get all my reading done.

We're already polygamists, *and* we're having affairs with other manuscripts. In terms of the dating metaphor of this chapter, editors and agents are usually involved in anywhere from four to forty relationships at a time. Books under contract, requested revisions, projects in development, other submissions ... we'd like to be exclusive with you, really, but we're cheating all over town. Further to that:

Reading, editing, writing, and publishing well requires time. The books I already have under contract are my existing marriages, on an official schedule, with deadlines the authors and I have to meet, while manuscripts on submission aren't under such pressure. I want to do my best editorial work for those authors under contract so we can create great books together and keep those marriages going. I have relationships with agents, and I want to give them smart feedback on projects so they'll keep submitting to me even when I say no—as I must, nine times out of ten. When I read manuscripts, I feel very aware that some part of the writer's soul lives in the pages—like a good Horcrux, say—and if I'm turning one down, I need to do so with thoughtfulness and respect. In a world that grows ever more rushed and demanding, spending considered time on *anything* is a compliment, and I want to pay that compliment to the writers who are important to me.

~

The beautiful and difficult thing about both dating and publishing is that they're one-to-one endeavors: one person making a connection with another, or one writer connecting to one reader at a time. And because everything is individual, there are absolutely no solid rules in either sphere, beyond, "Have a sense of humor" and "Don't be a jerk." Each author is different; each manuscript is different; each editor is different; each agent is different; each publishing house is different. No matter how many books an editor and author have worked on together, each new manuscript has to be considered on its own strengths, with its own problems.

This utter lack of certainty extends to the business side of publishing as well. Aesthetically terrible books get published and make a ton of money; aesthetically brilliant books win the National Book Award; other aesthetically terrible books cost their publishers piles of cash with very little return; other aesthetically brilliant books disappear completely. In adult publishing, Alice Sebold, Charles Frazier, Audrey Niffenegger, and Sara Gruen (to pick four names in a very common pattern) all experienced incredible success with early novels, leading to advances for their next books in the multiple millions; and not one of those newer novels achieved the success of their previous titles. Markus Zusak and *The Book Thief* ended up on *Good Morning America* because a smart Knopf publicist sent a copy directly to then-host Charlie Gibson. Gibson happened to open his own mail that day, became fascinated with the book, and took it home to read over the weekend. There's no way to guarantee that happening again, and thus it illustrates my point: Every book is individual, and success is not easily replicable.

Given this, we publishers have to weigh the aesthetic and financial factors that go into a book at every step in the process. Once, during my first year as an editorial assistant, I fell in love with a picture-book submission and brought it to my afternoon check-in meeting with my boss. "I love this manuscript," I said to him. "Will you read it?"

"Sure, leave it with me," he said.

"It's not even two complete pages," I said. "Can't you just look at it now?"

"No, I can't," he said patiently. "Leave it here and we'll talk about it tomorrow."

Now that I've been that editor facing an intern with a great manuscript in hand, I understand where he was coming from. Because each manuscript—even a two-hundred-word picture book text—presents an editor with a series of questions to be answered, to wit:

1. Is this any good in an aesthetic sense?
2. Is it of any interest in a publishing sense? (That is, does it have some reader appeal?)
3. Is it appropriate for our publishing house?
4. Do I like this enough to work on it for a year (at minimum)?
5. If it is some good aesthetically, but not perfect, what parts aren't working?
6. Can those parts be made to work?
7. Assuming yes to question #6: Are the good parts good enough, and the publishing interest strong enough, to justify the editorial time and energy it would take to try to get it to work?
8. Assuming yes to question #7: Is this manuscript strong enough as it is to try to acquire it now? Or should I request a noncontractual revision?
9. Is the author capable of revising it?
10. Is s/he someone we'll want to work with for the long term or just for this book?
11. How many copies do we think the book will sell in hardcover? Paperback? E-book?

12. Following on #11, how much should we pay for it?
13. Assuming no to question #7: How should I reject the book?

Sometimes the answers come very quickly: If I respond to the first four questions with "No," everything else is simple. But thinking through and naming the nonworking parts takes time; writing a letter to the author for that noncontractual revision takes time; figuring out whether the book is of publishing interest or whether, say, five other books on the same topic have just been published takes time. And all of that means this process can be slow.

If a manuscript works for me, it is actually very much like falling in love, where I just want to spend all my time with the book and ignore my other responsibilities. I'll read it on my lunch breaks; I'll rush home from work to pick it up again; and sometimes we'll stay in bed together *all weekend*. I love finding books like that.

So suppose I have your manuscript and we've been dating for a while—a few weeks or months. I've read your work. Now comes the crucial time— will we make a commitment? In making a decision, I weigh all the factors in my list above, especially those first four, and then . . .

An Offer and Contract: Going to the Chapel

If it's a yes, then we'll start the process of getting married . . . and it *is* a process, as an editor usually has to get permission to even make a proposal. Again, we come back to the fact that every publisher is different: Some publishers have an editorial meeting where a book needs to be read by a couple of other editors and receive the approbation of the overall group. In these houses, the editorial meeting is usually followed by an acquisitions meeting, where the editor presents the manuscript to a committee that can include heads and/or representatives of the sales, marketing, publicity, and rights departments, as well as the editor-in-chief, president, or publisher. The attendees assess the manuscript's publishing prospects and projected finances, then decide whether the house wants to pursue the project. If so, they'll also discuss how much the initial advance offer should be (and often a maximum offer if the project is going to auction), what rights the house wishes to procure, sometimes even how a book might be positioned within a season, relative to the other titles on that publishing list. Some houses don't have an editorial meeting and go straight to the acquisitions meeting; other publishers don't have an acquisitions meeting at all, and an editor just needs to convince the head of the division that the house should take the book on. Your agent will generally know the process at each publisher.

Once the permission to make a proposal is secured, the editor makes an offer to the agent, who, with the author, weighs all the offers they've received from various suitors. Smart authors and agents know that just as you shouldn't marry for money in your love life, the biggest financial offer in publishing isn't always the best one. The editorial fit and the house's commitment to the book also make a huge difference. To get a sense of this fit, ask to speak to any editors who make offers for your manuscript. What do they like about the book? What do they want to work on within it? Do their artistic instincts jibe with yours? What is their editorial style like generally—are they mostly big-picture people, or are they very hands-on the whole way through? Do you *like* this editor? (If not, and you sign a contract with her anyway, it could be a long eighteen to twenty-four months until your book comes out.) As much as possible, you want to find an editor who understands your vision for the manuscript and can help you improve it, backed up by a house that has a track record of turning books like yours into successes.

Of course, you can't forget the finances. A standard publishing contract includes:

- **Advance:** This is money guaranteed to the author up front, with one portion usually paid on signing the contract and the balance on delivery and acceptance of the final manuscript. For a children's or YA novel from a reputable publisher, advances can run anywhere from a few thousand to tens of thousands of dollars for a quiet but beautiful middle-grade novel, to a cool million for a hot YA series. (Hope for the latter; expect the former.)

- **Royalties:** A percentage of the book's selling price. The publisher keeps all initial royalties until the book's advance has been fully recouped, at which point the book has "earned out." These days, most houses offer both print and e-book royalties.
- **Territory:** In what countries can this book be sold? Standard territories include World, World English (meaning the United States, Canada, the United Kingdom, and Australia/New Zealand), or North America.
- **Subsidiary rights:** Rights can include reprint/reproduction (the right to create a paperback, or sell the paperback rights); electronic reproduction (the right to reproduce the text in an electronic format, or sell said rights); serial (the right to reprint a portion of the book in a magazine); audio; dramatic (the right to create a stage or film adaptation of the book); commercial (the right to create merchandise based upon the book or any associated dramatic productions; it's usually sold or retained in concert with dramatic rights); and international (the right to sell the book's publication rights in other countries; some publishers distinguish between "foreign" or "open-market" rights, for selling the book in English overseas, and "translation" rights, for selling it in other languages). When a publisher retains any of these rights, the monies earned from them are split between you and the publisher, and any money you earn from rights sales by the publisher will be applied against your advance until the book earns out.
- **Term:** How long the publisher retains the right to sell the book. Most children's and YA publishing contracts grant the publisher a term of copyright. (If the book goes out of print, however, you can request that the publishing rights revert to you.)
- **Due date:** The date the absolute final manuscript and all permissions clearances must be turned in. (Authors are generally required to clear their own permissions.)
- **Option:** The terms under which a publisher gets to see material from the author's next project.

There is no one right set of terms for all manuscripts. Rather, you, your agent, and your publisher will work out the best mix of money, rights, and splits for the nature of the particular project and everyone's connections and capabilities. And indeed, that last sentence holds true for pretty much everything at the contracts stage: Just like a marriage, the two parties must negotiate the happiest and most productive way to work together for a long-term fulfilling relationship.

Rejection: What Becomes of the Brokenhearted?

All of that said, when I'm looking at a manuscript, far more often than not, it's not something I feel I can take on. I'll likely say one of two things to the author at this point: "It's not your manuscript, it's me," or in standard agent/editorspeak, "It's not right for my list at this time." This means the manuscript could be fine, but it's just not something I'm excited to acquire right now, for a multitude of possible reasons: It isn't to my personal taste; it's too similar to something I've already published; it's a book that might be better served by another editor. You really do want to find an editor who is genuinely enthused about your work, because in-house excitement always starts with the editor, and if an editor isn't enthusiastic, then it's doubtful she can inspire anyone else to be energetic about it, either. (Would you marry someone who proposed by saying, "You're okay, I guess"?) If you hear this "not right for my list" line, you simply need to find the editor or agent who *will* be excited for your book. (In passing, do not ask the person who's rejecting the book to recommend someone else, as it's like asking an ex to recommend a friend you could date. The editor or agent's job is only to know their own taste, not everyone else's.)

However, I might also say, "Actually, it *is* your manuscript"—that, in my opinion, something in it isn't working. In that case, I hope you consider my feedback carefully. From what you can see in my response, did I pretty much grasp what you were trying to do in the book? If so, and if my criticism is useful in helping you better accomplish those ends, then you should take it seriously and revise the manuscript accordingly. If I didn't get what you were doing, then you should still take a hard look at the project, because obviously I wasn't approaching your book the way you expected your readers to approach it. How might this have happened? What can you do to improve that approach for your next reader?

In both cases, just as in a real breakup, remember that both dating and getting published take time. It's not something you can expect to happen instantaneously, and if you're lucky enough that it does, you'll still need to work on growing that relationship over the long term. Beyond that, the best revenge for rejection is writing well. Revise awesomely, or write a new book to make that agent or editor regret the pass.

Why We Write: Our Love Is Here to Stay

I've been talking here about the methods of getting published and getting married—the how. But after a breakup, particularly, it's a good time to step back and think about the *why*—why you want to be published; why you want to fall in love. Of course, there are many reasons, most of them excellent ones. (Although I have to say, if you're looking for financial security in love or in children's books, you need to rethink your strategy.)

But there's also a dangerous trap that you have to watch out for. I think some people seek to get married for recognition and affirmation: "Out of all the people in the whole world, someone has chosen *me*—and that provides proof I am good, whole, and worthy." The danger in this is that the entire process is focused upon getting that recognition, not maintaining it; gratifying one's own ego, rather than growing with a partner. That means both sides miss out on the rewards of a real relationship: the pleasures of getting to know someone and being known the same way; companionship in joy and trouble; the small things that create a life together. It can be the same way with publishing. If writers focus too much on getting published, on those rules I mentioned earlier, what "the market" wants, or what the latest trends are, they can get distracted from the most important and powerful part of creating a book.

And that is the writing. Telling your truth. Telling yourself the story you've always wanted to hear, the story you've never read anywhere else, the one that scares you with the pleasure of writing it. Being as honest as you can—creating a new reality, the artist's highest aim—where you get to inhabit and share a world you build from the ground up. You must treasure the joy of the work, because it is hard work, but when you can find that just-right word, that perfect plot twist: There are very few greater pleasures.

Now, that does not mean what you write will be *good*.

And that does not mean what you write will be published.

But you will have the story you always wanted. You will have preserved a little bit of yourself forever in the world. You will have a true thing. And then you look for people who respond to your truth: the truth of what you've written in publishing, or the truth of who you are in love.

E. B. White, the author of *Charlotte's Web*, once wrote, "All I hope to say in books, all that I ever hope to say, is that I love the world." And I think that's what it's all about: the way writing, or love, or a good book can open you up to know and experience and indeed love more of the world. I'm in this business to publish world-opening books. You're in this business to create them. I wish us all the very best of luck at finding our perfect matches.

Recommended Reading

All of the titles mentioned in the text are compiled here for easy perusal. (The exceptions are the titles in Chapter 15, "Worlds and Wonders," which constitute their own booklist.) Books with a (‡) indicate titles I edited. Again, I suggest the American Library Association's annual selections of Notable Children's Books or Best Fiction for Young Adults; bookseller Elizabeth Bluemle's "A World Full of Color" database on LibraryThing; and the booklists on my website for more recommendations.

Chapter Books

Clara Lee and the Apple Pie Dream by Jenny Han, illustrated by Julia Kuo
Clementine by Sara Pennypacker, illustrated by Marla Frazee
Captain Underpants by Dav Pilkey
Bobby vs. Girls (Accidentally) by Lisa Yee, illustrated by Dan Santat (‡)

Middle-Grade Realistic and Historical Fiction

The Crossover by Kwame Alexander
The Penderwicks by Jeanne Birdsall
The Secret Garden by Frances Hodgson Burnett
The Saturdays (The Melendy Quartet) by Elizabeth Enright

George by Alex Gino

Best Friends for Never (A Clique Novel) by Lisi Harrison

Out of the Dust by Karen Hesse

The Great Greene Heist by Varian Johnson (‡)

Diary of a Wimpy Kid by Jeff Kinney

From the Mixed-Up Files of Mrs. Basil E. Frankweiler by E. L. Konigsburg

Day of Tears by Julius Lester

To Be a Slave by Julius Lester (nonfiction)

Anne of Green Gables by L. M. Montgomery

A Single Shard by Linda Sue Park

Bridge to Terabithia by Katherine Paterson

Jacob Have I Loved by Katherine Paterson

Criss Cross by Lynne Rae Perkins

The Westing Game by Ellen Raskin

Stealing Air by Trent Reedy (‡)

Words in the Dust by Trent Reedy (‡)

Ninth Ward by Jewell Parker Rhodes

8th Grade Superzero by Olugbemisola Rhuday-Perkovich (‡)

The Encyclopedia of Me by Karen Rivers (‡)

Okay for Now by Gary D. Schmidt

Goodbye Stranger by Rebecca Stead

One Crazy Summer by Rita Williams-Garcia

P.S. Be Eleven by Rita Williams-Garcia

Brown Girl Dreaming by Jacqueline Woodson

Millicent Min, Girl Genius by Lisa Yee (‡)

Middle-Grade Speculative Fiction

The Peculiar by Stefan Bachmann

The City of Ember by Jeanne DuPrau

The Graveyard Book by Neil Gaiman

Ella Enchanted by Gail Carson Levine

Where the Mountain Meets the Moon by Grace Lin

Grounded: The Adventures of Rapunzel by Megan Morrison (‡)

The Borrowers by Mary Norton

The Golden Compass by Philip Pullman

The Lightning Thief by Rick Riordan

Harry Potter and the Sorcerer's Stone by J. K. Rowling

When You Reach Me by Rebecca Stead

The Real Boy by Anne Ursu

Young Adult Realistic and Historical Fiction

Speak by Laurie Halse Anderson

The Astonishing Life of Octavian Nothing, Traitor to the Nation by M. T. Anderson

Hush by Eishes Chayil

The Perks of Being a Wallflower by Stephen Chbosky

The Chocolate War by Robert Cormier

If I Ever Get Out of Here by Eric Gansworth (‡)

The Fault in Our Stars by John Green

Glory O'Brien's History of the Future by A. S. King

Openly Straight by Bill Konigsberg (‡)

The Porcupine of Truth by Bill Konigsberg (‡)

Nick and Norah's Infinite Playlist by David Levithan and Rachel Cohn

We Were Liars by E. Lockhart

Yaqui Delgado Wants to Kick Your Ass by Meg Medina

Cut by Patricia McCormick

The Year of Secret Assignments by Jaclyn Moriarty

Slam! by Walter Dean Myers

Shine by Lauren Myracle

I'll Give You the Sun by Jandy Nelson

Hatchet by Gary Paulsen

A Room on Lorelei Street by Mary Pearson

Ball Don't Lie by Matt de la Peña

Gabi, A Girl in Pieces by Isabel Quintero

Divided We Fall by Trent Reedy (‡)

When I Was the Greatest by Jason Reynolds

Eleanor & Park by Rainbow Rowell
Between Shades of Gray by Ruta Sepetys
Cleopatra's Moon by Vicky Alvear Shecter (‡)
Young Man with Camera by Emil Sher (‡)
Irises by Francisco X. Stork (‡)
Marcelo in the Real World by Francisco X. Stork (‡)
The Memory of Light by Francisco X. Stork (‡)
The Spectacular Now by Tim Tharp
The Killer's Cousin by Nancy Werlin
The Kidney Hypothetical by Lisa Yee

Young Adult Speculative Fiction

Feed by M. T. Anderson
Shadow and Bone by Leigh Bardugo
Chime by Franny Billingsley
Above by Leah Bobet (‡)
Graceling by Kristin Cashore
Tam Lin by Pamela Dean
Twilight by Stephenie Meyer
The Knife of Never Letting Go (The Chaos Walking Trilogy)
    by Patrick Ness
Shadowshaper by Daniel José Older (‡)
Divergent by Veronica Roth
The King of Attolia by Megan Whalen Turner

Adult Fiction

Americanah by Chimamanda Ngozi Adichie
Emma by Jane Austen
Pride and Prejudice by Jane Austen
Pride and Prejudice and Zombies by Jane Austen and
    Seth Grahame-Smith
Gone Girl by Gillian Flynn
For Whom the Bell Tolls by Ernest Hemingway
The Aubrey/Maturin novels by Patrick O'Brian

Writing Craft and Literary Theory

Poetics by Aristotle

Voice Lessons by Nancy Dean

Feeling Like a Kid: Childhood and Children's Literature
by Jerry Griswold

The Power of Point of View by Alicia Rasley

Acknowledgments

I extend enormous gratitude to the following people:

Brianne Johnson, for her immediate excitement and ongoing encouragement, and finding this the right publishing home; Amy Cherry, for her wise guidance, from which I learned much as both a writer and editor; Remy Cawley, for her assistance, and Rebecca Homiski, for her patience with a writer who *loves* to edit; James Monohan, for his patience, steadiness, and role as a sounding board on matters of character and plot; Alan and Becky Klein, for being great parents, and especially for the years of support for *Second Sight*; Melissa Jackson, for sisterly excellence and Argentina; Katy Beebe, for honesty, sympathy, talking everything through, and two decades of best friendship; Melissa Anelli and Rachel Griffiths, for pep talks when I needed them and inspiring awesomeness at all times; Mallory Kass, for writing the Madison scene much better than I could; all of my friends, but especially Emily Clement, Donna Freitas, Jill Santopolo, and Stefanie Woodbridge, for cheering, enthusiasm, and faith; Linda Urban, for her generosity in reading and responding to the text, and particularly her thoughts on voice; Eric Gansworth, Anne Sibley O'Brien, Daniel José Older, Linda Sue Park, and Trent Reedy, for their contributions to and commentary on various drafts of Chapter 9, "Power and Attention"; Justina Ireland, Nisi Shawl, and Daniel, for permission to quote their material in that essay; Stacy L. Whitman, for her excellent advice on Chapter 15, "Worlds and Wonders"; Francisco X. Stork, Lisa Yee, Eric, and Trent, for the use of material from their novels and editorial processes, and their general greatness as writers and people; Olugbemisola Rhuday-Perkovich, Bill Konigsberg, and Neil Connelly, for their useful responses to the initial outline of the text; Pablo Cartaya and the Betsy Hotel in South Beach, for four idyllic days in the Writers' Room; all of the authors I've worked with at Arthur A. Levine Books/Scholastic, for the honor of editing their wonderful books, and from whom I learn something new every day; Arthur A. Levine, for an initial incredible opportunity to be part of the children's/YA publishing world, and a terrific education in it; Weslie Turner, Kait Feldmann, and my other marvelous colleagues at Scholastic, past and present; organizers throughout SCBWI, for inviting me to speak about these topics at conferences across the country; the child_lit listserv and online children's and YA literature communities, which likewise prodded me to write about and provided an education in ongoing issues in the topic; my friends and followers on Facebook and Twitter, who provided many excellent insights and suggestions; and everyone who read and supported *Second Sight*.

No thanks go to Marley, the most distracting cat in all the land, and also the handsomest.

Index